Meditation and Judaism

Meditation and Judaism

Exploring the Jewish Meditative Paths

DOVBER PINSON

ROWMAN & LITTLEFIELD PUBLISHERS, INC.
Lanham • Boulder • New York • Toronto • Oxford

ROWMAN & LITTLEFIELD PUBLISHERS, INC.

Published in the United States of America
by Rowman & Littlefield Publishers, Inc.
A wholly owned subsidiary of The Rowman & Littlefield Publishing Group, Inc.
4501 Forbes Boulevard, Suite 200, Lanham, Maryland 20706
www.rowmanlittlefield.com

PO Box 317
Oxford
OX2 9RU, UK

Copyright © 2004 by Rowman & Littlefield Publishers, Inc.

British Library Cataloguing in Publication Information Available

Library of Congress Control Number: 2004113244

ISBN 0-7657-0006-9 (cloth : alk. paper)
ISBN 0-7657-0007-7 (paperback : alk. paper)

Printed in the United States of America

⊖™ The paper used in this publication meets the minimum requirements of American
National Standard for Information Sciences—Permanence of Paper for Printed Library
Materials, ANSI/NISO Z39.48-1992.

Dedication

This book is dedicated in loving memory of
my grandfather,
Reb Yehoshuah Ben Nachum Yitzchak Pinson.
He took great pride in the study of Torah
and inspired the same in others.

HB\XNT

Contents

Acknowledgment

Many thanks to a dear friend,
Alex Goldring
whose friendship means the world.

Introduction

Fundamental to any discipline for effective living is the concept of integration. This is the alignment of will, purpose, and goal. Most of us operate inefficiently and ineffectively by being out of integrity, and not orchestrating harmoniously our physical, mental, and spiritual energies. We are at odds with ourselves.

Meditation is derived from the Latin word *medi*–center. To meditate is to discover and align our center of being with the actions that express who we are in life. It is to get in touch with the true self that animates our life and not the false self that manifests as the ego and derives its identity from the externals, that is, material things, titles, and so on. Through meditation life can be lived more authentically by discovering our potential and by relating to the external from the internal. Ostensibly, if one's ground of being is outer directed then it is logical to infer that the only interaction with the outer world is the external carapace that one has put in place, minimizing the role of the self.

The most elementary use of meditation is to relax the mind and the body. In a stress-filled life and world, it is a welcome tool for relief. There are derivative salubrious effects from meditation, including the treatment of migraines, lowering blood pressure, decreasing stress on the heart, and strengthening the immune system.

Through meditation our human potentiality is augmented. Being in touch with ourselves, we become closer to other people and to life itself. Our capacity to love and our enthusiasm for life is enhanced. We coalesce with the world surrounding us and thus feel less alienated and detached. We begin to view ourselves as an integral part of something infinitely greater than what we had perceived ourselves to be.

In addition, meditation promotes concentration and the ability to focus by dispelling the distorting veil of man's internal and external prejudices. Spiritually, meditation is used as a device to attain spiritual liberation and to loosen our intrinsic bond with that which is physical. It is both a medium to encounter the divine and experience transcendence, while serving as a spring-board, propelling future spiritual growth. In its most elevated form it is used as a vehicle through which one ascends into higher realms and dimensions.

The Hebrew word most commonly used to connote meditation is *hitbodedut*—translated as isolation, being alone, drawing inward. Given the way we operate, we are filled with the noise of the world to the point that we derive our sense of being alive from it. To be alone and to have stillness is frightening for most people. Meditation weans one from the dependency on the external and redirects the focus inward. Jewish meditation is designed to focus on the center of all reality, the Creator, and to forge a connection between the self and God.

A focal point of Judaism and the very foundation of the Jewish experience is the concept of mitzvot. The root of the word mitzvah is *tzavta,* meaning to connect. With each mitzvah a human being connects and deepens his relationship with the Ultimate partner. Through doing a mitzvah a shift of consciousness occurs, and one attains an awareness of living in the presence of the Infinite. More to the point, each individual mitzvah is another form of meditation. For example, the mitzvah of immersing oneself in the mikvah—ritual bath—is a total body meditation. One becomes fully submerged and enveloped in the waters of the mikvah. The mitzvah of ushering in the Shabbat by lighting candles is a visual, light meditation.

There are also various methods of Jewish meditation that are purely contemplative. Jewish meditations vary, and there are perhaps dozens, if not more, methods of meditating. They range from simple meditations such as replacing mundane thoughts with loftier reflection, to the more sophisticated meditations whence one reaches an expanded state of awareness and consciousness. The scope of Jewish meditation encompasses intellectual meditation to heart meditation, body movement meditation to transcendental meditation, and many more.

Choosing the suitable technique and meditation is key for the success of the meditation. Not every soul is energized by the same tune. An assiduous and devout Chassid once implored his master to teach him *the* way to God. It was not, as he explained to his master, that he did not know what he was required to do; rather his request was that his master should direct him in the one most inspiring and effective path. What is *the* way? The master replied: "There is not *one* way." For each unique individual there is his singular road. One may find connection through prayer, another through study; one may feel closest to his creator through self-denial, while yet another finds his connection through the pleasures in life. While one meets the Infinite with love, another conjoins with fear. Each of us, concluded the master, should search within our hearts and find that which draws us closest to our source, and then follow that unique path with all the strength of our being.

CHAPTER
1

Meditation . . .
A Jewish Concept?

Meditation and its attendant techniques has become extremely popular in the past few decades. Inevitably, meditation, as is with so many other mystical, or intangible practices, becomes a veritable junkyard of useful and equally useless information. Meditation groups are ubiquitous, and each one is led by an "expert" in the field. Some may truly be masters in meditation, while others have some expertise in altered states of consciousness, or merely know of various relaxation techniques. Meditation is a vast plain, encompassing countless experiences. To most, the word meditation brings to mind a magical experience capable of generating profound effects.

But what precisely is meditation? What is a meditative experience? More pointedly, is meditation a concept found in Jewish thought? If the answer is in the affirmative, then what types of meditative techniques are exclusively Jewish? Is there a Jewish prototype of meditation, a meditation that correlates to the Jewish outlook on life?

Med • i • tate me-de-tāt *vb -tated; -tating* 1: to focus one's thoughts on: reflect, or ponder over 2: to plan or project in the mind: INTEND, PURPOSE.

Meditation is interpreted as an intellectual cognitive vocation, which entails developing a thought completely and gaining a greater understanding of the idea in mind, and intention, a thought-out plan.

What exactly is intention? An aspect of intention is that one does something with a goal or aim in mind. In Hebrew, intention, mindfulness is called *kavanah,* which literally means to straighten and direct the mind and to keep one's eye on the goal. In Jewish thought, a person doing a mitzvah (a Godly commandment, a good deed) must have *kavanah,* intentionality and mindfulness.

There are two components that should be present at the performance of a mitzvah. One is the awareness of the mitzvah itself. The other is the awareness of the Commander of the mitzvah. Hence, *kavanah* is more than just a presence of mind, a direction in thought; rather, it is the redirection of the whole human being toward God. For this reason, the sages of the Talmud concluded that *kavanah* is an integral part of a mitzvah.[1]

---

1. In the Talmud there are opinions that assert that the performance of mitzvot must include intention, and without the proper intention a mitzvah is not considered done. See: Talmud *Berachot,* 13a; *Eruvin, 95b; Pesachim,* 114b; *Rosh Hashanah,* 28. In *halacha* there is the opinion that differentiates between a mitzvah mentioned in the Torah, a Biblical law, and a mitzvah instituted by the sages. A mitzvah of the Torah is not complete without intention, while a mitzvah of the sages, though intentions are important, is considered done even without intention. See: *Shulchan Aruch, Orach Chaim,* chapter 60; Rabbi Avraham Gombiner (1634–1682) *Magen Avraham,* 31 [In the name of the *Radbaz*]; see also: *Shulchan Aruch, HaRav, Orach Chaim,* chapter 60; *Eishel Avraham, Orach Chaim, 60: 3.* Rabbi Tzvi Elimelech of Dinav (1785–1841), *Derech Pikudecha* (Jerusalem: Eshkol), *Hakdamah.*

For a detailed discussion of the various opinions with regard to intention, see: Rabbi Chaim Chizkiah Medini (1832–1904) *Sdei Chemed: Klalim* (New York: Kehot, 1959), *Mem Klaal,* 61. Rabbi Moshe Ben Maimon (1135–1204), the Rambam writes very strongly regarding performing mitzvot with intention. See: *Moreh Nevuchim* (Jerusalem: Mossad Harav Kook, 1977), part 3, chapter 51.

The Kabbalists assert that a mitzvah without *kavanah*, is as a body without a soul.[2] Every action a person does should be permeated and imbued with mindfulness and love. Fear and love, it is written, are wings, which allow the mitzvah, ostensibly a simple mundane act, to soar to the heavens. Without love, this same mitzvah is a fledgling, unable to fly.[3] *Kavanah*, in its literal translation, can also allude to a window.[4] It is only with *kavanah*, that one opens a window to the soul,[5] releasing its

---

There are the opinions that maintain that a mitzvah is relevant even without proper *kavanah*, that is, without having any intention at all. Nonetheless, even those opinions maintain that when a mitzvah is done with an improper intention, the mitzvah is not valid. See: Rabbienu Yona of Gerondi (1194–1263) on *Berachot*, 12a; Tosefot on *Sukkah*, 39a, titled *"Over,"* Tosefot on *Pesachim*, 7b, titled *"Latzeit,"* *Shulchan Aruch HaRav, Orach Chaim*, chapter 489:12. See: Rabbi Yoseph Enge (1859–1920), *Athvan Deoraitha*, "Klaal," 23; Rabbi Yoseph Caro (1488–1575), *Bent Yoseph Orach Chaim*, chapter 489.

2. Rabbi Yizchak Luria (1534–1572), *Likutei Torah LeArizal*, *"Parshat Ekev"* [In the beginning]; Rabbi Yeshayah Halevi Horowitz (1570–1630), *Shenei Luchot Habrit* (Jerusalem: 1963), Vol. 1, p. 249b; Rabbi Schneur Zalman of Liadi (1745–1813), *Tanya* (New York: Kehot, 1965), chapter 38.

Rabbi Chaim Ibn Attar (1696–1743), writes in the name of the Ari Zal (Rabbi Yitzchak Luria) that actions without intentions are analogous to empty vessels. See: *Or HaChaim*, Leviticus, chapter 26, verse 3 (33).

The idea of intention in regard to the wholesomeness of a mitzvah had been expressed in Jewish thought centuries earlier. Rabbi Bachya Ibn Pakudah (1050–1120) writes that prayer (without proper intention) is like a body without a spirit. See: *Chovot Halevavot* (Diessen, 1946); *Shar Cheshbon Hanefesh*, chapter 3, part 9. See also: *Safer Hayashar* (Author anonymous) (Bnei Brak: Mishar, 1989), *shar* 13, p. 124. *Shenei Luchot Habrit. Toldot Adam*, p. 6.

3. Rabbi Chaim Vital (1543–1620), *Shar HaYichudim*, chapter 11; Rabbi Schneur Zalman of Liadi, *Tanya*, chapter 40. Note: according to the Talmud the mitzvot themselves are called wings. Talmud *Shabbat*, 49a.

4. In the book of Daniel the word *vichivin*, the root of the word *kavanah*, is used in reference to a window. (Daniel, chapter 6, verse 11).

5. Rabbi Yoseph Yitzchak, the sixth Chabad rebbe (1880–1950), at a Chassidic gathering on the twelfth of Tammuz 5692 (1932).

energy and giving it the opportunity to express itself fully and freely.

Once, the Baal Shem Tov, founder of the 18th century Chassidic movement, remained standing at the threshold of a house of prayer, unwilling to enter. "I cannot enter this room," he exclaimed, "for it has been filled to capacity with prayers." Upon hearing this, his students were puzzled. One would think that there could be no greater praise and no more worthy a reason to enter. The Baal Shem Tov explained, "The people who have come to pray speak words without devotion, love, or intention; the words they utter are entirely without wings. The prayers drop to the floor and slowly gather layer upon layer, until the entire house of prayer is filled with empty words."[6]

Meditation, while practiced universally, has been associated in people's thinking with Eastern philosophies. They promote heightened states of awareness, transcendence, and the like, which finds resonance in Judaism. However, is meditation actually sourced in the Orient, or is it intrinsically a Jewish concept? If so, are there indigenously Jewish practices that promote the same benefits? *Kavanah,* those types of meditations defined as a state of being, which is intentional and mindful, is quite visibly a Jewish concept. The question remains, however, with regard to other meditations that are transcendent.

Upon examination of the Torah, it is intriguing to note that there is not one word in the entire canon that can be literally translated as meditation. There is no single Hebrew word, that solely translates as *meditation.* This does not mean, however, that meditation itself is not found within the Torah. On the contrary, meditation, and meditative states of consciousness are replete throughout.

The entire Bible, known as the TaNaCh (Torah—Pentateuch,

---

6. See: *Ba'al Shem Tov Al Ha Torah* (Jerusalem: 1999), "Parshat Vaetchanan," p. 523.

Nevi'im—*prophets,* Ketuvim—writings, also known as the Hagiographa), was written by people of prophetic insight, who were themselves masters in various meditative techniques. The Torah uses numerous expressions to express the idea of meditation. The most common term used is *hitbodedut*—literally translated as physical seclusion and isolation.[7] Figuratively, the word *hitbodedut* can be used to imply mental and psychological isolation, drawing into oneself, internal seclusion.[8] There is another commonly found term and that is *hitbonenut,*[9] which connotes contemplation and intellectual cognitive concentration.

In the Torah the first mention of meditation is in conjunction with the Patriarch Isaac. The Torah states. ". . . Isaac came from the way of *Be'er Lachai Roi . . .* and Isaac went out to *speak* in the field toward evening."[10] The term used for *speaking,*

---

7. The root of the word *hitbodedut is badad,* which means physical isolation. See: Leviticus, chapter 13, verse 46; Lamentations, chapter 1, verse 1.

8. See: Rabbi Avraham Ben HaRambam (1186–1237), *Sefer Hamaspik Leovedei Hashem* (Jerusalem: Sifrei Rabbanei Bavell, 1984), *"Erech, Hitbodedut,"* p. 177; Rabbi Levi Ben Gershon, the Ralbag (1288–1344), *Melchemet Hashem* (Israel: Books Export), *maamor 2,* chapter 6, p. 19; Rabbienu Yona of Gerondi speaks of practicing *hitbodedut* in the chambers of one's spirit. See: *Sharei Teshuvah* (Israel: Eshkol, 1978), *shar 2,* chapter 26, p. 51. Rabbi Chaim Vital writes of practicing *hitbodedut* of one's thoughts. See: *Sharrei Kedusha* Jerusalem: Eshkol), part *3, shar 8.* See also: Rabbi Klunimus Kalman (1751–1823), *Maor Vashemesh* (Jerusalem: Even Yisrael, 1992) *"Parshat Terumah,"* p 253.

9. In the Torah this word is used to connote contemplation, or gazing. See: Psalms, chapter 37, verse 10; chapter 107, verse 43; chapter 119, verse 95; Job, chapter 31, verse 1; chapter 32, verse 12; chapter 37, verse 14. The Talmud and Midrash is replete with this term. See e.g.: *Toraht Cohanim, parsha* 1:5. *Midrash Rabbah,* Numbers, parsha 14, chapter 21. See also: Rabbi Moshe Ben Maimon, Rambam *Hilchot Yesodei Hatorah,* chapter 2, halacha 2; Rabbi Yehudah HaChassid (1150–1217) *Safer Chassidim,* chapter 14.

10. Genesis, chapter 24, verses 62–63.

is *la'suach,* which according to Talmudic lore infers prayer.[11] He specifically chose to pray at *Be'er Lachai Roi* because it was at that very location that an angel revealed itself to man.[12] The commentaries construe that this site became a shrine where Isaac would meditate *(hitboded)* daily.[13] In the Torah, a few portions further, we find Isaac's son Jacob meditating in solitude prior to confronting his brother, Esau.[14]

The period in Jewish history, between the giving of the Torah, over 3,300 years ago, and the destruction of the first Temple, some 2,500 years ago, was known as the time of the Prophets. In that era, prophecy was a flourishing commodity, the prophetic experience was, in fact, quite a common affair. In the Torah there is mention of forty-eight prophets and seven prophetesses.[15] The Talmud teaches that in addition to those mentioned, there were literally millions of people, in this

---

11. See e.g.: Talmud *Berachot,* 26b; *Avodah Zarah,* 7b. *Midrash Rabbah,* Genesis, parsha 60, chapter 14; *Pirkei De'rebbe Eliezer,* chapter 16.

12. See: Genesis, chapter 16, verse 14.

13. The commentary known as the *Malbim,* Rabbi Meir Leibush Ben Yechiel Michel Weiser (1809–1897) on Genesis, chapter 24, verses 62–63 (Jerusalem: Menorah, 1973), p. 239. The *Malbim* writes that Isaac meditated daily. Other commentaries assert that he prayed at that site daily. See Ramban, Rabbi Moshe Ben Nachman (1194–1270), Genesis, chapter 24, verse 62. (See also Rabbi Ovadyah Seforno (1470–1550) ad loc.)

14. "Jacob was left alone" (Genesis, chapter 32, verse 25). Many commentaries assert that he was meditating in solitude. See: Rabbi Avraham Ben HaRambam in his commentary on this verse (Jerusalem: Sifrei Rabbanei Bavell, 1984). See also: Rabbi Yisrael, the maggid of Koznitz (1773–1814), *Avodat Yisroel* (Jerusalem: Mochon Sifrei Tzadikim, 1998), p. 59; Rabbi Simchah Bunem of Pshischah (1765–1827), *Kol Simcha* (Jerusalem: 1997), p. 37.

Thus, we find throughout the Torah that prior to experiencing a prophetic vision the prophet would meditate in isolation. For example, before Moses saw his first vision, at the burning bush, he was meditating in isolation. See: Rabbeinu Bachya, Rabbi Ovadyah Seforno on Exodus, *"Parshat Shemot,"* chapter 3, verse 1.

15. Talmud *Megillah,* 14a. Rashi (Rabbi Shlomo Yitzchaki) (1040–1105), ad loc.

particular era, who had actually experienced prophetic visions.[16] These millions of prophets did not include the trainees, known as "children of prophets," who were being disciplined in prophetic methods, and had not yet personally experienced prophecy.[17]

Earlier civilizations, in fact, seem to have been very spiritually involved and for a large part, their culture was centered on ethereal matters. Mankind in general appears to have been more spiritually attuned than we are, as a western, modern civilization.

The common assumption is that as time moves forward, so does knowledge. When modern man looks upon earlier civilizations, he observes them as primitive and unsophisticated. History is read as an evolving mechanism, with continuous intellectual growth. This may indeed be the case in a material and physical sense, especially with regard to the sciences. What we know today about the nature of the universe and human biology was perhaps never known to primitive man, and yet, when it comes to spiritual knowledge, it seems they were our masters. They were considerably more receptive to spirituality than modern man. The history of mankind can perhaps be read as a gradual regression of spiritual attachment and involvement.[18]

Perhaps, due to the ubiquity of prophecy, the prophets neglected to document their methods for attaining these prophetic states. Nonetheless, there are hints and allusions through-

---

16. Talmud *Megillah,* 14a; *Midrash Rabbah,* Lamentations, the end of chapter 4; *Midrash Rabbah,* Ruth, on chapter 1, verse 2; *Midrash Rabbah,* Song of Songs, on chapter 4, verse 11.

17. See, e.g.: Kings 1, chapter 20, verse 35; Kings 2, chapter 2, verses 3, 5, 7, 15, etc. See also: Rambam, *Hilchot Yesodei HaTorah,* chapter 7, *halacha* 5.

18. See: Rabbi Schneur Zalman of Liadi, *Maamorei Admmur Hazoken, Haktzorim* (New York: Kehot, 1986), pp. 480–481. See also: Rabbi Nachman of Breslov, *Sichot HaRan* (Jerusalem: Netzach Yisroel), chapter 60.

out the Torah for the various techniques they would employ to arrive at such expanded states of consciousness.[19] The practice of *hitbodedut,* for example, which requires total physical and psychological isolation and seclusion, was an essential prerequisite for prophetic revelation.[20] This form of meditation appears to have been a major factor in reaching these states. Playing music is also mentioned as an introduction to the prophetic state of mind.[21] As is attaining a level of stoicism, indifference to all physical and materialistic sensations and

---

19. Rabbi Avraham Ben HaRambam elaborates extensively on the various techniques mentioned in the Torah. *See: Sefer Hamaspik Leovedei Hashem Erech Hitbodedut, Erech Hitbodedut,* pp. 177–187.

20. Isolation of consciousness from imagination, where the mind is no longer disturbed by imaginary images. Rabbi Levi Ben Gershon, *Melchemet Hashem maamor 2,* chapter 6, p. 19. See also: Rabbi Avraham Ben HaRambam, *Sefer Hamaspik Leovedei Hashem, Erech Hitbodedut,* p. 177. See also: Rabbi Yehudah Chayit (1462–1529) in his commentary on *Ma'arechet Elokut* (Jerusalem: Mokor Chaim, 1963), chapter 8, p. 96a. Physical *hitbodedut is* also needed in order to enter a prophetic experience. See: Rambam, *Hilchot Yesodei Ha Torah,* chapter 7, *halacha* 4. Ramban, Deuteronomy, chapter 13, verse 2; Rabbi Moshe Alshich (1508–1600), Numbers, chapter 23, verse 3. See also: Rabbi Menachem Recanti (1223–1290) Parshat Balak, *Levush Malchut,* vol. 7 (New York: Gross Bros., 1965), p. 41a. Rabbi Moshe Corodovero (1522–1570) writes that the prophet would also employ various divine names and through them reach elevated levels of meditation. *See: Pardess Rimonim* (Jerusalem: 1962), *shar* 21, chapter 1.

21. Chronicles 1, chapter 25, verse 1. See also: Kings 2, chapter 3, verse 15. Music played an important role to bring the prophet to the level of prophecy. See: Rambam, *Hilchot Yesodei Ha Torah,* chapter 7, *halacha* 4. *See* also: Rabbi Yitzchak Aramah (1420–1494), *AAkeidot Yitzchak, Parshat Shemot,* shar 35. For example, by playing or vocalizing a repetitive melody in the form of a mantra, it could assist the prophet in reaching a loftier state of consciousness.

We find that King David danced as a form of meditation to be in the fitting mood for prophecy. See: Samuel 2, chapter 6, verse 14. See: the Lubavitcher Rebbe, *Likutei Sichot,* vol. 1 (New York: Kehot, 1964), pp. 228–229.

necessities.[22] Mention is also made of a physical position assumed by the prophet during his prophetic experience. He would put his head between his knees while in an alternate state.[23] Needless to say, these are only snippets and bits and not a comprehensive detailed guide on how the prophet would attain his prophetic state. Alas, the methods used remain a mystery to modern man.

With the destruction of the first Temple, in the year 586 BCE the age of the prophets came to a close. Since that time, prophecies became rare.[24] The next important era in Jewish history is that of the Talmudic sages. It began with the period of the Tannaim, and later the Amoraim. The word *tanna* means to teach, or to repeat. The Tannaim were the transmitters of the oral tradition. The word *aurora* translates as speakers, interpreters, for they were the ones who deciphered and expounded on the teachings of their predecessors, the Tannaim. The era of the

---

22. See: Kings 2, chapter 4, verse 29 as interpreted by Rabbi Avraham Ben HaRambam, *Sefer Hamaspik Leovedei Hashem, "Erech Hitbodedut,"* p. 177.

Rabbi Yitzchak of Acco (1250–1340) writes that *only* by attaining a level of equanimity can the prophet experience a prophetic vision. *Meirat Einayim* (Jerusalem: 1993), *"Parshat Ekev"* 11:18. See also: Rabbi Chaim Vital *Sharrei Kedusha,* part 3, *shar* 4.

23. See: Kings 1, chapter 18, verse 42. The commentaries explain that this position was used as an introduction to prophecy. See: Rabbi Dan Yitzchak Abarbenal (1437–1508), ad loc.

24. Though the idea of prophecy in its highest state came to a close, it did not vanish completely. See: the Lubavitcher Rebbe, *Likutei Sichot,* vol. 14 (New York: Kehot, 1978), pp. 72–73. Throughout history, even following the destruction of the Temple, there were individuals who experienced prophecy in Talmudic times. See: Talmud *Baba Batra,* 12b, commentary by Rashi. For post-Talmudic sages see: Talmud *Menachot,* 109b, commentary by Tosefot, ad loc; Talmud *Eruvin,* 60a, commentary of Tosefot, ad loc. Talmud *Gittin,* 88a, commentary of Tosefot, ad loc. Talmud *Shevuot,* 25a, commentary of Tosefot, ad loc, commentary Mardechai (1220–1298) at the end of the tractate *Yevamot.* Rabbi Avraham Abulatia (1240–1296), *Ve'zot L'yehudah* (Jerusalem: 1999), p. 29. See also *Zohar* part part 2, p. 154A.

Tannaim lasted for a period of around two centuries, coming to a close with the death of Rabbi Yehudah HaNassi, in the year 219 CE. The next era was that of the Amoraim. The title *amora* applied to all teachers of Judaism, who flourished over a period of three hundred years. The era of the Talmudic sages came to a close with the completion and publication of the Talmud some fifteen hundred years ago, in the year 500 CE.

The Talmud is replete with countless sages and saints who experienced the ascension to higher spiritual realms.[25] In fact, many of these sages attained a level of awareness that was close to the prophetic experience.[26]

There is an ancient mystical text dating back to the first century known as the *Heikhalot*. The text describes the methods that the Talmudic sages, particularly Rabbi Yishmael and his colleague Rabbi Akiva, would use to reach exalted states of awareness, and how they would utter various chants to clear the mind, and assist them in their spiritual journey.[27] The Talmudic sages used these means, as well as others, to aid in their ascension. These techniques involved the purification of the mind as well as the body. The purifying ashes of the red heifer were no longer available, since sometime in the middle of the fifth century,[28] and the sages of the Talmud ceased to use these methods for ascension.[29] It was deemed inappropriate to employ these methods without the proper purification, which required the ashes of the red heifer.

The Talmud tells of a group that it refers to as "The early

---

25. E.g., *Berachot*, 7a; *Berachot*, 51a, *Chagigah*, 14b.

26. Rabbi Yehudah Halevi (1075–1141), *The Kuzari* (Israel: Hadran, 1959), *maamor 3*, chapter 65.

27. *The Heikholot*, recently reprinted (New York: Gross Bros., 1966).

28. Talmud *Chagigah*, 25a.

29. Rabbi Chaim Vital, *Sharrei Kedusha*, part 3, shar 6; *Shar HaMitzvot*, "*Parshat Shemot*." See also: Rabbi Pinellas Eliyohu Ben Meir of Vilna (1743–1821), *Sefer Habrit*, part 2, *maamor* 11, chapter 1, p. 480.

Chassidim."[30] The custom of these Chassidim was "to spend an hour before prayer, in order to direct their hearts to their father in heaven."[31] These Chassidim would meditate for nine hours each day. One hour prior to the prayers, one hour of actual verbalization of the prayers, and one hour following the prayers. They would follow this routine three times daily.[32] In each prayer session they would operate on a heightened state of consciousness, a state of greater awareness and understanding for three hours at a stretch.[33]

Sho'in is the term the Talmud uses to describe this intense meditation. *Sho'in* literally means waiting, the act of being still. Maimonides, the great 12th century Jewish philosopher, writes that they would settle their minds and quiet their thoughts, and only then commence to pray.[34] In modern Chassidic thought, the idea of *sho'in* represents *bitul,* or self-negation. These early Chassidim would still themselves, silencing their *yeshut,* that which causes them to experience physical consciousness and sensations.[35] In other words, they reached a level *of hitpashtut*

---

30. In the Talmud these Chassidim are mentioned for their numerous acts of kindness, e.g., Talmud *Baba Kamma,* 30a; *Nedarim,* 10a; *Niddah,* 38a. Indeed, these Chassidim are known as tzadikim—righteous people. See: Midrash Rabbah, *Bereishit, parsha 62,* chapter 2, commentary by Rabbi David Luria; *Radal* (1798–1857), ad loc. 2.

31. Talmud *Berachot,* 30b.

32. Talmud *Berachot,* 32b.

33. See: Rabbi Chaim Vital, *Olat Tamid* (Jerusalem: Or HaSefer, 1975), *"Shar HaTefilah,"* p. 6a; Rabbi Yakkov Emdin (1697–1776), *Sidur Beit Yakov, "Limud Achar Tefilah,"* p. 95b.

34. Rambam, *Pirush HaMishnayot, Berachot,* chapter 5, Mishnah 1. See also: Rambam, *Moreh Nevuchim,* part 3, chapter 51. Rabbi Bachya Ibn Pakudah writes that when a person is engaged in duties of the heart, for example, prayer, he should first empty his heart from all distracting thoughts. See: *Chovot Halevavot, "Shar Cheshbon Hanefesh,"* chapter 3, part 9. See also: Talmud *Sanhedrin,* 22a; Rambam, *Hilchot Tefilah,* chapter 4, halacha 16.

35. Rabbi Menachem Mendel of Vitebsk (????–1788), *Pri Ha'aretz* (Jerusalem: HeMesorah, 1989). *"Parshat Vayakhel Pekudei,"* p. 70; Rabbi

hagashmiyut—divesting themselves of all materiality and physicality, a spiritual state where they were removed and detached from all bodily sensations. A truly lofty plane and one that is analogous to the prophetic experience.[36]

Kabbalah has developed through the ages in a series of evolutionary stages. After the (final) completion of the Talmud, there began a period known as the Gaonim. In those Gaonic times, Kabbalistic literature was scarce, for the masters of this particular discipline did not record any of their teachings. There are, however, remnants of the Kabbalah associated with Rabbi Hai Gaon (939–1038) and his school of thought. Kabbalistic texts and manuscripts began to be disseminated in the late twelfth century. The first Kabbalistic text, published in the year 1176, was the *Bahir—the Book of Illumination.* Following this, in the year 1290, the *Zohar,* which is the fundamental book of the Kabbalah, was published and made accessible to all. A further development in Kabbalah was brought about through the teachings of Rabbi Moshe ben Nachman, the Ramban (1194–1270) and the school of Kabbalah associated with his teachings. The Ramban, being a staunch advocate and supporter of the Kabbalah, prompted further growth in its evolution. Medieval Kabbalah reached its zenith in sixteenth-century Safed. That particular period in history is commonly referred to as the "Great Kabbalistic Renaissance." The movement was steered by the teachings of Rabbi Moshe Corodovero, known as the Ramak (1522–1570), and especially by the teachings of Rabbi

---

Yisrael, the Magid of Koznitz, *Avodat Yisroel, p. 164;* Rabbi Yisrael Dov Ber of Vilednick (1788–1839), *Shearith Yisroel* (Israel: M'Chon Ohr Yisroel, 1998), p. 3.

36. Rabbi Yaakov Ben Asher (1270–1343), *Tur, "Orach Chaim,"* chapter 98; Rabbi Yoseph Caroa, *Shulchan Aruch, "Orach Chaim,"* chapter 98. See also: Rabbi Yeshayah Halevi Horowitz, *Shenei Luchot Habrit,* Asarah Hilulim, p. 319. Rabbi Chaim of Volozhin (1749–1821), *Nefesh HaChaim* (Bnei Brak: 1989), shar 2, chapter 14.

Yitzchak Luria, whose sobriquet was the Ari-Zal, (1534–1572). Ultimately, with the birth of the Chassidic movement, Kabbalah has come to full fruition. Chassidism is the mystical movement founded by Rabbi Yisrael ben Eliezer (1698–1760) known as the Baal Shem Tov, the Master of the Good Name.

Within the vast literature of the Kabbalah, there are numerous methods outlining the techniques and objectives for meditation.[37] In the following chapters many of these techniques proposed and exercised by the great masters of Kabbalah will be illustrated and examined. By examining these methods, one will come to understand why so many of these techniques have entered into mainstream Judaism, and conversely, why many have not. The reader will be able to differentiate between a meditative mode, which has become an integral part of the Jewish experience, and a meditative experience, which remains peripheral, practiced by a few, singular mystics, and not explored by the masses.

Many practices executed by the great sages and saints throughout history, have been exercised as singular, private, and therefore isolated, behaviors, and were not meant to be emulated by the general populace. For example, Judaism affirms and sanctifies the institution of marriage. In Jewish thought, to become a complete being is to share one's life experiences with a life partner.[38] Yet, there have been notable saints throughout Jewish history, who lived their entire lives in celibacy. Two of the greatest prophets of all time, Elijah and Elisha, were never

---

37. Incidentally, by examining the works of the Kabbalist, one may have a glimpse into the world of the prophets. It is believed that the Kabbalists are the carriers of the traditions of the prophets. See: *Safer Haplia* (an ancient Kabbalistic text attributed to the first-century saint Rabbi Nechuniah Ben HaKana) (Israel: Books Export), part 1, p. 60a. See also: Rabbeinu Bachya, *Genesis,* chapter 2:17.

38. Talmud *Yevamot,* 63a.

married.[39] The eminent Talmudic sage Ben Azzai proclaimed that he, personally, could not ever marry.[40] Although his behavior may have been revered as an act of piety, it was simultaneously viewed as idiosyncratic, and not relevant to the general congregation. For the masses, marriage is essential, elevated, and holy.[41]

The same holds true with the concept of vegetarianism. Classically, -Judaism believes that every human being has the innate capacity to elevate all of creation; therefore, the consumption of meat is potentially a mitzvah.[42] And yet, despite this

---

39. See: Rabbi Avraham Ben HaRambam, *Sefer Hamaspik Leovedei Hashem,* "*Erech HaPirishut,*" p. 125.

40. There are various opinions in the Talmud on whether Ben Azzai married then divorced, never married, or was engaged and later broke up. See: Chapter 7 Footnote 17.

41. See: Rabbi Avraham Ben HaRambam, *Sefer Hamaspik Leovedei Hashem,* "*Erech HaPirishut,*" p. 128.

42. The Torah says: "You shall *rejoice* on your festival" [*Deuteronomy,* chapter 16, verse 14]. There is a positive mitzvah to rejoice on Yom Tov—on the festivals. In the times of the Temple one would rejoice by eating sacrificial meat. (See: Talmud *Pesachim,* 109a.) The sages write that there is no rejoicing without the consumption of meat and wine. Thus, there is the ruling that even today, when there is no Temple there *is* a mitzvah to eat meat (and drink wine) on Yom Tov. (See: Rambam, *Hilchot Yom Tov,* chapter 6, halacha 18; *Tur* "*Orach Chaim,*" chapter 529; *Shulchan Aruch,* "*Orach Chaim,*" chapter 529; *Magen Avraham,* 3. (There are also opinions that argue that today there is no biblical commandment to rejoice on Yom Tov. See: Talmud *Moed Katan,* 14b; Tosefot ad loc "*Shagas Aryei,*" chapter 65, "*Minchat Chinuch,*" mitzvah 485.) There are also opinions that argue and assert that there is *no* mitzvah to eat meat today on Yom Tov. See: *Beit Yoseph* on the *Tur Orach Chaim,* chapter 529. See also: *Pischei Teshuvah,* "*Yore Deah,*" chapter 18:9, where he offers proof from the Talmud that one is *not* obligated to eat meat on Yom Tov. See: *Chullin* 11b. On Shabbat, where the mitzvah is to have pleasure rather than to rejoice, it is assumed that most derive pleasure by eating meat d thus, the ruling is that one (who enjoys meat) should eat it on Shabbat. (See: Rambam, *Hilchot Shabbat,* chapter 30, halacha 10; *Shulchan Aruch Harav,* "*Orach Chaim,*" chapter 242:2.)

premise, there have been many revered Torah personalities throughout the ages who were vegetarians. A prime disciple of the great Kabbalist Rabbi Yitzchak Luria, was himself a vegetarian.[43] The same is so with the various forms of meditation and meditative techniques. Indeed, many of the meditation styles developed in Eastern schools, can also be found within Jewish thought. It is even assumed by many scholars that many Eastern philosophies can be traced to Judaism as their original source. The question posed is whether these types of meditation have been incorporated into practices performed by the multitude, or have these meditative experiences remained the domain of a select few mystics? Essentially, the question remains whether meditation is consonant with the mainstream concepts of Judaism.

---

43. See: Rabbi Chaim Chizkiah Medini, *Sdei Chemed, Asifat Dinim, Ma'arechet Achilah, Ot Alef.*

CHAPTER
2

Defining Meditation

MEDITATION AS CONTROLLED THINKING

The first definition the dictionary provides for the word *meditate* is: to focus one's thoughts on: reflect, or ponder over. Meditation as a cognitive intellectual endeavor.

The accurate Hebrew term for such meditation is *hitbonenut*. The most elementary type of *hitbonenut* would be to replace one's everyday mundane thoughts with loftier, transcendent thoughts. Simply, to think, and be God-conscious.

Most people believe that they *think,* when in fact their thoughts merely *occur.* What is more, there is no control over these random thoughts, and even more calamitous, to a degree these thoughts control them. The declaration *Cogito ergo sum*— I *think* therefore I am—is not quite accurate. We are not because we think; rather we are what our reactive thinking invents us to be. This automaticity can be a tyrant, and the quest is to liberate ourselves from it.

A prevailing objective of meditation is to have hegemony over one's thoughts. A person meditates to experience *controlled thinking,* which, simply put, is to master one's thoughts and retain the ability to consciously decide what one will think about, and for how long that thought will be maintained.

Meditation as such, trains the mind to control its thoughts. This is far easier spoken of than accomplished.

Observe, if you will, the difficulty of concentrating for a protracted period of time on any given subject. Notice the way extraneous thoughts interfere with your focus, as if they have a mind of their own. If you were to resolve to focus your attention on an object in front of you, within a minute or two at the most, your mind would slowly begin to drift to other areas of the room. At best, you may find yourself thinking of the focus that you should be experiencing. One thing is certain, however; you will not be thinking about the object itself. The mind burps up unrelated ideas to the matter at hand. It distracts and exhausts itself by straying and then needing to be reengaged.

The human being is a complex and intricate creature. There is more to the human mind and psyche then the naked eye perceives. There are layers upon layers of consciousness operating within each one of us. Perhaps it is true that man is able to control the conscious elements of the mind, for this most external component of human consciousness is indeed subordinate to man's will. This translates to mean that if one truly intends to dwell on a matter, whatever it may be, it is the conscious mind that will be doing the thinking. There are, however, deeper elements in the mind, buried levels in the subconscious, which cannot be as easily controlled. The subconscious seems to have an agenda of its own, erratic and chaotic as it may be.

This chaos can invade at the most inopportune moments. Whether it is internal dialogue, or simply random thoughts that serve to interrupt the concentration of an individual. The result is distraction and often confusion. It takes an act of concentrated will to return the focus to the agenda of the moment. Most people suffer from this phenomenon, to a greater or lesser degree. We are all at times forced to think about something, although we wish to dwell on something else.

A principal result that is sought in meditating is to gain

control of the thinking process on the conscious and subconscious levels, so that thinking and focusing can be prolonged on any specific issue. At first it may be for just a few minutes, but the more one practices, the longer the duration increases. With time and practice, one's entire being can be mastered, and full control of the self may be achieved. In this condition, one will be able to concentrate fully without any distractions, for longer periods of time. There are two types of writing.[1] One is with an implement, such as pen or pencil on paper. Another is engraving into an object, such as stone. In the case of writing on paper, the letters imprinted will always remain separate from the paper. Not so with engraving into rock. Once the letters are carved, both the stone and the letters become one permanently. Further-more, poetically it could be argued that the letters were always contained within the stone's substance, waiting to be revealed and released. Michelangelo said, upon completing his now famous sculpture of Moses, that he did not sculpt the form of Moses so much as he liberated it. There are similarities in contemplating a thought: when the person and the thought, the knower and the known, remain separate, and a deeper level in study, when one becomes one with the thought. At this state there appears to be a blur between the knower and the known.[2] The thoughts become engraved and made part of the consciousness. Even when not actively contemplating, one is permeated with knowledge.[3]

Maimonides recognizes in his writing, that just as a wise

---

1. Rabbi Schneur Zalman of Liadi, *Likkutei Torah*, *"Parshat Bechukotai,"* p. 45a.

2. See: Rambam, *Moreh Nevuchim*, part 1, chapter 68. Once the knower knows a knowledge, than the knower, the knowledge and what is known become one.

3. Therefore, there is a mitzvah to respect scholars even while they are not studying. See: Rabbi Schneur Zalman of Liadi, *Likkutei Torah, Parshat Kedoshim,* p. 30d.

person is acknowledged in the wisdom he has procured, he is also identifiable as a scholar in his everyday manner. The way in which he walks, speaks, eats, and so forth, betray his mind and stature.[4] The wisdom that occupies his mind permeates his entire existence as well. His entire being becomes wisdom itself, they art one and the same.[5]

This wise person is operating in a higher meditative state. The very thoughts that occupy his mind become one with his existence. The thoughts are now lodged into his consciousness. Close your eyes for a moment and you will notice that there are myriads of colors, lights, and flashing images that appear in front of your eyes. The images, which you detect when your eyes are closed are still very much there when your eyes are open. It is only that these images are very faint compared to the images that enter the mind from external sight. These are the inner images that emanate from one's innermost psyche. The Kabbalah teaches[6] that by closing the eyes and visualizing the letters of the name of God (the tetragrammaton), one can discern the source of his soul. The clearer and more transparent the colors are, the loftier the soul.[7] Since these colors are images that exist when the eyes are open, therefore, even when one concentrates exclusively

---

4. Rambam, *Hilchot De'ot,* chapter 5, halacha 1.

5. To a degree a wise person's entire being becomes wisdom. See: The Lubavitcher Rebbe, *Likutei Sichot,* vol. 18 (New York: Kehot, 1982), p. 155. The Talmud says that anyone who would hold onto the cane of Rabbi Meir (the brilliant Talmudic sage, who was renowned for his great intellectual capabilities [See: Talmud *Sanhedrin,* 24a and Talmud *Eruvin,* 13b]) would gain (from the cane) intellectual insights. (Jerusalem Talmud *Nedarim,* chapter 9, halacha 1; *Moed Katan,* chapter 3, halacha 1.) The wisdom of Rebbe Meir permeated his entire being, even the most external. Any person or object that came into contact with this great sage became imbued with his wisdom. Thus, his cane was a piece of wood infused with wisdom. See: *Likutei Sichot,* vol. 4 (New York: Kehot, 1974), p. 1096.

6. Rabbi Chaim Vital, *Shar Ruach Hakodesh.* See also: *Shulchan Aruch Ariza* (Jerusalem: 1998), p. 195.

7. On a simple level this has to do with the colors one is most drawn to.

on an object, one will not experience its beauty in its entirety, for the external image passes and is funneled through the internal images of the mind. The beauty of an object is thus mixed and diluted with the inner images of the mind.

Meditation is a way in which one can achieve control of one's inner images and colors. In a higher meditative state it is possible to turn off these interferences and to block them from the mind. When the meditator has gained dominance of his inner images, and stilled them, he can then experience an objective reality in all its true beauty, without the distortions of the internal imagery.

There is a theory that by nature the mind of a human being is selective rather than indiscriminate.' This theory proposes that the mind of a human being observes much more than it actually thinks it does, and has a much broader scope and vision than we would imagine. An analogy could be made to a motion picture camera that records everything the lens is aimed at. However, when played and viewed not everything that has been

---

There is a science called gemology, the theory of stones. There are those who claim that there are healing powers contained within stones. They believe that every human being has a particular color they are associate with, and their stone (with its distinct colors) they feel most attracted to. (See: Rabbeinu Bachyah, Exodus, "Parshat Tetzaveh," chapter 28, verse 15 where he explains that each of the twelve tribes of Israel had their own stone, wit its own distinct color that they were associated and connected with.) For the healing powers in stones see: Rabbi Gershon Ben Shlomo (thirteenth century, father of the Ralbag), Shar HaShamaim (Israel: 1968), maamor 2, shar 3, p. 16. See also: Rabbi Shem Tov ben Shem Tov (????–1430), Sefer Ha'emunot (Jerusalem: 1969), shar 5, chapter 1. Rabbi Eliyahu HaCohen (????–1629), Sheivet HaMusar (Jerusalem: Or Hamusar, 1989), chapter 6:10, p. 100. Rabbi Moshe Isserles, the Ramah (1530–1572), Machir Yayin (Bnei Brak: 1999), p. 44.

8. A theory purposed by Henri Bergson. See for example, The Creative Mind: An Introduction To Metaphysics (New York: Carol Publishing, 1992), pp. 135–137. See also: William James, On Psychical Research (New York: Viking Press, 1960), p. 292. Malcome M. Moncrieff, The Clairvoyant Theory of Perception (London: Faber & Faber, 1951), p. 7.

recorded is observed by the viewer. The selection process that
the brain exercises is paradoxically a creative act even though it
is automatic. Its creativity lies in the process of weeding out a
specific something from the everything that was recorded, and it
is automatic in that the selection process is based on the viewer's
predisposition, past experiences, bent, mood and so on, that sets
him to resonate and see one thing before another. The selectivity
of the mind, of course, extends beyond the visual. In the domain
of ideas the same selective process is extant, the mind choosing
what it considers important or not, and this selection process
includes values. So this is a primary benefit derived from
meditation. It allows us to gain hegemony over the automatic
and selective mind so that we can deliberately choose what to
focus on and for what duration. From the above we see that a
primary use of meditation is to achieve the freedom to focus and
to liberate the conscious mind from the tyranny of habitual
random thinking. By reaching this level of mastery, the meditator can turn his attention to whatever he chooses with greater
efficiency and clarity. A known observer of states of consciousness writes that a person in such a state may say "I have heard
that said all my life, but I never realized its full meaning until
now."[9] When one has achieved this type of mastery, one's
perceptions (even the old ones) take on new dimensions. In fact,
it allows one to be more in the present, dealing with the here and
now more effectively. Perhaps for the very first time.

MEDITATION FOR SELF-EXAMINATION

To truly understand and know one's inner self is perhaps the
most essential element in the quest for character refinement.

---

9. William James, *The Varieties of Religious Experience*, lecture on
Mysticism (New York: Penguin Classics, 1985), p. 382. He writes this with
regard to the mystical state.

A person operating within the parameters of normal consciousness, builds around himself a protective veil of the ego.[10]
This serves as an obstacle in the path of self-examination. It is
near impossible for an individual to view himself objectively,
namely, to observe and evaluate his own nature and character
traits, and see clearly that which needs to be corrected. He
thinks subjectively and thus cannot judge his own behavior
precisely and truthfully. In the Mishnah it is written that a
person cannot see his own blemishes."

With this knowledge that we are all subjective and cannot
see ourselves as we truly are, is there any conceivable way in
which a person may critique himself objectively? Is it possible
for a person to have a purely objective view about himself,
which he could then utilize in proper self-evaluation, and
ultimately self-perfection?

Meditation is a road to self-awareness. The ego is tamed
and the meta state can be achieved, in which one becomes the
observer of one's own life and life in general. From this vantage
point the meditator can deconstruct the patterns and traits that
dominate his life, and can then correct them. At times the
positive can also be enhanced, the alteration then is the
removal of its automatic quality.

---

10. There are three kelipot—literally shells—that surround and cover
over one's Godly self. According to Rabbi Eliyahu ben Moshe Di Vidas
(sixteenth-century Kabbalist) these three *kelipot are* manifested in the form of
haughtiness, stubbornness, and anger. The source of all these negative attributes is the ego. See: *Reshit Chachmah, Shar HaYirah,* chapter 4; Rabbi
Eliyahu HaCohen, *Sheivet HaMusar,* chapter 12:12, p. 186.

11. Mishnah *Negoim,* chapter 2, mishnah 5. Though this law refers
specifically to physical blemishes, nonetheless, as the commentaries explain,
this premise extends also to mental as well as spiritual imperfections. See:
Rabbi Menachem ben Shlomo, *Meiri* (1249–1316) and Rabbi Shemuel De
Uzeda (1540–1605), *Midrash Shemuel* on *Avot,* chapter 1, mishnah 6; Rabbi
Eliyahu HaCohen, *Sheivet HaMusar,* chapter 40:24, pp. 576–577. In the
words of the Talmud, "A person is close to himself." Talmud *Sanhedrin,* 9b.

An additional by-product is that self-assurance and self-esteem are made to grow. Through increasing inner directedness one is less at the mercy of external forces and whims. One becomes more sensitive to what *he* wants and what makes *him* happy, as opposed to what makes other people feel happy. Through self-knowledge one avoids becoming what one needs not be, and allows oneself to become what one truly is. Paradoxically, by learning to take a stand in one's own life, more of the person is available to himself, to others, and to life.

Though the results of self-knowledge are rewarding, the way to reach this knowledge is difficult. The Talmud tells of a saintly sage, who upon laying on his deathbed, began crying with bitter tears, saying: "In the afterlife there are two paths my soul can journey on. One is the path leading to heaven, and the other the path leading to hell. I do not know on which one of these paths I will be led."[12] A puzzling tale indeed. How was it possible for this great sage, a man well-known for his piety and nobility, to be uncertain of his ultimate destiny?

Most of us are so preoccupied with doing right and well in the external world that we tend to neglect our internal world. Our inner spiritual calculus is ignored, along with the proper self-evaluation.[13]

It is conceivable that one could go through life, doing all the right things, at all the right moments, being known throughout as a man of piety and holiness, and yet remain empty in the core of one's being. Everything is done right, yet it is only on the surface level, limited to the domain of action. The actions are transcendent and noble, and yet his innermost being, his internal subconsciousness is completely in a state of alienation and estrangement. In Kabbalistic terms, it is possible that his extremities, the *garments* of the soul, namely, the conscious

---

12. Talmud *Berachot,* 28b.
13. For a similar interpretation of why this sage cried see: the Lubavitcher Rebbe, *Likutei Sichot,* vol. 5 (New York: Kehot, 1978), p. 304.

thoughts, speech, and actions, are indeed holy, while the inner essence of his soul lies within the depth of kelipot—unholiness.[14]

It is for this reason that the saintly sage wept. How was he to know for certain that he had transformed his entire existence, external as well as internal being, to Godliness? He may have feared that perhaps there were hidden parts within him that had not been elevated."

There is a fascinating concept appended to the idea of *teshuvah,* popularly translated as repentance, although the accurate translation would be *return.* The Torah law states that an individual who has done an accidental misdeed, in the times of the temple, was obligated to bring a *karban*—sacrifice.[16]

It seems strange that the law requires a sacrifice for a nondeliberate act. Why should a person do *teshuvah* for an act that was committed unintentionally? Yet that is precisely the point. The Torah aspires to educate man how to live life deliberately rather than haphazardly, consciously as opposed to accidentally.[17] The Torah requires man to take control of life,

---

14. See: The sixth *Chabad* Rebbe, Rabbi Yoseph Yitzchak, *Sefer Hamaamorim,* 5696–5697 (New York: Kehot, 1989), pp. 55–56. The Lubavitcher Rebbe, *Sefer Ha'maamorim,* "*Meluket,*" vol. 4 (New York: Kehot, 1993), p. 386.

15. See: Rabbi Schneur Zalman of Liadi, *Likutei Torah,* "*Parshat Vayikrah,*" *Hosofot,* p. 50d; *Maamorei Admur Hazoken, Haktzorim,* p. 309.

16. *A karban chatas,* for even an unintentional act needs correction. See: Talmud *Shevuot,* 2a; Rashi, *Toleh,* Genesis, chapter 9, verse 5; Rashi, *Meyad Aish.* (See also: Talmud *Makkot,* 10b.) There is an argument about whether or not transgressing unintentionally a mitzvah of the sages also needs rectification. See: Rabbi Yoseph Engel, *Athvan Deoraitha,* klaal 10; Rabbi Chaim Eliezer (Shapira) of Munkatsch (????–1937), *Menchat Eliezer,* part 3:12; Rabbi Schneur Zalman of Lublin (1730–1802), *Toraht Chesed,* "*Orach Chaim,*" chapter 31.

17. See: *Rabbeinu Bachya* in his commentary on Leviticus, chapter 1, verse 9; Rabbi Yitzchak Aramah, *Akeidot Yitzchak,* "*Parshat Vayikra,*" shar 57. Rabbi Moshe Isserles (1530–1572), the Ramah, *Toraht Ha'olah* (Tel Aviv: Yeshivath Chidushei Harim, 1999), part 2, chapter 1, p. 14.

and not allow life to take control over him.[18] "To a righteous man no accidents occur."[19] A person who follows the dictates of the Torah, and is rigorously involved in the discipline of the Torah, will rarely encounter mishaps.

Most of us however, do not live life in a disciplined, deliberate, and integrated fashion, and we often find ourselves at the effect, and result of internal and external forces that we are not even conscious of, and which at times may be conflicting in nature. We may surprise ourselves by our own actions. Occasionally, we will look back at our day and wonder how we even said something, or acted in a particular manner. An action, a thought, or an emotional outburst from a moment ago, may at times seem to us to be completely uncharacteristic of our true nature.

It is this lack of integrity (not to be confused with honesty, a derivative of integrity), resulting in a disalignment between the varied aspects of the same person's character and personality, that the Torah is strenuously calling our attention to, by demanding a sacrifice for accidents. *Teshuvah* here means a return to wholeness. A transformation from the fragmented self is required. In doing *teshuvah,* by bringing an offering, one is returning and becoming whole again. In this way, an unintentional, instinctive act, in a certain sense, needs greater *teshuvah,* than an act which was intentionally committed.[20]

A person who wishes to understand himself in an internal way, and objectively observe his spiritual standing, should note

---

18. When there is no Temple, one can use the advice given by Rabbi Yisrael the Magid of Koznitz, who writes that if one transgressed unintentionally, he should aspire to do as many mitzvot possible, even if they are done unintentionally. See: *Avodat Yisrael, "Rosh HaShana,"* p. 251. (See also: Midrash. Leviticus *Rabbah,* 25:5.)

19. *Proverbs,* chapter 12, verse 21.

20. See: Rabbi Schneur Zalman of Liadi, *Tanya, "Igeret Hakodesh,"* epistle 28; the Lubavitcher Rabbe, *Likutei Sichot,* vol. 3, p. 944.

how it is that he acts instinctively. What is his immediate reaction when faced with a challenge? What are the first thoughts and feelings that spring to mind? That which is instinctively, immediately felt and observed, is that person's true self (at that particular time in life), relating to the moment at hand.[21]

A dream, as Freud once said, is the royal path to the subconscious. If a person wants to know what is happening within him, that which is occurring in his inner consciousness, he may wish to evaluate his dreams. By examining one's dreams, one achieves a glimpse into one's inner being. The real self is discovered, as is the status of one's spiritual development.[22] It is perhaps for this very reason that many of the great sages throughout the ages meticulously recorded their dreams.[23] There are meditations designed to achieve within the meditator a dreamlike state. Once the meditator has entered into this state, it becomes an opportune time for him to tap into the inner essence of his being. When the external trappings of the conscious mind are quieted, there becomes more room for the inner consciousness of the mind to express itself. This demonstrates yet another reason why many people find meditation so necessary—so that they can discover who they really are, and what it is that requires improvement.

---

21. Rabbi Schneur Zalman of Liadi, *Maamorei Admur Hazoken,* "*Maarazal,*" p. 31.

22. Rabbi Nachman of Breslov (1772–1810), *Sefer HaMidot* (Brooklyn: Moriah, 1976), "*Emet,*" pp. 6–7.

23. Rabbi Chaim Vital, *Safer Chizyonot;* Rabbi Moshe Chaim Ephraim of Sudylkov (????–1800), Degel *Machanah Ephraim* (Jerusalem: Mir, 1995), "*Likkutim,*" p. 259; Rabbi Tzodok HaKohen of Lublin (1823–1900), *Kuntres Divrei Chalomot* (Bnei Brak: Yehadut, 1973). Rabbi Eliezer of Komarna (1806–1873), *Safer Chizyonot* (Israel: Heichal Habracha, 1997), pp. 21–24. Rabbi Shimon Agassi (1782–1814), *Safer Toraht Hagilgul* (Jerusalem: Ahavaht Shalom, 1982), *Chizyonot Ve'Giluy Eliyahu*, pp. 3–13.

MEDITATION—REACHING EXPANDED
STATES OF AWARENESS

If one carries the hypothesis of the mind as selective (rather than indiscriminate) to its logical conclusion, then one may argue that the brain is not productive in its function, but rather eliminative. This means to say that potentially a person could perceive everything that is beheld, but the impact would be overwhelming and would overload the system. For the sake of self-preservation, then, much of the information is filtered out.[24]

The screening of the mind has such a pervasive effect on the majority of people, that they believe that the only reality that exists is that which they see and perceive, the three-dimensional. There are those, however, whose minds and nervous systems are not as eliminative, and these people can actually experience and perceive other dimensions. They are capable of experiencing a reality in which space and time, though they still exist, have lost their importance. A reality where the mind is primarily concerned not with measures and locations of the tangible but with the ethereal. This is the hallmark of an expanded state of consciousness, in which one comes to the realization that physical reality is but a veil, concealing that which is beyond it. Meditation can be utilized to reach this expansive state of awareness. It is believed that one can also reach such states of consciousness through narcotics and other substances.[25] There are those who aspire to attain higher states of awareness and attempt to achieve this through nonnatural causes, external stimuli.

The purpose of the Torah is facilitate and empower man to

---

24. See: Aldous Huxley, *The Doors of Perception: Heaven and Hell* (New York: Harper Perennial, 1990), p. 22.

25. Aldous Huxley was a proponent of using narcotics to reach higher states of consciousness. See: Ibid. The problems with this (other than addiction and that some drugs are harmful) is that they are unnatural, and they bring one to that state whether one is equipped for it or not.

exist within the natural state.[26] As will be illustrated further
on, rather than neglecting the natural, encountering whatever
it is that one aspires to experience *through* and *within* nature.
The goal is to reach this elevated and expansive state through
utilizing the mind, and not through disregarding it. Once this
state is achieved, one will be strong enough to manage it, and
simultaneously be capable of integrating the experience into
one's daily lifestyle, engendering and empowering spiritual
growth.

Observing those who avail themselves of substances such
as drugs or alcohol, we are compelled to conclude that normal
waking consciousness or rational consciousness, is but one, singular type of awareness. In truth there exists within man layers upon layers of consciousnesses.[27] There are other states of
awareness looming deep within our being, waiting to be
revealed. We may also conclude that it is quite possible for a
human being to go through life without ever suspecting that
these layers exist. However, by applying the appropriate stimulus, a person can awaken these higher states from the deepest
levels. According to the Kabbalah a human being can reach
these expanded states of consciousness through the appropriate
meditations.

Many schools of meditation speak of meditation as a means
of attaining extrasensory perception, ESP. (This includes, for
example, mental telepathy, clairvoyance, the ability to predict
the future, and the like.) These opinions assert that a human
being in a normal state of consciousness is not properly attuned
to these modalities. ESP is ubiquitous and available, according to

---

26. See: *Midrash Tanchumah*, *"Parshat Naso,"* chapter 16. The purpose of
the creation is to create a dwelling place for God within this world. Meaning,
the objective is not transcendence, but to hallow the mundane—to bring
heaven down to earth.

27. See: William James, *The Varieties of Religious Experience*, lecture on
Mysticism, p. 387.

this trend of thought, in a normal state. However, the signals that may come to the mind are overshadowed by the continuous conventional, rational information entering the mind. Conversely, these signals may be blocked out by the mind's perpetual static, the internal images discussed previously. However, in a meditative state, the conventional, rational apparatus is quieted down, and there is no extraneous information entering the mind. The mind is completely quieted; the meditator has silenced the information processor. It is then conceivable, they maintain, for the human being to tap into the domain of ESP.

Consequently, meditation can be utilized to attain this extrasensory perception. It is believed that within every one of us there is the power and potential to have an authentic mystical experience, to attain a heightened state of awareness.[28] Being in such a state has a twofold advantage. First, life takes on a new and fresh meaning. Through a mystical experience, the meditator gains new insights and deeper understanding of the realities of life. And additionally, through reaching advanced stages of higher consciousness, the meditator can acquire extrasensory perception, in which he can predict the future, and the like.

Man, since the beginning of time, has been fascinated with the future, the unknown. Those who were able to tap into the future and predict what would occur the next day, were and are still regarded by many with the greatest admiration.[29] The modern fascination with what we call psychics goes back thousands of years. The assumption that everyone has within them the potential to acquire extrasensory perception is inviting

---

28. Though, as Carl Jung accurately points out, the unconscious is not a synonym for God, "it is the medium from which the religious experience seems to flow." Carl G. Jung, *The Undiscovered Self* (New York: Mentor, 1958), chapter 6, p. 102.

29. See: Rabbi Yoseph Albo (1380–1435), *Sefer Haikkarim, maamor* 3, chapter 8. See also: Rabbi Moshe ben Nachman, Ramban, Deuteronomy, chapter 18, verse 9.

to many. It becomes tantalizing and tempting to achieve the power and gifts of ESP by entering into meditative practices.

This raises the much-deliberated question of the Torah's perspective on the mystical, or more precisely, the magical, experience. The term magic is a loose term, and not used to indicate black magic, for that is clearly forbidden according to the Torah, but rather, a magical, otherworldly experience. Does such an experience, this mystical *personal* experience find any place within the general context of the Jewish experience? What is the role of the mystical experience in Judaism and taking this one step further, how does Jewish thought speak of the super-natural abilities, and psychic powers that many people seem to have been born with?

To begin with, the mystical experience must be clearly defined. It appears that every mystical experience, in whichever culture or era, has two distinct qualities. The first would be ineffability—the experience defies all expression—which means to say, that no report of how it feels can be adequately transmitted with words, and it is intensely personal. The second quality would be the noetic quality. It seems to the person experiencing it as a state of knowledge, in addition to it being a state of feeling, a state of insight into depths of truth unplumbed by discursive intellect, an illumination and revelation of significance and importance.[30] The person undergoing a mystical experience feels as if everything is charged with meaning and relevance. They feel surrounded by ultimate truths. They are filled with a consciousness of meaning and order. They feel how everything makes sense in the greater scheme of reality.

This experience creates a dilemma. One cannot go to such a place of power and not be radically energized and transformed. This energy, however, can go in one of two directions. The individual can either come through with profound humility,

---

30. William James, *The Varieties of Religious Experience,* pp. 380–381.

realizing and recognizing the magnificence of what is. Or, it can become the ultimate ego trip with side effects of arrogance and contempt toward those who have not yet attained these levels. The former becomes a manifestation of transcendence, allowing the infinite's energy to manifest within him, enriching life and existence. The latter becomes a metaphysician who is able to manipulate physical and spiritual reality to serve his own ends and benefits. He exploits the energy for his own self-indulgence. In the Torah, just as the former is revered with the greatest esteem, the latter is looked upon as thoroughly forbidden and is strongly condemned.

In Jewish thought, it is asserted that every human being has the potential to connect with the upper/inner worlds, those worlds that exist within/above this physical plane. The Creator desired, so to speak, that while humans operate within the confines of the physical dimensions of time and space, they will also have ways of accessing the spiritual and experiencing the divine intimately.[31] In fact, an authentic mystical experience is one of the sources of Kabbalistic literature. It has been documented that the prophet Elijah revealed himself through visions, throughout the ages, to various great masters, and transmitted through the aforementioned visions, the deepest secrets of the creation.[32] This revelation of the prophet can occur in a different form as well. The master would experience a divine revelation (a

---

31. Rabbi Nisan Ben Reuven (c.1290–c.1375), *Derashot HaRan* (Jerusalem: Mochon Sholom, 1977), *derush* 5, "In the beginning"; Rabbi Moshe Metrani (1500–1580) *Beit Elokim* (Jerusalem: Otzer Hasefarim, 1985), "*Shar Hayesodot,*" chapter 19; Rabbi Moshe Chaim Luzzato (1707–1747), *Derech Hasher,* part 3, chapter 2: 3. See also: Rabbi Chaim Vital, *Share Kedusha,* part 3, shar 3.

32. The very foundation of the Kabbalah, the *Zohar,* was authored by Rabbi Shimon Bar Yochai, who received these teachings from divine inspiration and via a revelation of the prophet Elijah. See: Rabbi Chaim Vital, *Eitz Chaim,* "In the *Hakdamah*"; Rabbi Naphtali Hirtz Bacharach (seventeenth century), *Emek HaMelech, hakdamah* 2. See Rabbi Yoseph Ergas

prophetic vision) in the consciousness of his mind.[33] Following his revelation, he would transmit these teachings to his disciples, who in turn would write it down and transmit it to their disciples.

Creation was arranged in such a manner so that all existences are interconnected. Each entity is interlaced with the next. The course of events in the lower worlds are a manifestation of the happenings in the spiritual worlds above. The sages taught that there is no blade of grass that does not have its angel (energy) above it in heaven, striking it and commanding it to

---

(1685–1730), *Shomer Emunim* (Jerusalem: Bepirush U'Beremez, 1965). The second *Hakdarah*, part 2, p. 47.

The Kabbalists who chronicled the development of modern Kabbalah assert that it all began with a revelation by the prophet Elijah. See: Rabbi Menachem Recanti in his commentary to the Torah, *Parshat Naso;* Rabbi Shem Tov Ibn Shem Tov, *Sefer HaEmunoth* (Jerusalem: 1969), shar 4, chapter 10, p. 36b; Rabbi Meir Ben Gabbai (1480–1547), *Avodat Hakodesh* (Jerusalem: Shivilei Orchot HaChaim, 1992), part 2, chapter 13; Rabbi Yoseph Shlomo Delmedigo, known as the Yashar of Candia (1591–1656), *Metzareph Le-Chachmah,* p. 15a; Rabbi Chaim Yoseph David Azulay, *Sher Hagdalim Marrechet Gedolim Aleph* (10).

The same is true, with the teachings of the holy master, the Arizal, Rabbi Yitzchak Luria. It is told that he too received many of his insights by means of revelation. See: Rabbi Yoseph Ergas, *Shomer Emunim,* part 1, number 17; Rabbi Chaim Vital, *Eitz Chaim,* "In the *Hakdamah,*" *Olat Tamid* (Jerusalem: Or HaSefer, 1975), *Inyon HaTefilah,* p. 46b; Rabbi Pinchas Eliyohu Ben Meir of Vilna, *Sefer Habrit,* part 2, maamor 12, chapter 5, p. 499.

Chassidic legend has it that the teacher of the Baal Shem Tov, the founder of Chassidism, was the master prophet Achiya Ha'Shiloni. *See: Keter Sher Tov,* chapter 143, p. 18a; Rabbi Yaakov Yoseph of Polonnye (d. 1784), *Toldot Yaakov Yoseph,* "*Parshat Balak,*" p. 575. The Lubavitcher Rebbe, *Likutei Sichot,* vol. 2, p. 512, *Hayom Yor, Chai Elul.*

33. A revelation by the master prophet Elijah can also occur within the consciousness of a human being. See: *Tikunei Zohar,* The *Hakdamah.* See also: Rabbi Yehudah Loew (1526–1609), *Netzach Yisrael* (Bnei Brak: Yehadut, 1980), chapter 28, pp. 136–137; Rabbi Nachum of Chernobyl (1730–1787), *Meor Einayim* (Brooklyn: 1975), "*Parshat Vayyetze,*" p. 45.

grow.[34] The Kabbalah speaks of parallel universes. This physical realm is but one of many worlds. The creation of this universe, the world of the finite, is through a process of transmutation. Divine infinite light was first projected into higher spiritual worlds, until, in the later stages of the process it turned into something defined, limited, and finite, as this physical world. This is what the Kabbalah calls *seder hishtalshelut,* order of progression. This means that there is a continuous thread of light weaving through the entire creation, from the most integrated worlds above to the furthest of worlds below.

Consequently, when a human being elevates to a higher spiritual reality and connects with the spiritual entities (angels, spirits, souls, and the like) above, he unites with a world in which the dimension of time has no relevance. He can therefore experience extrasensory perception, and perhaps even observe the future. The soul of man, that is, the spiritual life force residing within every human being, has clairvoyant perception. It can observe the future as it perceives the present. Yet, owing to the limitations of physicality, this perception remains shut out from one's consciousness. If, however, one divests oneself of the physical and the mundane, one will then be able to possess this higher, otherworldly perception.[35] The preeminent connection a human being can attain with the divine is through the attainment of prophecy. The sign of a true prophet is the accurate prediction of future events.[36] When a prophet experiences a prophetic vision, his physical being becomes entwined with the higher reality of an angel.[37] Accordingly, as he enters a world of

---

34. *Midrash Rabbah,* Genesis, *parsha* 10, chapter 6; *Beit Hamidrash,* 2:27. *Zohar,* part 2, p. 171a. *Zohar,* part 3, p. 86a.

35. Rabbi Shimon Ben Tzemach Duran (1361–1404), *Magen Avot* (Livorno: 1785), part 3, p. 88a; Rabbi Chaim Vital, *Sharrei Kedusha,* part 3, *shar* 7 (1).

36. Rambam, *Hilchot Yesodei HaTorah,* chapter 10, *halacha* 1.

37. Rambam, *Hilchot Yesodei Ha Torah,* chapter 7, *halacha* 1. According

timelessness he can foresee future events. This extrasensory perception can also occur as *ruach hakodesh*—a holy spirit, or alternately translated divine inspiration.[38] When a person has reached this lofty level (albeit, lower than prophecy[39]) he may also attain extrasensory perception, expanded awareness, and it is even possible for him to predict future events much as the prophet would.[40] Human souls are inherently connected with higher realms, and when a human being who has reached a level of perfection becomes involved in meditation, it is then conceivable for him to foretell future events.[41]

Herein lies the difference between that which is an authentic mystical experience, and that which is merely a delusional experience. A genuine mystical experience occurs when the meditator experiences the divine. He is encountering something more than himself, a moment of transcendence. It may be that he experiences an angel, or spirit. Or, it may even be that he experiences a revelation of his very own soul, the transcendent part of the soul, which is still intrinsically connected to the upper/inner worlds.[42] In addition, the mystic who encounters an authentic experience does not seek to attain supernatural

---

to the Rambam all prophetic visions are experienced through an angel. See also: Rambam, *Moreh Nevuchim,* part 2, chapter 34; Rabbi Avraham ben HaRambarn, Exodus, chapter 7, verse 1.

38. See: Rabbi Moshe Chaim Luzzato *Derech Hashem,* part 3, chapter 2:5.

39. The Rambam enumerates eleven levels of divine inspiration, ranging from prophesy through experiencing a vision of an angel. *Ruach hakodesh* is the second highest level. See: *Moreh Nevuchim,* part 2, chapter 45.

40. Rabbeinu Bachya on Leviticus, chapter 8, verse 8. See also: Rabbi Yitzchak Aramah, *Akeidot Yitzchak,* "*Parshat Bereishit,*" *shar 6.*

41. Rabbi Hai Gaon (939–1038), quoted by Rabbi Moshe Botril in his commentary to *Sefer Yetzirah,* chapter 4, mishnah 2. It is possible for the soul of the person to reveal future events through a dream. See: Rabbi Shimon ben Tzemach Duran, *Magen Avot,* part 3, p. 88a.

42. Rabbi Shimon ben Tzemach Duran, *Magen Avot,* part 3, p. 88a.

powers for his own gain or benefit. For him the sole objective of the experience is to touch the divine, and become absorbed by it.

An inauthentic experience, on the other hand, produces feelings that are derived from within. A mystical experience, whence the outcome is ego-centered and delusional, occurs when the meditator searches deep within and finds himself. He reaches deep down and reveals a deeper level of ego, that is, of the instinctual/selfish self.

The nature of the inauthentic experience is egotistic and selfish. It is ego driven and plays on the feelings of the meditator. By contrast, the authentic mystical experience is of a different order, totally selfless and altruistic. The self is engaged with the divine and not the ego.

In addition to the Godly authentic and the selfish-inauthentic meditational experiences, there is a third mystical experience that is neither revelatory nor ego-centered. It is an experience in which the meditator is sincere and on an honest quest for truth, and is not merely looking for answers to justify the ego, or validate some preconceived notions. Through the mystical experience, on his own, absent of any revelation, the meditator discovers and develops profound insights into life, and perhaps manages to gain a glimpse into the ultimate reality. Yet, since it is an experience sans revelation, he is operating in a void. He can only progress insofar as a finite creature can move within his own limited (finite) capacity. His realizations are ultimately circumscribed by human subjectivity and his own biographical input, and is therefore either humanly verifiable, which means to say that his discoveries are self-evident truths, or his epiphanies are merely speculative truths, which may indeed be true but can never be proven with certainty. However, a prophetic or *ruach hakodesh* revelational experience, which is derived from above, is more an objective truth, for it is a truth that is revealed from a higher source other than one's ego.

As it pertains to *ruach hakodesh,* meditation is but one of the numerous steps required to achieve it. On its own meditation is not sufficient. To reach even the lowest level of *ruach hakodesh* is an extremely difficult task, and one must be on an elevated spiritual state to achieve it. In fact, the Talmud mentions a ten-step protocol that one must master before one can even aspire to attain this elevated lofty condition of *ruach hakodesh*.[43] There have been various works in Jewish thought dedicated to piety and devoted to explaining each of these ten requisite steps.[44]

Previously, a question was raised regarding the Torah's perspective on the mystical and psychic experience. All the above mentioned experiences were encounters that were achieved by devotion and diligence. These are the mystical experiences. A psychic is one who possesses an innate sensitivity toward the nonphysical (spiritual) forces, to the degree that he is able to glimpse and even to predict the future. There is no doubt that there exists people who seem to posses these powers; the question, however, remains, how are these powers to be regarded? Are they to be looked upon with reverence or trepidation? Does the fact that one possesses an inborn tendency towards spirituality indicate that this person is inherently holier than others?

In Judaism, the prophet, one who is able to foresee future events with absolute accuracy and unmatched precision, is regarded with the greatest admiration; in fact, he is considered a person of stature.[45] Yet the psychic, possessed of the seemingly identical ability, is, at best, regarded with impartiality.

The difference lies in the source of these spiritual powers. A

---

43. Talmud *Avodah Zarah,* 20b. For a similar text see also: The end of the Mishnayot, tractate *Sotah,* chapter 9, *mishnah* 14.

44. Rabbi Moshe Chaim Luzzato writes that his entire work known as *Mesilat Yesharimk* is dedicated to explaining these spiritual steps. See: *Mesilat Yesharim, Hakdamah.* Rabbi Eliyahu ben Moshe Di Vidas elaborates with great detail on these ten steps. See: *Reshit Chachmah, Shar Ha'Ahavah,* chapter 11.

45. Rambam, *Moreh Nevuchim,* part 2, chapter 36.

prophet's powers do not stem from within him. It is an abundance, a divine influx that comes from without, from above. A prophetic experience occurs independent of the prophet, excepting the fact that he is a conduit. The powers are generated and initiated by the will of the Creator.[46] The prophet must prepare himself for the eventuality, but ultimately he is but a vehicle for the manifestation of the divine influx. The source of a psychic's abilities, on the other hand, is from within. Their spiritual intuition originates from within themselves. Because of the dissimilarity, there exists a marked distinction of quality between the psychic and the prophet, while the prophet is distinguished as a person of extreme humility and humbleness,[47] prevalent character traits of many psychics, though this is not always the case, are self-centeredness, ego, and at times, even arrogance.

In a sense, the innate psychic power is a talent like any other talent, much like a musical ability, an artistic sensitivity, and the like. Being that it is an inborn talent, a natural gift and not a revelation from above, it is subject to free will. Prophecy or any other form of divine inspiration is a direct expression of the spirit, an emanation originating from above. Consequently, it is intrinsically divine and noble.

Being that the psychic power is a human potential, like any

---

46. Rambam, *Hilchot Yesodei Ha Torah*, chapter 7, *halacha* 5; Rambam, *Moreh Nevuchim*, part 2, chapter 32. Rabbi Yoseph Albo, *Safer Haikkarim, maamor 3*, chapter 8, chapter 10; Rabbi Moshe Metrani, *Beit Elokim*, "*Shar Hayesodot*," chapter 19; Rabbi Meir Ben Gabbai, *Avodat Hakodesh*, part 4, chapter 20; Rabbi Yitzchak Aramah, *Akeidot Yitzchak*, "*Parshat Vayera*," shar 19; Rabbi Yakov Emdin, *Migdal Oz, Even Habochen*, p. 65.

47. Talmud *Nedarim*, 38a. Although the Rambam does not enumerate humility as a prerequisite to prophesy (Rambam, *Hilchot Yesodei Ha Torah*, chapter 7, halacha 1), nonetheless, as the commentaries explain, even according to the Rambam humility is an integral ingredient for prophesy. See: the Lubavitcher Rebbe, *Likutei Sichot*, vol 23, pp. 82–91. Humility is greater, and is the source of any positive quality trait the prophet needs to attain prophetic vision. See Rabbi Nisan Ben Reuven, *Derashot HaRan, derush* 5, p. 62.

other human potential it is amoral, that is to say, neither moral nor immoral. It can be utilized in a positive direction or used in a negative manner. The power itself has no intrinsic value; it is neither good nor bad. The psychic, spiritual powers given to man is subject to man's own free will.

CHAPTER
3

Extraordinary Phenomena Encountered Through Meditation

In the heightened meditative state or awareness, the boundaries of time and space are dimmed and it becomes possible for the meditator to experience phenomenal encounters otherwise unexplored.

One such phenomenon that can occur during meditation is *panoscopic vision.* In an ordinary state of consciousness, a person viewing an object will see but one side of the object at a time. Likewise, when one visualizes in one's mind a physical object that was previously seen, the object will appear in the mind in the manner in which it is viewed, namely, each side separately. When one meditates, and a higher state of consciousness is achieved, it is feasible to attain panoscopic vision, whence one can observe an object with all its sides and dimensions simultaneously. For example, one can visualize a cube and actually see all six sides at the same time.

There is a school in modern art called analytic cubism. This method of art was popularized by Pablo Picasso and Georges Braque. The objective of this style of art is to depict three-dimensional objects on two-dimensional surfaces. This was accomplished by means of overlapping the planes with strokes of the brush. In order for them to depict such an idea on canvas, they must have experienced this type of vision for themselves.

When one learns to control one's mental capacities, one can then visualize objects with a totally new and original perspective.

When the prophet Ezekiel describes his prophetic vision, he says that he saw angels with four distinct faces on each one of their sides: "The face of a man, and the face of a lion to the right . . . the face of an ox to the left . . . and the face of an eagle . . ."[1] He further emphasizes the fact that although they were in motion, "they did not turn as they went."[2] He was able to visualize, during his prophetic vision, all four sides of the angels simultaneously.

The mechanism of a prophetic experience resembles that of a dream. In both of these states of awareness the regular conventional state of consciousness is quieted. It is for this reason that at times prophecy is described in the Torah as a dream.[3] As a dream is marked by symbolism and metaphor, so is a prophetic experience. The prophet sees visions in the form of metaphor,[4] and owing to their similarities, and being that a dream is "a sixtieth of prophecy"[5] one can, during a dream (as in a state of prophecy), have a paradoxical experience.[6] While

---

1. Ezekiel, chapter 1, verse 10.

2. Ezekiel, chapter 1, verse 9, 12, and 17.

3. See: Numbers, chapter 12, verse 6; Job, chapter 33, verse 15.

4. See the following commentaries on the verse in Numbers, chapter 12, verse 6, Rashi; Rabbi Shlomo Yitzchaki, *Daat Zekeinim (A* collection of comments by the twelfth- and thirteenth-century Tosofists). Rabbi Chaim Ibn Attar, *Or Ha Chaim.*

All prophets (other than Moshe) received their prophetic vision without clarity. See: *Midrash Rabbah,* Leviticus, parshah 1, chapter 14; Rambam, *Hilchot Yesodei HaTorah,* chapter 7, halacha 2; Rambam, *Moreh Nevuchim,* part 2, chapters 41–45.

5. Talmud *Berachot,* 57b. See also: *Midrash Rabbah,* Genesis, parshah 17, chapter 5; *pariah* 44, chapter 17.

6. The Sixth Chabad Rebbe, Rabbi Yoseph Yitzchak, *Safer Hamaamorim 5700,* "Purim," p. 8.

dreaming, one has the potential to imagine an elephant passing through the eye of a needle.[7] When dreaming, it is conceivable for one to observe a physical three-dimensional object in a totally new light. The panoscopic vision, visualized by the prophet in a prophetic state, can also be seen in a meditative dreamlike state of awareness. If a dream state is reached while the person is awake, then this phenomenon can be experienced.

Another fascinating occurrence one may experience during meditation is *synesthesia,* during which a synthesis of the senses occurs. There are meditators who will characterize tastes as colors, and in recounting sights seen, may describe what they had seen as very loud, or perhaps, exceedingly quiet. In such a

---

7. Ibid. This assertion seems to contradict a well-known Talmudic assumption. The Talmud cites as proof that dreams stem from a person's thoughts during the day, from the fact that no one has ever seen (in a dream) an elephant passing through the head of a needle, since it cannot be imagined in a waking state. (Talmud: *Berachot,* 55b. See also: Rabbi Shimon Ben Tzemach Duran, *Magen Avot,* part 3, p. 70a.) The answer is that there are two types of dreams, dreams that stem from the dreamer himself, the person's subconscious wishes and desires, and dreams that come from above, in the form of a minor prophecy. (Talmud: *Berachot,* 57b; Midrash Rabbah, Genesis, parshah 17, chapter 5.) See for post-Talmudic sources: Rambam, *Moreh Nevuchim,* part 2, chapter 36 and chapter 45. Rabbi Levi Ben Gershon, *Melchemet Hashem, maamor* 2. Rabbi Chasdai Cresces (1340–1410) *Or Hashem* (Jerusalem: Sifrei Ramot, 1990), *maamor 2, klall* 4, chapter 3; Rabbi Menasha Ben Israel, *Nishmat Chaim,* (Jerusalem: Yerid HaSefarim, 1995), *maamor* 3, chapter 5; Rabbi Schneur Zalman of Liadi, *Shulchan Aruch Harav,* "Orach Chaim," chapter 288:7. The reason why some people have prophetic dreams while others don't solely depends on what level of spirituality the dreamer is on. If during the day a person is preoccupied with materialistic gain, their primary focus is on the physical, then in their dreams they will see their wishes being fulfilled. Their dreams will project in actuality their subconscious desires. However, if a person is more spiritual, then their dreams will also be more spiritual, and thus their dreams will be a sixtieth of prophesy. (Talmud *Berachot,* 57b.) Rabbi Avraham Ben HaRambam, *Sefer Hamaspik Leovedei Hashem,* "Erech Ha'Prishut."

state there is a blurring of the senses, and the person may describe tastes by color and colors by shape.[8]

Generally, the senses tend to be compartmentalized. Each sense is associated with its own compartment in the brain. However, in an expanded state of consciousness, the barriers between the senses blur, fusing together, so the sense of sight can perceive sounds, and vice versa, the auditory sense can hear colors.

This can actually occur in a normal state of consciousness as well. For instance, upon hearing a melody being played, a feeling of color and texture can be evoked. Hearing a mellow tune, one may identify the tune with lighter colors, and upon hearing a powerful tune, a forceful song, one may associate the tune with darker colors.[9] The reason for this is because the barriers are never truly absolute, and in an expanded state of consciousness the barriers become porous, until they nearly meld. A person may hear a piece of music, and simultaneously see music in visual patterns. A noted author writes of a future culture, a civilization in which the elite intellectuals are engaged in a game made up of symbols, namely, beads, which contain all of culture and knowledge. They arranged the beads as musical notes, and instead of actually playing music, the patterns of the beads substitute for the sounds of music.[10]

In describing the historic scene at Mount Sinai, the Torah says: "The entire nation *saw* the thunder."[11] They saw what one ordinarily hears, and they heard what is normally seen.[12] At the

---

8. See: Dr. Richard E Cytowic, *The Man Who Tasted Shapes* (Bradford: 1998).

9. Rabbi Shlomo Zalman of Kapust (1830–1900), *Magen Avot, "Parshat Yitro."*

10. Herman Hesse, *The Glass Bead Game (Magister Ludic)* (Canada: Henry Holt, 1990).

11. Exodus, chapter 20, verse 15.

12. Spiritual synesthesia. See: Exodus, chapter 20, verse 15; Rabbi

height of the Sinaic moment, the greatest collective mystical
encounter ever experienced, there was a total blurring of the
senses.[13]

The 18th century Chassidic master, Rabbi Shlomo of Karlin
would hod in his hands a sugar cube while drinking his tea. His
son once questioned him regarding this. "Father," he asked, "if
you wish to sweeten your drink, why keep it in your hand, and
if you don't enjoy the tea sweetened, then why hold the sugar at
all?" His father did not reply, but merely smiled. Later, upon fin-
ishing his tea, he placed the sugar cube on the table and asked
his son to taste it. His son did so, and was amazed to find that

---

Shlomo Yitzhaki, Rashi on this verse; Midrash Mechilta on this verse. See also:
Targum Yonothan Ben Uziel, ad loc. In the Midrash *Mechilta* there is an argument
on whether they saw the sounds and heard what was usually seen, or not. Rabbi
Akiva is of the opinion that they did see the sounds. In Talmudic tradition
Rabbi Akiva is known, as a great mystic. (See, e.g., Talmud *Chagigah*, 14b.)
And perhaps he spoke of this phenomenon (spiritual synesthesia) from person-
al experience, from mystical experiences he once had. In the same vein, Rabbi
Yonothan Ben Uziel (who also interpreted this verse to mean that they saw the
sounds and heard what is usually seen) was also a great mystic. (See: Talmud
Sukkah, 28a; Talmud, *Megillah*, 3a.)

Another explanation for this phenomenon, the seeing of sounds, is as follows: Just like when it is cold, the words you utter create a visible affect, at the
giving of the Torah, a thick, dark cloud descended upon Mount Sinai. Thus, it
caused the words of God to be (so to speak) seen. See: Rabbi Bachya Ibn
Pakudah, *Torat HaNefesh* (Paris: 1896), chapter 3; Rabbi Menachem Recanti
Parshat Vayera, *Levush Malchut*, vol. 7 (New York: Gross Brosl, 1965), p. 26a.
Rabbi David Ben Zimra (1470–1572), *Magen Dovid* (Jerusalem: Da'at Yoseph,
1992), Ot Tet, pp. 19–20. Rabbi Meir Ben Gabbai, *Tolaat Yakov* (Jerusalem:
Makor Chaim, 1967), "*Sod Tefila Meumad*," p. 33. Alternatively, they saw the
angels that were created through the words of God. See: Rabbi Moshe Alshich,
Exodus, chapter 20, verses 15–6.

13. Rabbi Ze'ev of Zhitomir (????–1800), *Or HaMeir* (Israel: Even Israel,
1994), Megilat Ester, p. 199; Parshat Ekev, p. 184. See: Rabbi Michal of
Zlotchov, *Malchei BaKodesh* (Israel: Mechon Zechut Avut, 1998), "*Chamisha
Arazim*." Parshat Yitro, p. 20. See also: Rabbi Klunimus Kalman, *Maor Vashemesh*
(Jerusalem: Even Yisrael, 1992), *Parshat Mattot*, p. 506.

the sugar was not at all sweet anymore. When his father left the room, the son understood the phenomenon as follows; being that his father was so completely absorbed in the oneness of God, his human faculties had also merged into a unified oneness; consequently, his sense of taste was no longer limited to the taste buds in his mouth. Rather, all his senses had joined as one, and therefore he was able to absorb taste through his fingers as well.[14]

There are various types of meditations whose primary goal is to experience *nothingness*. This may seem strange to a novice who has little experience with meditation. Why, they wonder, would a person want to reach a state of nothing?

Interestingly, seekers of truth will report that often, in their quest for answers, in their search for a something, they have instead found an emptiness, a feeling of nothingness. Yet, paradoxically, it is in this state of nothingness, that they have found what they were looking for. They encounter solace and comfort in the discovery of this nothingness.

But what is it that they have found? The Kabbalah tells us that the world was created *yesh m'ayin, ex nihilo*—something from nothing.[15] The "nothing" being the Creator. The reason we call God *ayin*—nothing—is simply that God cannot be grasped or characterized.[16] God is beyond all definition, beyond

---

14. See: Eliezer Shtainman, *Be'er HaChassidut, Chachmei Ha'Chassidut* (Israel: Mochon Kemach), pp. 63–64.

15. The word *barah*—created—connotes a creation out of nothing. See: Midrash *HaGadal*, Genesis (in the beginning), Ramban, Genesis, chapter 1, verse 1; Rambam, *Moreh Nevuchim*, part 3, chapter 10; Rabbi Avraham Abulafia, *Chayay Olam Habah* (Jerusalem: 1999), p. 48. Rabbi Schneur Zalman of Liadi, *Tanya, Shar Hayichud VaHaEmuna*, chapter 2; Rabbi Dan Yitzchak Abarbanel, Genesis, "In the Beginning," "Explanation of the word created." *Mifalot Elokim* (Jerusalem: Otzer Hapaskim, *1993), maamor* 2, chapter 5; Rabbi Chaim of Volozhin, *Nefesh HaChaim*, shar 1, chapter 13, in the note.

16. Rabbi Moshe Corodovero, *Pardess Rimonim* (Jerusalem: 1962), shar

even the definition of being beyond definition.[17] Accordingly, God is best described as being *ayin*. Reaching the *ayin* means to pierce the coarse veil of physical reality and go beyond the surface, and in this manner, encounter the divine.

One may experience this sensation of nothingness on a cognitive level or on an emotional level, and perhaps even by visualizing nothingness.

Experiencing nothingness in the mind and heart is accomplished by being able to still the mind, encountering a complete withdrawal from all perceptions both internal as well as external and thereby reaching a level of emptiness, nothingness. To reach nothingness is to achieve a state where one's mind is emptied of all thoughts, perceptions, and sensations, whether physical or spiritual, and in which all one feels and perceives, is nothingness.

A more advanced level would be to conceptualize nothingness. The 19th-century Chassidic Master, Rabbi DovBer of Chabad, was lying ill in bed, and overheard his doctor saying that the reason for his illness was that he aspired to reach a level of transcendence that is otherworldly. He attempted to touch and visualize that which is beyond the veil of the physical. Upon hearing this, the Rebbe sat up and asked the doctor, not ungently, "How do you presume to know of such aspirations, when you cannot even imagine that which is beyond the mere surface lever" (The Rebbe knew the character of the physician well.) In an attempt to prove to the Rebbe that he was capable of relating to his dilemma, the doctor replied, "I can imagine what is beyond. For example," he said, and he pointed to a table in the room, "you see, Rebbe, this table in front of us. I am now imagining the table lifting above the ground and twirling in empty space." The Rebbe smiled and replied, "It is indeed true

---

23, chapter 1. See also: Rabbi Yoseph Gikatalia (1248–1323), *Shaarei Orah*, (New York: Moriah, 1985), shar 5, p. 87, shar 9, p. 185.

17. See: Rabbi Schneur Zalman of Liadi, *Tanya, Shar HaYichud VeHaEmunah*, chapter 9.

that what you are imagining is to an extent a transcendent thought, yet, this is not the real transcendence. You see," he continued, "both the table and the space it occupies exist in a physical dimension. What you envisioned was a transcendence within the parameters of space. What I wish to encounter is beyond that. A level of nothingness that surpasses all physical dimensions. A conceptualization of what is beyond."[18]

All that exists in this world is defined by physical dimensions, and being that everything is comprised of time and space there is no true emptiness or nothingness in our world as we know it. In our attempt to conceptualize nothingness, we may visualize a black empty space, a complete vacuum of nothingness. However, black is itself a color and thus a definition. The color black and space are both a something by their very definition; thus, blackness, or empty space, cannot be the accurate description of nothingness. We entrap it within our physical domain, as we attempt to envision it. In our ordinary way of thinking about anything, we tend to reify things, including that of nothingness. At a more advanced level, one may envision pure transparent emptiness,[19] that is, without any coloring whatsoever. The highest level, however, is the experience of pure nothingness.

Parenthetically, on a level much closer to our mundane state of mind, the depiction and visualization of nothingness has been, and continues to be, a predominant feature in Oriental art. Void and emptiness are often the most prominent features on the

18. See: *Otzar Sipury Chabad,* vol *16* (Israel: Kehot, 1997), p. 134.

19. The Torah says that under God's feet the Israelites saw *livenath hasapir.* Exodus, chapter 24, verse 10. Traditionally, *livenath hasapir* is translated as a "brickwork of sapphire," but it can also be translated as "transparency of crystal," transparent without any color, i.e., pure empty space. See: Rabbi Ovadyah *Seforno,* Exodus 24:10. Rambam, *Moreh Nevuchim,* part 1, chapter 28. See also: Rambam, *Hilchot Yesodei HaTorah,* chapter 3, *halacha* 1.

artist's canvas.[20] The concept of empty space is depicted in today's contemporary American design. A trend of advertisement design in America today is to place a small image of the product one wishes to sell upon a large span of negative space. However, this type of art is truly visual and registers in our normal perception of reality.

Superconscious meditation is another possible phenomenon of the meditative state. It occurs when the meditator becomes unified with nature. The meditator experiences a complete oneness with nature, a place where object and subject, observer and observed, cease to exist separately and merge as a whole. We feel sometimes that perhaps we can observe our surroundings in a completely subjective manner, yet scientifically it has been proven that this is not possible. There is no truly objective observer. There has even been a suggestion put forward by some scientists to erase the word *observer* from our vernacular and exchange it for the word *participator.*[21] For there is no true objectivity in this world, only participators.[22] When one meditates on nature, one is participating in the wonders surrounding him, and through this participation, one attains the sensation of being an indivisible part of the nature that envelops him.

The incredible beauty and wondrous, intricate details of nature has inspired meditation throughout the ages.[23] Rabbi

---

20. See: Rudolf Otto, *The Idea of the Holy* (Oxford University Press, 1958), chapter 9, p. 69.

21. A suggestion by John Wheeler; quoted by Fritjof Capra, *The Tao of Physics* (Boston: Shambhala, 1991), p. 141.

22. William James writes that the superconscious state is when one's soul has lost its finite form and becomes one with the universal soul, becoming immortal and omnipotent. See: *The Varieties of Religious Experience,* lecture on mysticism, p. 400.

23. Rabbi Bachya Ibn Pakudah writes of the necessity to meditate on nature and through the meditation recognize the Creator's greatness. See: *Chovot Halevavot, "Shar Habechinah,"* chapter 2. Rabbi Eliyahu ben Moshe Di Vidas writes that it is a mitzvah to gaze on the beauty of nature. See: *Reshit*

Nachman of Breslov, the famed Chassidic Master, was an advocate of meditation in the open fields.[24] He speaks of nature as being alive. The winter, he writes, is a time of impregnation, and all the nature, the grass, and the trees are asleep. Spring, he says, is a time of birth and rebirth, when all are awakened. It is then, in the joyous springtime, the most opportune time to meditate in the open meadow, for nature in its entirety, the grass, and the trees, join the meditator in his prayers and inspiration.[25] All of nature is meshed in the experience of meditation. Yet the objective of joining with nature, is not an end for itself, nature for nature's sake. Rather, it is to be unified with the source of nature, to connect with the Creator of those very wonders, to unite with the source of all reality.

A human being innately requires the companionship of other creations[26] and particularly the friendship of other human beings.[27] Rabbi Tzodok of Lublin, a 19th-century Chassidic Master, writes that a person who is lacking in companionship and finds himself to be lonely, should contemplate Torah. Torah is the fountainhead and blueprint of all creation[28] and thus

Chachmah, "*Shar HaKedusha,*" chapter 8, p. 161. See also: Isaiah, chapter 40, verse 26; Psalms, chapter 8, verse 4.

24. Rabbi Nachman of Breslov, *Likutei Moharan* (Jerusalem: Toraht HaNetzach, 1997), part 2, chapter 25; *Chayei Moharan* (Jerusalem: 1995), part 2, chapter 230; *Likutei Aytzot* (Brooklyn: Moriah, 1976), "*Hitbodedut,*" chapter 12, p. 59. *Sichot Haran* (Jerusalem: Netzach Yisroel), chapter 227.

25. Rabbi Nachman of Breslov, *Chayei Moharan,* part 1, chapter 72.

26. See: Talmud *Berachot,* 6b.

27. See: Rambam, *Moreh Nevuchim,* part 2, chapter 40; part 1, chapter 72. "Man cannot survive alone." See also: Rambam *Hilchot De'ot,* chapter 6, *halacha* 1. Rabbi Shimon Ben Tzemach Duran, *Magen Avot,* part 2, chapter 1, p. 8b. Thus *a metzora*—a leper—is considered not alive (Talmud Nedarim, 64b) for a *metzora* must live alone (Leviticus 13:46). The Talmud says friends or death. Talmud *Taanit,* 23a.

28. "God looked into the Torah and created the world accordingly," *Zohar,* part 2, p. 161a. See also: *Midrash Rabbah* Genesis, parsha 1, chapter 1; *Midrash Tanchuma, Bereshit,* chapter 1.

through meditating on Torah (the origin of nature), one connects with the totality of creation. Through the study of Torah one's loneliness will subside.[29] By way of the Torah meditation, one connects and joins with nature via their source, through the eyes of the Infinite. One eventually attains by this means, a deep and internalized understanding of the nature and structure of reality. The uniqueness of such a connection is such that one's perception of reality is not limited to that of a human, which is a confined and finite perception. Rather, the reality of the physical world is seen through a transcendent perspicacity, which is infinite and limitless. In this way, when our doors of perception are cleansed and thrown wide open, we perceive everything as it really is, infinite.

There are other fascinating phenomena attainable in advanced stages of meditation. In the following chapters many of these phenomena, particularly those that are pertinent to the Jewish experience, will be illustrated.

---

29. Rabbi Tzodok of Lublin (1823–1900), *Resisei Layla* (Bnei Brak: Yehadut, 1967), chapter 1. For this reason the Talmud says that when one is traveling alone one should study Torah. Talmud *Eruvin*, 54a.

CHAPTER
4

Preparing for the
Meditative Session

The meditational experience is one that highly involves the mind and psyche of the person who meditates. Being that one's mindset and mood is greatly persuaded by both external and internal influences, it becomes apparent that for the ultimate success of the meditative experience one must be properly primed to achieve a heightened state of awareness. This meditative temperament can be effected through various preparational techniques.

As mentioned previously, there are various preparations the prophets would undergo to enter a prophetic state of consciousness. They would practice *hitbodedut*—literal seclusion—as well as mental isolation (i.e., internal seclusion). They would play music. They would attain a degree of stoicism, indifference to all matters physical. Also mentioned is the position they would assume while receiving the prophetic influx. Now, although parallels can be drawn between the preparation for prophecy and the preparation for meditation, nonetheless, at some point the lines diverge, since prophecy and meditation are inherently dissimilar. Prophecy is a quest to receive a divine flow from above, and meditation is a very human venture, to expand human consciousness. Therefore, not every preparation for a prophetic experience is necessarily fitting for a meditative experience.

For example, the idea of playing music. According to the Talmud, the holy spirit rests only with one who is joyous.[1] For this reason, a prophet would play music to enter a joyful state fitting to receive the spirit of God.[2] Furthermore, it is said, that music is the language of the spiritual worlds, and it is through music that a prophet can communicate with the divine.[3] However, we have no indication that joy and its antecedent music is a requisite for meditation. Perhaps meditation can (also) be practiced when one is more somber and serious. Consequently, the preparations that will be discussed are those that have particular relevance to the meditative experience.

Every existence within creation, Kabbalah teaches, has three dimensions—universe, year, and soul.[4] In modern terms, these would be space, time, and energy. Coincidentally, the preparations for meditation can be divided into these three

---

1. Talmud *Shabbat*, 30b.

2. Rambam, *Yesodei HaTorah*, chapter 7, *halacha* 4; Rabbi Avraham Ben HaRambam, *Sefer Hamaspik Leovedei Hashem*, "*Erech Ha'Prishut*," p. 129; Rabbeinu Bachya, Exodus, chapter 18, verse 12; *Kad Kemach, Roth Hashanah* 2, p. 379; Rabbi Shimon Ben Tzemach Duran, *Magen Avot*, part 2, chapter 2, p. 15b; Rabbi Moshe Corodovero, *Shiur Komah*, "*Nevuah*," p. 60; Rabbi Chaim Vital, *Sharei Kedusha*, part 2, *shar* 4; Rabbi Meir Ben Gabbai, *Avodot Hakodesh*, part 4, chapter 23; Rabbi Yehudah Muscato (1520–1590), *Nefutzhot Yehudah* (Israel: Mishot, 2000), pp. 4–5; Rabbi Yonathan Eibechuvetz (1690–1764), *Tifferet Yonathan*, "*Parshat Beshalach*," chapter 15, verse 20; Rabbi Yakov Emdin, *Migdal Oz*, "*Even Bochen*," p. 66; Rabbi Yisrael of Modzitz (1848–1920), *Divrei Yisrael*, "*Parshat Mikketz*," *Maamor Echad M'Remazei Chanukah*.

3. *Zohar*, part 3, p. 223b; Rabbi Meir Ben Gabbai, *Avodot Hakodesh*, part 3, chapter 10; Rabbi Nachman of Breslov, *Likutei Moharan*, part 1, chapter 3; *Likutei Aytzot, Neginah* 3.

4. In the ancient Kabbalistic text *Sefer Yetzirah* (a text that is mentioned in the Talmud *Sanhedrin*, 65b), it speaks of three dimensions, universe, year, and soul. See: *Sefer Yetzirah*, chapter 3, mishnah 3. See also: Rabbi Yehudah HaLevi,

categories. In the domain of soul, preparations must be made internally before meditation can occur. Also in this category is the question of with whom one should meditate. In the domain of time, the part of the day that is most conducive for maximum effect should be chosen. In universe, the location for meditation must be picked with care.

Souls

A prerequisite for any type of meditation is being in the proper mood to meditate, making certain that physically as well as mentally, one is comfortable and at ease, and in a fitting mental paradigm. For this reason, many find that playing or listening to music can be the appropriate device to cause relaxation.[5] Although it is not necessarily important for the meditator to be happy while meditating, nonetheless, if one is depressed the mind becomes cloudy and opaque.[6] Playing or listening to the right music, can relieve a person from a depressed mood, and cause them to become joyous.[7]

Once fully relaxed, one must make certain to be in a comfortable position. The manner in which one holds one's

---

5. Generally music is used to relax and calm. See: Rabbi Shem Tov Ben Yoseph Ibn Falaquera (1225–1290), *Safer Hamevakesh*. (This text was once printed with the endorsement of the *Chida*, Rabbi Chaim Yoseph David Azulay.) (Reprinted, Jerusalem: Mekorot, 1970) p. 12, p. 86. Therefore, music is used for therapeutic purposes. See: Samuel 1, chapter 17; Radak ad loc; Rambam, *Shemonah Perakim*, chapter 5; Rabbi Moshe Yichie Elimelech of Levertov, *Safer Shemirat HaDa'at*, "*Aimrei Tal, ma'amar Nigun*" (Bnei Brak: Ginzei MaHaritz, 1986), pp. 5–7. Rabbi Yehudah Muscato, *Nefutzhot Yehudah*, p. 5.

6. Rabbi Menachem Ben Shlomo, the Meiri, writes that when a person is depressed, his mind is closed. See his commentary on Talmud *Shabbat*, 30a.

7. Rabbi Schneur Zalman of Liadi, *Maamorei Admur Hazoken*, "*Inyonim*," p. 403; Rabbi Nachman of Breslov, *Likutei Aytzot, neginah* 8, p. 138; Rabbi Pinchas of Koritz, *Midrash Pinchas*, p. 89, chapter 14.

posture during meditation plays a significant role in the success
of the experience. Many people, when envisioning a meditation, imagine the meditator to be sitting in the lotus position
with his feet crossed beneath his body. However, it should be
noted that this posture originates in the East, where this position is quite customary. Strolling along the streets of the Far
East, one will observe groups of people sitting on the floor,
crouching for a game of checkers, or merely squatting for a
chat. People of the East are accustomed to sit lower than the
people of the West. The position they meditate in, the lotus
position, is for them a very comfortable posture. However, for
Westerners, who are not accustomed to sit this way, this position is usually uncomfortable. Therefore, the meditator should
find a position in which they are most comfortable. The
definition of comfortable is a position that will cause the least
distractions possible.

The Torah makes reference to a position where one places
the head between the knees. Elijah, the master Prophet, would
pray in this manner.[8] Again, the problem with this position is
that it may be extremely uncomfortable and for some perhaps
even painful. Interestingly enough, the commentaries explain
that the reason Elijah prayed in this position was not because of
its comfort, but to the contrary, precisely because it was
uncomfortable.[9] When Elijah prayed in this posture, he was
beseeching God for rain. It was a time of drought, the fields
were barren, the reservoirs were empty. Elijah felt that if he
prayed in this awkward position, his prayers would be answered

---

8. Kings 1, chapter 18, verse 42. The commentaries explain that this
position was used as an introduction to prophecy. See: Rabbi Dan Yitzchak
Abarbenal, ad loc. The Midrash says that he meditated and prayed in the position of his head between the knees, his head facing his privates, so to recall the
merit of the mitzvah of circumcision. See: *Midrash Rabbah,* Leviticus, parsha 31,
chapter 4.

9. See Rabbi Levi Ben Gershon, the Ralbag, on Kings 1, chapter 18,
verse 42.

quickly. He surmised that God would not want to see him in agony for too long.[10]

Another classic position mentioned in the Torah involves kneeling with the hands outstretched to the heavens above.[11] In the daily prayers there are segments of prayer where one prays standing, others parts where one prays sitting, while other portions, prostrating oneself.[12] By positioning ourselves in

---

10. This position, as well, has particular relevance in attaining prophesy. The knees represent the *sefirot* of *netzach* and *hod*, eternity and splendor (see: the introduction by the prophet Elijah to *Tikunei Zohar)*, which says that these *sefirot* are the source of prophesy. See: *Zohar,* part 3, p. 35a; Rabbi Yoseph Gikatalia, *Shaarei Orah, shar* 3–4, p. 70; Rabbi Yehudah Chayit on *Ma'arechet Elokut* (Jerusalem: Mokor Chaim, 1963), chapter 4, p. 65b; Rabbi Schneur Zalman of Liadi, *Tanya,* "*Shar HaYichud VeHaEmunah*," chapter 5; Rabbi Nachman of Breslov, *Likutei Moharan,* part 1, chapter 3. This position also represents a state of complete purity and integration. It symbolizes the position a fetus is in when it is in its mother's womb. See: Talmud *Niddah,* 30a.

This position is also mentioned in the Talmud with regard to prayer (Talmud *Berachot,* 34b) and with regard to study (Talmud *Niddah,* 30b) and with regard to repentance (Talmud *Avodah Zarah,* 17a). This position of the head between the knees is also favored by many post-Talmudic Kabbalists. See: Rabbi Hai Gaon (939—1038) quoted in *Ha'Ktov,* on *Eyin Yakov, Chagigah,* 14b, #11; Rabbi Yoseph Tzayach (1505–1573), *Even HaShoham,* the introduction.

11. See: Chronicles 2, chapter 6, verse 13; Ezra, chapter 9, verse 5. See also: Exodus, chapter 17, verse 11 as explained in Midrash *Pirkei D'Rebbe Eliezer,* chapter 44. In Kabbalah it is taught that spreading the hands (with the appropriate mystical intentions) has tremendous spiritual potential. (It alludes to one receiving spiritual energy from on high.) Thus, there are limitations for how long a person can stretch their hands. See: *Sefer HaBahir,* chapter 138; Ramban, Exodus, chapter 17, verse 11; *Rabbeinu Bachya,* Exodus, chapter 17, verse 12; Rabbi Moshe Cordevero, *Pardas Rimonim, shar* 15, chapter 3; Rabbi Yitzchak of Acco, *Meirat Einayim,* "*Parshat Beshalach*," chapter 17, verse 16; Rabbi Menachem Azaryah De Fano (1548–1620) *Asarah Maamorot* (Jerusalem: Yismah Lev-Torat Moshe, 1998), "*Maamor Chikur Din,*" part 1, chapter 22.

12. The Midrash says that Israel will be redeemed in the merit of prostrating in prayer. See: *Midrash Yalkut Shimoni,* Samuel 1, chapter 1:28.

these three postures during prayer, we are mimicking the three psitions we find in the Torah that Moses prayed in.[13] They are sitting,[14] standing,[15] prostrating himself.[16] In assuming these positions in prayer, we are copying Moses, thereby hoping to succeed as he did, in beseeching God, and at the very least, we are reminded of Moses, and we petition in his merit.

Many early Kabbalists would sit on the floor when studying and meditating on the Kabbalah. They did so in order to arouse their students to humility.[17]

However, comfort is key to meditation, lest the lack of it distract. Therefore, if one finds that standing is more comfortable, and enhances one's concentration, then stand. Conversely, it is also important to note, that the position one meditates in should not be overwhelmingly comfortable and relaxing. For example, using a recliner may be a bad idea for meditation. Being too comfortable may cause one to be drowsy, and perhaps even

---

The Talmud says that when Rabbi Akiva would pray alone, he would prostrate and kneel so often that if one were to see him in one corner of the room and would leave, upon returning, one would find him at another corner. See: Talmud *Berachot*, 31a; *Midrash Tanchuma*, "Parshat Chayei Sarah," chapter 5. Today, however, we do not actually prostrate during prayer. See: *Shulchan Aruch*, "Orach Chaim," chapter 131. (Though see: Rambam, *Hilchot Tefilah*, chapter 5, halacha 14; Rabbi Chaim Vital, *Shulchan Aruch Arizal* (Jerusalem: 1998), p. 33.)

13. Rabbi Yakkov Ben Asher, *Tur*, "Orach Chaim," chapter 131.

14. Deuteronomy, chapter 9, verse 9.

15. Deuteronomy, chapter 10, verse 10.

16. Deuteronomy, chapter 9, verse 18. (See also: Numbers, chapter 16, verse 4. According to the explanation by the Rashbam, Rabbi Shlomo Ben Meir (1085–1174). See also: Numbers, chapter 17, verse 10. As interpreted by Rabbi Avraham Ibn Ezra (1089–1164).

17. See: Rabbi Moshe Corodovero, *Or Ne'erav* (Israel: 1965), part 3, chapter 2, p. 23. It seems that general Torah study (not only the Kabbalah), was done sitting on the ground. See: Talmud *Megillah*, 21a; Rashi, *Shelo*; Rambam, *Hilchot Talmud Torah*, chapter 4, *halacha* 2; *Shulchan Aruch*, "Yoreh Deah," chapter 246:9.

fall asleep. (Incidentally, falling asleep during meditation can at times be dangerous.)

Just as there are physical distractions that must be taken into account, there are also mental, psychological diversions that must be quieted prior to meditating. Since human beings are social animals, we tend to be influenced by other people and seek their judgment and evaluation, as well as approval. How many times have you wanted to do something, which may seem somewhat bizarre, but you did not do it, because you were thinking, "What will the neighbors say?" Often behavior is controlled by other people's judgments. Many people would love to meditate, yet, they fear that if other people found out, they would be regarded as strange or at best, eccentric.

An important step to meditation is realizing that you are your own person, and reaching a level where you are indifferent to all criticism. The Psalmist sings, "I have set the Lord before me at all times."[18] The word the verse uses for "I have set" is *shivisi,* which in Hebrew can be translated as equanimity The Kabbalah tells us that in order for the prophet to receive the divine flow, he had to first attain a degree of equanimity. It was a crucial state of awareness that the prophet entered prior to achieving actual prophecy.[19] The Baal Shem Tov teaches that this elevated state is appropriate for every human being, and at all times.

But what is equanimity? The Baal Shem Tov describes it as a feeling that life is always as it should be. Whether people praise or condemn you, or if you are eating foods that you relish, or foods that you dislike, it is completely irrelevant to you. In a sense all of life's pettiness becomes totally insignificant.[20] You

---

18. Psalms, chapter 16, verse 8.

19. See: Chapter 1, footnote 22.

20. Rabbi Yisrael Ba'al Shem Tov, *Tzavos Horivash,* p. 1; *Keter Shem Tov,* chapter 220, p. 28b; *Likutei Yekarim* (Jerusalem: Yeshivat Toldot Aharon, 1974), chapter 179; *Or Haemet* (Brooklyn, 1960), p. 164; *Magid Devarav*

do not take any of these trivial judgments seriously. Neither the shallow superficial recognition, nor the apathetic frivolous criticism, makes any difference. You do what you know you have to do. This act of stoicism, so to speak, is an appropriate predisposition to meditation. In addition, being in this state of awareness can also assist one in the actual meditation. When one is in this lofty, elevated state, concentration is intensified, for there are no diversions.

With whom should one meditate? Generally, it is advised that a meditator should find a master, a teacher, who is well versed in the art of meditation, and himself a practitioner of meditation. A teacher can give you the suitable meditation, and the appropriate direction and goal for the meditation. But finding a teacher can be a tricky endeavor. The Talmud cautions a student to study Torah only from a teacher of the highest caliber.[21] A good measurement of a teacher's qualities is the degree to which the teachings are integrated into the teacher's life. The student should take note of spiritual stature as well as interaction with other people. Additionally, one should also take notice and see if the teacher is in it for an ego trip, or is truly a

---

Leyokav, Likutei Amorim, Or Torah, Psalms, 16:8, chapter 179. Rabbi Michal of Zlotchov, *Malchei BaKodesh,* p. 98.

The idea of equanimity in general divine service has been expressed throughout in Jewish thought. See: Rabbi Bachya Ibn Pakudah, *Chovot HaLevavot, "Shar Hakniah,"* chapter 7; *"Shar Yichud Hama'ase,"* chapter 5; Rabbi Yoseph Caro, *Magid Mesharim* (Jerusalem: Orah, 1960), *"Parshat Beshalach,"* p. 57a; Rabbi Alexander Zisskind (????–1794), *Yesod V'Shoresh Ha'Avodah* (reprinted Jerusalem: 1978) (when this work was first published it received an endorsement by the Chassidic rebbe, Rabbi Levi Yitzchak of Berdichov), *"Avodat H'lev,"* chapter 10.

21. Talmud *Moed Katan,* 17a; Rambam, *Hilchot Talmud Torah,* chapter 4, *halacha* 1. Today this ruling includes every student without exception. See: Rabbi Shabsai HaKohen, *Shach, Shulchan Aruch, "Yoreh Deah,"* chapter 246:8.

refined human being who wishes to help other people spiritually.[22]

If one cannot find a teacher, then a trusted companion may substitute. The Baal Shem Tov teaches that it is essential to have a friend to meditate with.[23] This directive echoes the opinion of the great Kabbalists throughout the ages, who have also advocated the idea of meditating with another person, a confidant.[24] With a trusted friend, one can freely discuss the meditation and its implications. The simple advantage of meditating with a partner, as opposed to meditating alone, is that after the meditation one can discuss and review what has transpired during the meditation. One can better assess what needs correction and improvement, and slowly work on perfecting the meditative techniques.

There is a Chassidic tale that illustrates the im portance of meditating with a partner. Once, two young 18th-century Chassidic masters, Rabbi Avraham the Angel, and 's colleague Rabbi Schneur Zalman of Liadi, were engaged in deep mystical study. All of a sudden Reb Zalman noticed that Reb Avraham was slowly drifting away. He realized that his companion was being swallowed in the ecstasy of his experience. Hurriedly, Reb Zalman rushed to the kitchen to retrieve a bagel with butter. Upon returning, he handed Reb Avraham the bagel and forced him to have a bite. Subsequently, Reb Avraham *returned* to the mundane materialistic domain. The consumption of a physical object, the bagel, forced a rejoining of soul and body. An ancient text of Kabbalah advises that "If your heart runs, return to the

---

22. The Talmud's description of a suitable teacher is one who is immaculate as an angel. Talmud *Moed Katan*, 17a.

23. Rabbi Yisrael Baal Shem Tov, *Tzavoas Horivash*, chapter 63; *Likutei Yekarim*, chapter 13; *Or Haemet*, p. 205.

24. See: Rabbi Eliyahu ben Moshe Di Vidas, *Reshit Chachmah*, "Shar HaKedusha," chapter 6, p. 141a.

place."[25] Focus on something physical. Eat something, drink something, smell a pleasurable fragrance, listen to a piece of music, and so on.

Rabbi DovBer, the early 19th-century Chabad Rebbe, had a musical ensemble play for him. His son-in-law, Rabbi Menachem Mendel, was once asked why his father-in-law had this ensemble. He answered that music was played to ground my father-in-law's soul from expiring. If not for the music, he might have drifted into the divine. The point is that in an advanced stage of meditation, when reaching a level of transcendence, and feeling that one is being carried away, swallowed up in the ecstasy, it is important to immediately shift the focus to something physical. Having a partner to meditate with will help one to concentrate on the meditation without having to worry about being swallowed up by it. Knowing that one is not alone in the room while meditating will give reassurance that if one begins to slip away, the companion will bring one back to reality.

Many Kabbalists encourage the study of an ethical text daily.[26] Reading and learning a practical moral code assists the

---

25. *Sefer Yetzirah,* chapter 1, Mishnah 8; Or as the Zohar says, "If your heart runs return to one," *Tikunei Zohar,* "*Hakdamah,*" 6a, meaning, if your heart runs and seeks to transcend the physical, return to "one," return to your destiny of creation, which is to inhabit and transform the physical to spiritual. See: Rabbi Schneur Zalman of Liadi, *Tanya,* chapter 50; *Likutei Torah,* "*Parshat Korach,*" p. 55b. See also: *Sefer Hamamorim Ranat* (5659) (New York: Kehot, 1984), p. 213, footnote. Rabbi Avraham Abulafia speaks of using pleasurable fragrance to ground one in meditation. See: *Chayay Olam HaBah,* pp. 146–148.

26. See: Rabbi Chaim Yoseph David Azulay, *Avodat Hakodesh, Tziparon Shamir,* chapter 4:53, p. 94. Rabbi Yisrael Baal Shem Tov, *Tzavoas Horivash,* chapter 1 and chapter 117; *Baal Shem Tov Al HaTorah,* "*Parshat Vaetchanan,*" p. 496; *Likutei Yekarim,* chapter 198; Rabbi Yonathan Eibeschuvetz, *Yarot D'vash* (Jerusalem: Levin-Epshtain), part 1, p. 73a; Rabbi Pinchas of Koritz, *Midrash Pinchas* (Jerusalem: 1971), chapter 31, p. 90; *Aimrei Pinchas* (Bnei Brak: Mishor, 1988), p. 193; Rabbi Elimelech of Lizhensk, *Noam Elimelech* (Jerusalem: Mesamchei Lev, 1999), "*Hanhagat HaAdam,*" 4; Rabbi

meditator in bringing focus and direction to the meditation. It, so to speak, reinforces the meditator's connection to earthbound reality.

Universe

Finding the right location to meditate in is an exceedingly important component for the success of the meditation. One must make sure that the space is conducive to meditation, with a minimum of possible distractions. For example, a room full of furniture can be a disturbance during meditation; hence the room should be as simple as possible. It is best to have a room dedicated to meditation.[27] The objective is to associate the room with meditation and to reflexively identify it with a meditative mood. There are those who feel that by practicing meditation in

---

Nachum of Chernobyl, *Meor Einayim* (Brooklyn: 1975), "Hanhagot *Yesharot*," p. 2 (5). See also: *Meio Sheorim* (New York: Kehot, 1975), p. 20b. Rabbi Yizchak Luria writes that it is an obligation to study *mussar* throughout the entire year. See: *Shulchan Aruch*, "*Orach Chaim*," chapter 603:1, *Be'er Heitiv* and the *Mishnah Berurah*, ad loc.

27. It is told that the Baal Shem Tov (prior to being revealed) would meditate daily in the mountains, in a specific cave. See: *Sheivchei HaBaal Shem Tov* (Jerusalem: Rubin Mass Ltd, 1991), p. 64. His disciple and successor, the Magid of Mezritch, would also often meditate alone in his room. See: *Magid Devarav Leyokav, Likutei Amorim, Or Torah, Hosofot*, p. 38b. Rabbi Nachman of Breslov would have a dedicated room where he would meditate for hours daily. See: *Shivchei HaRan* 1:14, p. 9. The founder of the *mussar* movement, Rabbi Yisrael Salanter, says that when people are evaluating themselves (i.e., meditating on their character refinement) they should do so in a special room dedicated for such meditations. See: *Or Yisrael* (Bnei Brak: 1969), in the introduction by Rabbi Yitzchak Blazer. Rabbi Yitzchak Blazer, *Sharei Or*, p. 36. See also: *T'nuat HaMsusar*, vol. 4 (Israel: Mofet, 1967), p. 205.

For an earlier source see: Rabbi Eliyahu ben Moshe Di Vidas, *Reshit Chachmah*, "*Shar HaKedusha*," chapter 6, p. 140b. See also: Rabbi Pinchas Eliyohu Ben Meir of Vilna, *Sefer Habrit*, part 2, *maamor* 12, chapter 1, p. 489.

a sacred place, such as a synagogue, or a house of study, their mood will automatically be in sync with their meditation.

The energy in a person's immediate environment is created through positive or negative acts. A positive action releases positive vibes in the environment, and the atmosphere becomes imbued with positive energy. A negative act produces negativity. An environment where people waste their time speaking idle words overflows with negative energy.[28] A place where people exchange words of meaning is saturated with positive energy. For this reason, many prefer to meditate in a place of worship[29] or, as mentioned previously, to meditate in a room the sole purpose of which is meditation. (Once a person has mastered the art of meditation, they can meditate at any time and in any place. The locations and the times become trivial.)

Rabbi Nachman of Breslov felt that a person should dedicate a secluded area in the fields, or a room in the home, as a sacred place for meditation.[30] This assigned space is an area where one can be alone with oneself and closed off from the turbulence of society. Having this sacred place where one's

28. The sixth Chabad Rebbe, Rabbi Yoseph Yitzchak, *Sefer Hamaamorim 5703*, p. 21. Rabbi Pinchas of Koritz said that he desired to pray in the early morning, before the world is filled with frivolity. See: Rabbi Pinchas of Koritz, *Midrash Pinchas*, p. 32, chapter 57.

29. See: Rabbi Moshe Corodovero, *Shiur Komah, 28*, p. 84. The Talmud teaches that one should attempt to study in a house of worship (Talmud *Berachot*, 6a). In addition, a person should have a designated place (in his own home or even in the synagogue) where he should pray (Talmud *Berachot*, 6b; Jerusalem Talmud, *Berachot*, chapter 4, *halacha* 4; Rambam, *Hilchot Tefila*, chapter 5, *halacha* 6; Shulchan Aruch, "Orach Chaim," chapter 90:19; *Magen Avraham;* ad loc.). The reason is because when one is accustomed to pray in a particular location, the place itself becomes more conducive for one's concentration during the prayers.

Rabbi Meir Leibush Ben Yechiel Michael Weiser, the Malbim. See also: Genesis, chapter 24, verse 62–63; Rashi, and Rabbi Ovadyah Seforno, ad loc.

30. See: Rabbi Nachman of Breslov, *Likutei Moharan*, part 1, chapter 52; *Sichot HaRan*, chapter 274–275.

worries are not granted entry, one will always have a space where one feels comfortable and sheltered. And once a person is alone and at ease, one can then think through the issues at hand with the clarity and the openness of mind needed, without feeling pressured and disempowered.

Hitbodedut, which is literally translated as seclusion, or isolation is the classic word in Hebrew for meditation. These two, meditation and seclusion, are frequently associated with each other, because meditation necessitates being left alone. Generally, study and intense concentration is best done when one is in a quiet, secluded area, in a state and in a place of *hitbodedut.*[31] True *hitbodedut* would mean to practice in complete solitude; nonetheless, as illustrated above, in the early stages of meditation, it is most appropriate to meditate with a partner. As one advances in the mastery of meditation, he can then meditate in complete isolation.

The discipline of seclusion has found great merit within all spectrums of Jewish thought.[32] The Kabbalistic masters

---

31. Rabbeinu Bachya, Kisvei Rabbienu Bachya, *Kad Kemach, Torah* (Jerusalem: Mossad Harav Kook, 1995), p. 427. Being alone is conducive for thinking. See: Talmud *Sanhedrin,* 40a; Rashi, *Kal HaLayla.* See also: *Likutei Yekarim,* chapter 175.

32. Rabbi Bachya Ibn Pakudah writes that since the majority of transgressions are committed with two or more people, it is a custom for some pious people to isolate themselves from society completely, to practice *hitbodedut* as a way of life. See: *Chovot Halevavot, "Shar Cheshan Hanefesh,"* 17.

The Rambam writes that a pious person should seclude himself and only interact with other human beings when necessary. See: *Moreh Nevuchim,* part 3, chapter 51.

Rabbi Eliyahu ben Moshe Di Vidas writes that the path to holiness and purity is *hitbodedut*—seclusion. *Reshit Chachmah, "Shar HaKedusha,"* chapter 6, p. 140b. See also: Rabbi Yeshayah Halevi Horowitz, *Shenei Luchot Habrit, "Shar Ha'otyot,"* p. 474; Rabbi Moshe Chaim Luzzato, *Mesilat Yesharim,* chapter 26; Rabbi Eliyahu HaCohen, *Sheivet HaMusar,* chapter 19:6, p. 171; Rabbi Moshe Sofer Chatam Sofer (1762–1839) responsa, *Yoreh*

point out[33] that the acronym of the verse *"Bechal D'rachecah Da'ayhu"*[34]—"In all your ways shall you know Him," a verse that in Talmudic lore is a foundation of Torah,[35] is *BaDaD,* the root of the word *hitbodedut,* seclusion. Practicing isolation is an integral part of religious worship. Only when a person is alone, says a Chassidic master, and is at one with himself, can he truly connect with the real oneness, that is God.[36]

Yet, despite the positive qualities of seclusion and isolation, it is not a way of life envisioned by the precepts of the Torah. Though living on "Walden Pond" is most suitable for contem-

---

Deah, introduction, *"Petuchei Chotom;"* Rabbi Alexander Moshe Lapidus, *Divrei Emet,* chapter 13.

The secret to attain a love for God is to procure a love for *hitbodedut*— seclusion. Rabbi Eliyahu ben Moshe Di Vidas, *Reshit Chachmah,* "Shar Ha'Ahavah," chapter 3, p. 59a.

The Baal Shem Tov says that to achieve *Daveikut*—being one with God—one needs to practice *hitbodedut; Tzavoas Horivash,* chapter 82.

One of the greatest proponents of *hitbodedut* was the Chassidic master Rabbi Nachman of Breslov; he strongly encouraged the idea of *hitbodedut,* especially in the fields. See: Rabbi Nachman of Breslov, *Likutei Moharan,* part 2, chapters 93–101; *Sefer HaMidot,* "Hitbodedut," p. 97; *Chayei Moharan,* "Ma'alat Hitbodedut,* pp. 463–471; *Likutei Aytzot,* "Hitbodedut," pp. 56–62; *Sichot Haran,* chapters 227–234.

The founders of the *mussar* movement advocated a love for *hitbodedut.* See: Rabbi Simcha Zissel Ziv of Kelm (1824–1898), *Kisvei Ha'Saba M'Kelm* (Bnei Brak: *Sifsei Chachamim,* 1984), p. 176; *Rabbi* Yitzchak *Blazer* (1837–1907), *Chocvei Or* (Jerusalem: 1974), p. 176; Rabbi Alexander Moshe Lapidus (1819–1906), *Divrei Emet* (Jerusalem: 1995), chapter 13, pp. 94–98. In regard to the costume of Rabbi Yoseph Zundal of Salant (1786–1866), see: *Or Yisrael,* p. 30. See also: *T'nuat HaMsusar,* vol. 1, p. 135.

33. Rabbi Chaim Yoseph David Azulay, *Avodat Hakodesh* (Brooklyn: Atereth Publications, 1987); *Tziparon Shamir,* chapter 4:51; *Midbar Kadmot* (Jerusalem: 1962), *Marrechet Hei,* p. 15; Rabbi Michal of Zlotchov, *Malchei BaKodesh,* pp. 85–86.

34. Proverbs, chapter 3, verse 6.

35. Talmud *Berachot,* 63a.

36. Rabbi Moshe *Chaim* Ephraim of Sudylkov, *Degel Machanah Ephraim* (Jerusalem: Mir, 1995), *"Parshat Ha'azinu,"* p. 242.

plation and meditation, it is not, and should not be, a permanent lifestyle.[37] "If a person conceals himself in a hidden place will I not see him?"[38] A celebrated Chassidic sage, Rabbi Elimelech of Lizhensk interprets the verse this way: If a person conceals himself from humanity, if he serves God in loneliness, secluded from the rest of the world, I will not see him. I will not reveal Myself to him.[39] A human being needs to experience life with other people. He must mingle and share his life's experiences with other people, so that the people around him can learn from him, and he, in turn, can learn from them. In the journey of life there is always room for positive criticism, and by listening to other people's observations and evaluations, one can aspire to attain genuine perfection of character.[40]

Hitbodedut, seclusion, can be also accomplished while one is involved and superficially immersed with the world. In fact, true *hitbodedut* is an activity of the mind rather than an exercise

---

37. Rabbi Yehudah Halevi, *The Kuzari, maamor 3,* chapter 1. See the commentary *Otzor Nechmad,* ad loc. Rabbi Moshe Sofer, *Chatam Sofer Al HaTorah,* "Parshat Kedoshim," "In the beginning"; The sixth Chabad rebbe, Rabbi Yoseph Yitzchak, *Likkutei Diburim,* vol. 1, p. 272. (See by the same author: *Igrot Kodesh,* vol. 3, p. 539.)

Rabbi Moshe Chaim Luzzato cautions one not to take the idea of *hitbodedut* to the extreme. See: *Mesilat Yesharim,* chapter 14.

Rabbi Yakov Emdin writes that *hitbodedut is* a beneficial practice when it is done periodically. He writes that when one lives a life in *hitbodedut* he cannot perform many of the Mitzvot. See: *Migdal Oz* (Israel: Eshkol, 1978), "Aliyot Habadidut," pp. 156–157.

38. Jeremiah, chapter 23, verse 24.

39. See: Rabbi Klunimus Kalman, *Maor Vashemesh,* "Parshat Kedoshim," p. 364. See also: Eliezer Shtainman, *Be'er HaChassidut HaMaggid VeTalmidav* (Israel: Mochon Kemach), p. 91.

40. Rabbi Yoseph Yavatz (1434–1507) writes that at times *hitbodedut* is unsuitable behavior, for when one is alone and is his only judge of character, he may err. See: Rabbi Yoseph Yavatz's commentary on Psalms, chapter 29, verse 1.

of the body. When one has trained in the art of seclusion, one can achieve *hitbodedut* even while being among other human beings. While physically they are, so to speak, involved, mentally they remain alone.[41] A known Kabbalistic master once said: "One should practice *hitbodedut* while being in the company of other men."[42] A person exists where his thoughts exist, and wherever one's thoughts wander, that is where one really is.[43] Therefore, if one is in control of one's thoughts, and one can focus his attention at will, then, in a sense, it is completely irrelevant where one is physically located. Wherever a person may find himself physically, he can transplant himself via his thoughts to another reality. Consequently, while he is engaged in mundane reality, he can focus his thoughts and attention on the moment and beyond. He can exercise the art of *hitbodedut*, of being alone, even while in the company of others. This is the type of *hitbodedut* one should aspire to master, where one can be involved and not be involved, concurrently.[44]

The efficacy of the meditation may depend on the direction

---

41. Rabbi Eliezer Ezcary (1522–1600), *Safer Cheraidim* (Jerusalem: 1990), chapter 66:32. See also: Rabbi Yisrael Baal Shem Tov, *Tzavoas Horivash*, chapter 63; *Or Haemet*, p. 205; *Likutei Yekarim*, chapter 13. Sut Meira, p. 51.

42. A teaching by the master Kabbalist Rabbi Shimshon of Ostropol, author of *Dan Yadin, Likutei Shoshanim*, and numerous other works of Kabbalah. The sainted Rabbi was killed during the massacres of 1648. This saying is quoted by Rabbi Yoseph Yitzchak, the sixth Chabad rebbe, *Sefer Hasichot 5703*, p. 191. See also: Rabbi Nachman of Breslov, *Chayei Moharan*, chapter 241, p. 322; Rabbi Elimelech of Lizhensk. See Eliezer Shtainman, *Be'er HaChassidut*, "*Hamagid VeTalmidav*," p. 91. Rabbi Moshe Sofer, *Chatam Sofer*, Responsa "*Yoreh Deah*," the introduction, "*Petuchei Chotom*."

43. Rabbi Yisrael Baal Shem Tov, *Keter Shem Tov*, chapter 56; *Tzavoas Horivash*, chapter 69. See also: Jerusalem Talmud *Berachot*, chapter 6, *halacha* 8.

44. In the words of Henry Thoreau, "The really diligent student in one of the crowded hives of Cambridge College is as solitary as a dervis in the desert." See: *Walden* (New York: Barnes & Noble, 1993), "Solitude," p. 112.

one faces while meditating. There are those who emphasize certain directions that should be faced during phases of the meditation. Initially, the meditator faces east, then west, and so on.[45] This is most appropriate for the advanced practitioners, but has less relevance for the uninitiated. There is no one specific direction to face while meditating. However, if parallels can be drawn between prayer and meditation, then it can be assumed that, as with prayers, one should face *mizrach*—east, toward Jerusalem.[46] There are quite a few laws and customs in Jewish practice, not necessarily connected to prayer, in which special emphasis is made to face east during their performance.[47] Facing east toward Jerusalem seems to evoke spiritual vibes within the person. By facing east one's focus and attention, and generally one's temperament for sincere meditation, is enhanced.

---

45. Rabbi Moshe Corodovero, *Pardess Rimonim, shar 21,* chapter 1, in the name of an ancient Kabbalistic text, *Safer HaNikud.* See also: Rabbi Avraham Abulafia, *Or HaSechel* (Jerusalem: Havad Lehotzahot Sefarim, 1999), part 8, p. 131.

46. Rabbi Avraham Abulafia writes of facing east in advanced meditations because it is from the east that the light enters the universe. See: *Or HaSechel,* part 8, p. 131.

47. For example, under the *chupa* the bride and groom stand facing east. See: *Aruch HaShulchan, "Even HaEzer,"* chapter 62:9; *Kitzur Shulchan Aruch,* chapter 147:5. There is the opinion that says that the rabbi who recites the blessings under the *chupa* should be the one facing east. See: *Machzor Vitri,* p. 475; Rabbi Yakov Emdin, *Siddur Beit Yakov, "Birchat Erwin VeNesuin,"* p. 124; *Kitzur Shulchan Aruch,* chapter 147:5, see also: *Shulchan Aruch, "Even HaEzer Be'er Heitiv,"* chapter 61:7. Additionally, there is also this concept in a negative sense. That one should not face east (toward the Temple) while performing certain actions (e.g., releasing extremities). See: Talmud *Berachot,* 61b; *Chidushei HaRashba Berachot,* ad loc; Rambam, *Hilchot Beit Habchira,* chapter 7, *halacha* 9; *Smag,* "Mitzvah Assei," 164; *Shulchan Aruch, "Orach Chaim,"* chapter 3:5 (while sleeping). See: Talmud *Berachot,* 5b; Rambam, *Hilchot Beit Habchira,* chapter 7, *halacha* 9; *Shulchan Aruch, "Orach Chaim,"* chapter 3:6.

Year

The obvious time for meditation is when one would feel the least possible distractions during meditation. For this reason, many find night[48] or the early hours of the morning as the most fitting time for introspection and quiet meditation. During the waking hours of the day, the world is preoccupied with the "sounds of Rome," the cacophony of culture. People are engrossed and immersed in the mundane. The energy generated in the atmosphere is that of a rush for materialistic accumulation. At night, however, all is still, the noise is silenced and quieted, and perhaps for this reason, it is the most fitting and opportune time for meditation.[49]

Meditating at night has been strongly advocated by the Kabbalists throughout the generations.[50] Rabbi Avraham the Chassid, a staunch proponent of meditation in darkness, says

---

48. Particularly past midnight. See: Rabbi Moshe Corodovero, *Or Ne'erav,* part 3, chapter 1, p. 21.

49. See: Rabbi Nachman of Breslov, *Likutei Moharan,* part 1, chapter 52.

50. Rabbi Avraham Abulafia, *Chayay Olam HaBah,* p. 146. Rabbi Avraham Ben HaRambam, *Sefer Hamaspik Leovedei Hashem,* "Erech hitbodedut," p. 185. Rabbi Menachem Ben Shlomo, the Meiri, writes that night is the most appropriate time to study and to meditate on the lofty mysteries of creation. Meiri on Talmud *Baba Batra,* 10b (Jerusalem: Kedem, 1971), p. 70. Rabbi Eliezer Ezcary writes about meditating at night. See: *Safer Cheraidim,* chapter 65. Rabbi Nachman of Breslov teaches that the best time to meditate is at night. *Likutei Moharan,* part 1, chapter *52; Likutei Aytzot,* "Hitbodedut," (7–8) p. 58. Breslover Chassidim today meditate in the early hours of the morning, before daylight.

Interestingly, according to the commentaries when the Torah says "Jacob remained alone, and an angel wrestled with him" (Genesis, chapter 32, verse 25) it means that he was in a state of external as well as internal isolation (i.e., meditation) and thus he had this angelic experience. This incident, incidentally, occurred during the night hours. See: the commentary by Rabbi Avraham Ben HaRambam (Jerusalem: Sifrei Rabbanei Bavell, 1984), *"Parshat Vayishlach,"* chapter 32, verse 25.

that this is alluded to by the master prophet, Isaiah. "Who among you fears God obeying the call of his servants? Such a man walks in darkness without light. He trusts in the Lord and relies on his God."[51] According to Reb Avraham, walking in darkness is interpreted as someone who meditates in the darkness of the night.[52] As the verse says: "Arise. Cry out at night,"[53] which means to meditate at night.[54]

The advocacy for meditation at night is not restricted to mystical thought. The Talmud speaks in admiration of King David, for he would awaken each night at midnight to contemplate Torah.[55] In Talmudic lore, studying Torah and contemplating the mysteries of the creator during the night is regarded in high esteem, and one who does so, the Talmud asserts, will be blessed with an aura of charm and kindness that will accompany him throughout the day.[56] In fact, according to Talmudic tradition, most of a person's wisdom is acquired at night.[57]

---

51. Isaiah, chapter 50, verse 10.

52. Quoted by Rabbi Avraham Ben HaRambam, *Sefer Hamaspik Leovedei Hashem*, "*Erech Hitbodedut*," p. 185.

53. Lamentations, chapter 2, verse 19.

54. Rabbi Avraham Ben HaRambam, *Sefer Hamaspik Leovedei Hashem*, "*Erech Hitbodedut*," p. 185. This verse is interpreted in the Talmud to mean that one should study Torah at night. Midrash Rabbah, Exodus, *parsha* 47, chapter 5. Rambam, *Hilchot Talmud Torah*, chapter 3, *halacha* 13. See also: Talmud *Tamid*, 32b.

55. See: Talmud *Berachot*, 3b. Midrash Rabbah, Ruth, *parsha* 6, chapter 1; *Midrash Tanchuma*, "*Parshat Behaalotecha*," chapter 10. Parenthetically, there is an ancient custom practiced by many Kabbalists to meditate on the destruction of the Temple at midnight. See: *Zohar*, part 1, p. 242b and 295b; Rabbi Asher Ben Yechiel Rosh on Talmud *Berachot*, 3b; *Shulchan Aruch*, "*Orach Chaim*," chapter 1; *Magen Avraham*, ad loc.

56. Talmud *Chagigah*, 12b; *Avodah Zarah*, 3b; *Zohar*, part 1, p. 194b; *Tikkunei Zohar*, "*Hakdamah*," p. 2b. Rambam, *Hilchot Talmud Torah*, chapter 3, *halacha* 13.

57. Rambam, *Hilchot Talmud Torah*, chapter 3, *halacha* 13, See also: Talmud *Eruvin*, 65a; *Tur*, "*Orach Chaim*," chapter 238.

These types of night meditations involve awakening and leaving one's bed but there are also meditations that can be executed while lying in bed. The most basic meditation while lying in bed would be to meditate and think about our love for God,[58] for the opportunity to meditate on our love and relationship with God is present at all times.[59]

One of the more intense meditations recommended for bedtime is from the Chassidic Rebbe, Rabbi Elimelech of Lizhensk. He says that if you find yourself lying in bed unable to sleep, envision a flaming fire burning in front of you, reaching to the heart of heaven, and for the sake of sanctifying the divine's name, resolve that you are now willing to overcome your instincts and cast yourself in the flaming fire.[60]

Meditation during the night is also done in order to generate a unification and fusion between night and day. By awaking at midnight, and spending time in study or prayer until day breaks, the meditator creates a union of night and day,[61]

---

58. See: Rambam, *Moreh Nevuchim*, part 3, chapter 51; Rabbi Yisrael Baal Shem Tov, *Tzavoas Horivash*, chapter 133; *Or Haemet*, p. 201; Rabbi Nachman of Breslov teaches that while laying in bed one has the opportunity to speak his heart to God. *Sichot HaRan*, chapter 68.

59. Rabbi Yisrael Baal Shem Tov, *Tzavoas Horivash*, chapter 8; *Likutei Yekarim*, chapter 38.

60. *"Tzetal Katan,"* 1, printed in *Noam Elimelech*, in the beginning; Rabbi Alexander Zisskind writes that when one accepts and envisions himself being self-nullified for the sanctification of God's name, it creates immense delight above. See: *Yesod V'Shoresh Ha'Avodah*, *"Avodat H'lev,"* chapter 11.

61. See: Rabbi Yehudah Ashkanazi (Germany, eighteenth century), *Be'er Heitiv* on *Shulchan Aruch*, *"Orach Chaim,"* chapter 238; Rabbi Eliyahu ben Moshe Di Vidas, *Reshit Chachmah*, *"Shar HaKedusha,"* chapter 7, p. 151a. Rabbi Yisrael Ba'al Shem Tov, *Tzavoas Horivash*, chapter 83. See also: *Likutei Yekarim*, chapter 189; Rabbi Alexander Zisskind, *Yesod V'Shoresh Ha'Avodah*, *"Shar Ha'ashmoret,"* chapter 6. Rabbi Eliyahu ben Moshe Di Vidas writes that the idea of unifying night with day is a spiritual remedy for sins that cause separateness. See: *Reshit Chachmah*, *"Shar HaKedusha,"* chapter 17, p. 210b.

thereby transforming the darkness of night into the brightness of day.[62]

The attention one is able to give to the meditative session is extremely important. A person's measure of alertness will also play an important role in the success of the meditation. There are times within the day when one is in the mood to be inspired, and there are times when one is fatigued, lethargic, and not in the mood. One should take into account the level of alertness one is in, before beginning the meditation.

One should also heed attention to mealtimes, when he has eaten, and also what he has eaten. Experiencing hunger pangs during meditation may cause considerable distraction. According to the Talmud, prior to one's eating, a person possesses two hearts.[63] A human being when hungry cannot think clearly and cannot focus properly. They have many opinions but no resolve.[64] Therefore, a person should make sure that he is not hungry when desiring to meditate.[65]

Conversely, it is also not ideal to meditate immediately following a meal. This is especially true following a heavy meal, because after you have eaten coarse foods, the mind tends to be cloudy and opaque.[66] Accordingly, the Talmud asserts that one

---

62. See: Rabbi Avraham Azulay (1570–1643), *Chesed LeAvraham* (Jerusalem: Yerid HaSefarim), part 2, chapter 15.

63. Talmud *Baba Batra*, 12b. Parenthetically, eating creates a joyous mood, which is a prerequisite in reaching higher prophetic states of consciousness. See: Rabbi Nisan ben Reuven, *Derashot HaRan, derush* 5, p. 74; Rabbeinu Bachya, Exodus, 18:12; Rabbi Yakkov Culi (1689–1732), *Me'am Lo'ez,* ad loc. See also: Rabbeinu Bachya, *Kad Kemach,* "Rosh Hashanah," 2, p. 379; Rabbi Yonathan Eibechuvetz, *Tifferet Yonathan,* "Parshat Yitro," chapter 18, verse 12; Rabbi Meir Simchah of Dvinsk (1843–1926), *Meshed Chochmah* (Israel: 1996), Parshat Toledot, p. 40.

64. Talmud *Baba Batra*, 12b; Rashi, ad loc.
See: Rabbi Yakkov Culi, *Me'am Lo'ez,* "Parshat Yitro," chapter 18, verse 12 (61).

65. The sixth Chabad rebbe, Rabbi Yoseph Yitzchak, *Sefer Hamaamorim:*

can not concentrate fully on their studies following a meal.[67] In addition to the mind difficulties one may experience following a meal, there are also the bodily disturbances, such as stomach pains, and the like. These aches and pains disturb the concentration needed for meditation.

Therefore, the best times for meditation are during the day somewhere between meals, in the early morning, when you are not yet hungry, or at night, with a proper interval after dinner. Many practitioners of meditation advocate focusing on breathing—closing the eyes and concentrating on the way one breathes. Imagine being filled with whatever you desire to be filled with, be it love, passion, or the like. You inhale positive energy and exhale negativity. Controlled breathing is also used to attain a fitting mood for a specific meditation. For example, when exhaling, one can visualize all the stress and uncertainties one has, being slowly expelled and drawn out of the body. And through inhaling, one can be filled with the proper temperament for meditation, becoming relaxed and at ease. It should be noted that there are breathing techniques mentioned in the Kabbalah, associated with advanced states of meditations, where the meditator meditates on a specific concept, and he is asked to pay attention to his breathing—how much and when he breathes.[68]

Kuntreisim (New York: Kehot, 1986), vol. 2, p. 918. See also: *Sefer Hamaamorim 5703* (New York: Kehot, 1986), p. 21. Coarse foods cause drowsiness. See: Rabbi Gershon Ben Shlomo, *Shar HaShamaim* (Israel: 1968), *maamor* 10, pp. 68–69; Rabbi Eliyahu ben Moshe Di Vidas, *Reshit Chachmah, "Shar HaKedusha,"* chapter 7, p. 153b. Generally, excessive eating causes tiredness. See: Talmud *Yuma,* 18a; Midrash *Tana Devei Eliyahu,* chapter 13.

67. Talmud *Nedarim,* 37b; Rashi, Rabbi Shlomo Yitzchaki; Ran, Rabbi Nisan Ben Reuven, ad loc.

68. Rabbi Avraham Abulafia, *Or HaSechel* (Jerusalem: Havad Lehotzahot Sefarim, 1999), part 8, pp. 130–131. Rabbi Moshe Corodovero, *Pardess Rimonim, shar* 21, chapter 1. In the name of an ancient Kabbalistic text, *Safer HaNikud.*

Yet, this type of meditation is quite different than meditating on the breathing itself. In this method of meditation, the focus is not on the breathing; rather, the breathing assists with the meditation.

CHAPTER
5

A Classification of
Jewish Meditations

In previous chapters meditation was divided into three, broad categories—meditation as controlled thinking, as self-knowledge, and as a means to reach an expanded state of awareness. These three uses of meditation are not necessarily related to Judaism; rather, they are universal. Notwithstanding, Jewish meditation can also be divided into these three categories, one being a meditation to gain a greater knowledge of oneself, another to attain a greater understanding of a concept and yet another to reach expanded states of awareness, a meditation in which the primary goal is for the meditator to catch a glimpse of the transcendent.

Type A

The first type of meditation is intrapersonal and transformational. Its use is to gain self-knowledge, to understand oneself better, and ultimately, to find a purpose and a destiny in one's life. This style of meditation is traditionally termed *cheshbon hanefesh*—taking stock of the soul, self-evaluation to reach self-perfection. Concomitant with a human being's spiritual growth is self-mastery and interpersonal relationships. One's relationship with oneself and with other human beings, is interrelated with one's relationship with God.

Cheshbon hanefesh can be achieved in various ways, and the most commonly used method is through extensive study. By meditating on a devotional work, such as a book on ethics, which speaks of the negativity of certain human traits,[1] a person reflects on each one of these traits to see if he possesses any of them. Then, in an effort to achieve self improvement, one attempts to make corrections. For example, meditating on a text that concerns itself with the negative implication of being arrogant, and then examining oneself, to see if one possesses this trait, and if need be, aspiring to rectify it.

The advocacy of this style of self-perfection, which is also known as the study of *mussar,* was further developed into a full-fledged movement by the 19th-century moralist, Rabbi Yisrael Salanter. The primary ambition of the *mussar* movement is the perfection of the self. Through *mussar* people are encouraged to improve and change their imperfections. Rabbi Yisrael recognized that what one knows intellectually does not necessarily translate into action. One may know the value of being virtuous, yet act differently. There are inner subconscious motivations, rooted in a place that is hidden from reason. Therefore, he speaks of focusing on a single negative trait that one feels needs the most correction, and pondering its negative

---

1. From the eleventh century there were already texts dedicated to self-evaluation and perfection. Rabbi Bachya Ibn Pakudah (1050–1120) wrote *Chovot Halevavot,* the first book of that genre. The author asserts that the purpose of *all* philosophy is to achieve self-knowledge. See: *Chovot Halevavot,* "*Shar Habechinah,*" chapter 5. Other classic works of *mussar* are Rabbeinu Yona (1194–1263), *Sharei Teshuvah;* Rabbi Asher Ben Yechiel, known as the Rosh (1250–1327), *Orchot Chaim; Orchot Tzadikim* (author anonymous); Rabbi Moshe Corodovero (1522–1570), Tomer *Devorah;* Rabbi Eliyahu ben Moshe Di Vidas (16th century), *Reshit Chachmah;* Rabbi Moshe Chaim Luzzatto (1707–1747), *Mesilat Yesharim.*

ramifications while simultaneously striving to perfect it.[2] One should meditate on each character trait in a specific and conscientious manner. Each individual trait should be dealt with as an isolated case. After extensive study one should then take the issue studied in the text and relate it to one's own personal life, with the intention of becoming a better person. The main point is the implementation following the meditation.[3]

Superficial study is insufficient; rather one must contemplate the issue at hand repeatedly, until the subject matter enters one's consciousness completely.[4] Recognizing the various levels of a person's consciousness and intentionality, a person may act (consciously) one way, while deep down—and one may not even know it—one may feel differently.[5] In this way, by contemplating these issues extensively, the ideas will crystallize and slowly penetrate, thereby causing an internal shift.[6] Rabbi Yisrael also speaks of studying the issue with detail and with imagination, reifying the issue, doing it with excitement and vigor.[7] In addition, one may find that at times putting the

---

2. Rabbi Yisrael Salanter, *Or Yisrael,* p. 82.

3. Rabbi Simcha Zissel Ziv of Kelm, *Kisvei Ha'Saba M'Kelm* (Bnei Brak: Sifsei Chachamim, 1984), pp. 151-153.

4. Rabbi Moshe Chaim Luzzato, *Mesilat Yesharim,* "*Hakdamah*"; Rabbi Yitzchak Blazer in the name of Rabbi Yisrael Salanter, *Or Yisrael,* p. 28. See also: *T'nuat HaMsusar,* vol. 1, p. 253.

5. Rabbi Yisrael Salanter, *Or Yisrael,* p. 49. This idea that what we show and feel on a conscious level is at times only a surface emotion is clearly illustrated according to Rabbi Yisrael in the following scenario. A wise man has a gifted student, whom he loves very dearly while he also has a child a rebel whom he dislikes. If the teacher were to be sleeping while a fire would break out in the homes of his beloved student and his child, and he would be awakened, Rabbi Yisrael says, that he would instinctively rush to the home of his child. See: *T'nuat HaMsusar, Vol.* 1, pp. 250–251.

6. See: *T'nuat HaMsusar,* Vol. 1, pp. 250–254.

7. Rabbi Yisrael Salanter, *Or Yisrael,* p. 43.

meditation to a tune will have a greater effect. Many find that reading an ethical text with a melody evokes a greater response.[8]

Rabbi Nachman of Breslov proposed another interesting method of self-improvement. He advocated a technique of speaking to one's body parts.[9] The objective is to explain to the body, in rational terms, that all the worldly desires it pursues are of no real importance. Each part of the body is associated with another human trait. In this type of meditation, one talks to the body part associated with the negative trait one wishes to negate. For example, if one desires to rid oneself from speaking slander, one may talk to the lips, reproving them for speaking slander.

Another form of self-perfecting meditation is a repetitive acknowledgment to oneself of the negativity one wishes to eradicate. For example, to rid oneself of depression one would repeatedly remind oneself of the negative implications of depression. Words create reality. The way one languages and interprets reality, is the way reality will be for them. Consequently, by languaging and continuously repeating to oneself how life is full of happiness and joy, one will ultimately cultivate a state of happiness.

These methods of self-improvement can only be effective when one knows what requires refinement. Knowing what one is lacking, one can then attempt to perfect it. However, people see and judge themselves subjectively, and not objectively.[10] We perceive ourselves through the distorting veil of our own ego. So, how is one to know for certain what it is that is in need of correction? Can one circumvent the ego to secure a true evaluation? Meditation may be the solution. By transcending the

---

8. Rabbi Yisrael Salanter, *Or Yisrael*, p. 33. See also: *T'nuat HaMsusar*, Vol. 1, pp. 258–259.

9. Rabbi Nachman of Breslov, *Chayei Moharan*, chapter 442. See also: Rabbi Eliyahu HaCohen, *Sheivet HaMusar*, chapter 8:4, p. 126.

10. See: Chapter 2, Footnote 11.

lower self and achieving a meta state from which one can view oneself more objectively. Meditation has the powerful ability to get the ego out of the way.

There is no one, single way of meditating through which one can reach such objectivity, although the most common method would be a mantra type of meditation.[11] Mantra meditation is generally unstructured, meaning it is only a stepping stone to reach higher spontaneous thoughts. A state of consciousness where the conscious mind is stilled, and thoughts occur spontaneously. At this level the meditator can listen to himself, and observe his inner reality.

A verbal mantra meditation occurs when the meditator repeats a word over and over again, until slowly one begins relaxing and feeling at ease. The word suffuses the mind completely, blocking extraneous thoughts from entering. Slowly the meditator feels his normal conventional state of mind being silenced and stilled. This can also be done with the sense of hearing by listening to a continuous sound.

Concentrating on an object for a fixed period of time and allowing it to fill the mind is a visual mantra meditation. This is also an unstructured meditation. One utilizes the technique as a sort of launching pad, a starting point, to reach an expanded state of consciousness. Rabbi Nachman of Breslov says that if a person wishes to meditate and does not know what to say, let him repeat *"Ribbono Shel Olam"*—"Master of the universe.[12] These words serve as a mantra bringing a person to a heightened state of awareness. It opens the meditator's consciousness to experiences that are beyond the ego allowing one feel the presence the Creator.

---

11. Rabbi Yisrael Salanter writes of repeating a saying *of mussar* many times over, until it is inscribed upon one's heart. See: *Or Yisrael,* p. 33.

12. Rabbi Nachman of Breslov, *Chayei Moharan,* chapter 440; *Likutei Aytzot,* *"Hitbodedut,"* chapter 16, p. 60.

One of the benefits of transcendent meditation is that it enables a person to connect with his subconscious. In a meditative state, one's inner, and perhaps even suppressed feelings, are revealed, thereby allowing the meditator to discern what needs purification and rectification on a deeper level. There are other ways, as mentioned earlier, through which a person can come to know the inner workings of his subconscious. A person can take note of his immediate, instinctive reactions,[13] or he can jot down his unintentional nonmeditated thoughts. If an idea appears to you, seemingly from out of the blue, immediately write it down, and you may thereby observe what is transpiring on a subconscious level.[14] Another way to uncover the subconscious would be through dissecting one's dreams, as they are wish fulfillments and projections of one's deep, inner feelings.[15] While the above-mentioned methods are valid, meditating may be the most efficacious and direct vehicle.

Rabbi Klunimus Kalmish, the Rebbe of Peasetzna, teaches yet another method in the quest for self-perfection. It is known as *hashkatah*. It is a technique wherein one silences the thought process. The conscious mind is constantly flooded with a continuous stream of turbulent thought. The objective is to drain the conscious mind of this deluge. Once the mind is cleared, the meditator is instructed to focus on a single sacred concept. Reb Klunimus offers as a sample thought for this method, meditations on one's faith, love and awe, or alternately,

---

13. Rabbi Schneur Zalman of Liadi teaches that in potential every person is in control of his conscious mind and can govern what thoughts to consciously think about. However, most people are not yet in control of their subconscious, their instincts. See: *Tanya,* chapter 12. Thus, by observing one's instinctive reactions (for the positive or negative) one can know where one's really holding. Is one's subconscious, selfish, instinctive, or selfless, Godly?

14. See: *T'nuat HaMsusar,* Vol. 1, p. 251, with regard to Rabbi Yisrael Salanter.

15. See: Chapter 3, Footnote 7.

the refinement of a negative quality such as laziness.[16] By emptying the mind and then filling it with a carefully selected thought, the thoughts become that much more powerful and will have an even greater impact on the meditator.

It is important to note that when one is aiming for self-perfection, one needs to work slowly and methodically,[17] taking one step at a time, without attempting to remodel and change oneself in a single day. Internal changes that come too suddenly, rarely endure. The moment the high, or the inspiration, is over, so is the transformation. This occurs to all of us at one time or another. In the heat of a moment we may decide to drastically change. Yet when the passion fades, the resolutions become mere memories. It is better to make small changes successfully, than fail in drastic ones. The rate of success for a resolution is greater when the resolution taken is not of monumental magnitude. A simple example, if one feels oneself to be slacking in prayers, one should resolve to pray with the proper concentration once a week, and uild on the success.[18] Success breeds success. When people feel successful in what they are doing they then feel empowered, which affords them the strength and courage to move forward, and become even better.

A classic book of *mussar* is divided into seven parts corresponding to the week cycle. Each day, the student reviews one part of the text, and attempts to purify and rectify what is discussed that day.[19] Every day one should aspire to become a

---

16. Rabbi Klunimus Kalmish (Shapiro) (1889–1943), *Derech HaMelech* (Jerusalem: 1991), pp. 406–407.

17. See: *Safer Hayashar* (Bnei Brak: Mishar, 1989), *shar* 6, p. 84. (The author of this classic work of *mussar* is anonymous. See: Rabbi Chaim Yoseph David Azulay, *Shem Hagdalim*, "Marrechet Siforim," *chof* 72.) Rabbi Nachman of Breslov, *Sichot HaRan*, chapter 27.

18. *See: Safer Hayashar, shar* 6, p. 87.

19. Rabbi Asher Ben Yechiel, known as the Rosh, *Orchot Chaim* (Bnei Brak: Mishor, 1989), pp. 155–168.

better person than he was the day before. Every day lived is another opportunity for growth.

A desired result of meditation, as previously mentioned, is to experience controlled thinking. The first and most basic form of meditation is to think for extended periods of time, without any diverting thoughts, about the existential issues of life.[20] The meditator asks himself, "What is the purpose of my being?" "Where is my life heading?" "How can I achieve a state of self-worth and happiness?" "What in life makes me feel fulfilled?" The meditator may then wish to extend the question to his own interpersonal relationships. Is there anyone, or anything, in this world of great value? Is there anyone, or any ideal, that is as important to me as life itself?

These internally directed meditations enable us to consciously reveal and contend with issues that lurk in the subterranean levels of our psyches. If we ignore these issues, they are apt to ambush us at the most unpredictable times. What's more, these issues have the power to run our lives by coloring our perception of reality. The objective of these meditations is to engage the true issues of life, preventing false perceptions from forcing themselves upon us.

Perhaps the Greeks were somewhat right when they said that "The unexamined life is not worth living." To sit down, occasionally, and do a rigorous examination of one's life, a *chesbon hanefesh,* is a vital element in one's spiritual development and growth.

This form of meditation is to a certain extent structured meditation. There is a definite agenda to the meditation, albeit an all-inclusive one, encompassing all of life's issues. The meditation is also in a sense unstructured, in that the meditation involves more than a single, isolated subject.

---

20. See: Rabbi Moshe Chaim Luzzato, *"Derech Eitz Chaim,"* printed in *Safer Hadrachim* (Bnei Brak: Mishor, 1989), p. 185.

A completely unstructured meditation occurs when one sits down without any defined plan or direction as to where one desires the meditation to go. Whatever arises spontaneously is observed. The meditator does not force the issues, but rather allows the issues to come forth on their own. This type of meditation can be practiced by simply sitting and focusing (not intensely) on a general area, for example, gazing at a sunset.[21] This spontaneity enables the meditator to get in touch with himself. It frees the mind from the everyday pettiness of life, and allows it to explore its inner universe. It empowers the meditator to see himself, and become open to himself.

There is a common custom among the mystically inclined to do *a chesbon hanefesh,* before going to sleep, each night,[22] while some practice this custom at the end of each week,[23] on Thursday night.[24] This *chesbon hanefesh* occurs during the recitation of the Shema. The first thing said is a prayer in which one wholeheartedly forgives anyone who wronged him, in this incarnation, or in a previous incarnation, intentionally, or unintentionally, by coercion or by will, and praying that no person should ever be punished on his accord. At this point one recites the Shema, affirming the oneness of the Creator, and expressing one's love and devotion. Then one envisions the entire day, and takes a brief reckoning of all actions, words, and thoughts throughout the day, observing if the day went as planned. When

---

21. It is a mitzvah to contemplate and gaze on the beauty of nature. Rabbi Eliyahu ben Moshe Di Vidas, *Reshit Chachmah,* "*Shar HaKedusha,*" chapter 8, p. 161. See also: Isaiah, chapter 40, verse 26. Rabbi Chaim Yoseph David Azulay, *Avodat Hakodesh, Tziparon Shamir,* chapter 11:164, p. 117.

22. The Zohar recomends that one should do a *chesbon hanefesh* each night before going to sleep. See: *Zohar,* part 1, p. 191a and pp. 198b–199a. See also: Rabbi Eliyahu HaCohen, *Sheivet HaMusar,* chapter 20:17, p. 290.

23. See: Rabbi Schneur Zalman of Liadi, *Maamorei Admmur Hazoken,* "*Haktzorim,*" p. 359; Rabbi Pinchas Eliyohu Ben Meir of Vilna, *Sefer Habrit,* part 2, *maamor* 12, chapter 1, p. 488.

24. The Lubavitcher Rebbe, *Likutei Sichot,* vol. 5, p. 362.

reviewing the day, one reflects upon thoughts, words, or actions of the day gone by, relinquishing all negativity and resolving to improve and spiritually advance.

Type B

Another objective of meditation is to acquire a greater comprehension of a concept. This is an intellectual cognitive pursuit, the aim of which is to understand a thought more thoroughly.

Torah study is the classic type of Jewish meditation that is practiced by virtually any person that contemplates Torah. By its very definition, meditation means to ponder, contemplate, and vigorously study. In Jewish tradition the contemplation of Torah has always been regarded as being of primary value.[25] It was and is a vital part of the Jewish experience. Hence, a person who studies Torah, and possesses Torah knowledge is accorded a high degree of respect.[26]

Nehege is the Hebrew word that is used to stress the importance of contemplating Torah throughout both day and night.[27] The root of the word *nehege* is *hagah,* which means to continually review, ponder, and investigate until the knowledge

---

25. The study of Torah equals all mitzvot. See: Mishnah *Peah,* chapter 1, mishnah 1; Rambam, *Hilchot Talmud Torah,* chapter 3, *halacha* 3; *Shulchan Aruch,* "Yoreh Deah," chapter 246:18. The Talmud teaches that the first thing judged when a person stands in front of the heavenly tribunal is in regard to Torah study. See: Talmud *Kiddushin,* 40b; Rambam, *Hilchot Talmud Torah,* chapter 3, *halacha* 5; *Shulchan Aruch,* "Yoreh Deah," chapter 246:19.

26. There are entire chapters dedicated in *Shulchan Aruch*—the code of Jewish law—to discussing the various laws of respect one must show for a Torah scholar (albeit, a God-fearing honest scholar. See: *Shulchan Aruch,* "Yoreh Deah," chapter 243:3). See: *Shulchan Aruch,* "Yoreh Deah," chapter 243–245; Rambam, *Hilchot Talmud Torah,* chapter 6.

27. Joshua, chapter 1, verse 8. See: Rambam, *Hilchot Talmud Torah,* chapter 1, *halacha* 8. See also: Talmud *Menachot,* 99b. (This term is used repeatedly with regard to Torah study. See, e.g., Psalms, chapter 1, verse 2.)

becomes part of one's existence.[28] It is not sufficient to have a superficial comprehension, but one must cogitate and contemplate the Torah, until it becomes completely ingrained. This vigorous style of study is called *hitbonenut*—intellectual meditation.[29] The student contemplates the thought until it becomes fully illuminated in his mind and heart.

The Torah of one who has never learned it, is called the Torah of God. Once however, one has studied and mastered his knowledge of Torah, the Torah is then called in his own name.[30] The student becomes, so to speak, a master of the Torah. A true student of Torah is one whose mind has been so thoroughly transformed that it has become operative in the modality of Torah. And thus, his own opinions and ideas are the same as the Torah.

Being that the Torah is part of the infinite,[31] when one studies Torahh, the mind grasps the Torah and by extension (figuratively speaking), the Infinite. This is the most fantastic and greatest unity a finite can achieve with the infinite. The mind grasps the subject of Torah and encompasses it, while concurrently being ensconced within the subject.[32] There occurs the ultimate fusion and integration between finite man and the Infinite Creator.

---

28. Rabbi David Kimchi, the Radak (1160–1235), *Sefer Sherashim "Erech Hagah,"* Rashi explains that the word *yehege* connotes a vigorous study, which involves questioning and finding answers, bringing one case as proof for another, and so on. See Talmud *Avodah Zarah,* 19a; Rashi, *Ve Achar Kach Yehege.* Both these interpretations connote a serious study, a comprehensive intellectual pursuit.

29. The sixth Chabad rebbe, Rabbi Yoseph Yitzchak, *Igrot Kodesh,* Vol. 3, pp. 525–529.

30. Talmud *Kiddushin,* 32b; *Avodah Zarah,* 19a; See Rashi, ad loc.

31. See: *Zohar,* part 1, p. 24a; part 3, p. 73a. In the words of the Talmud "I have given Myself in my writings (i.e., Torah)." Talmud *Shabbat,* 105a, *"Ayin Yakkov."* See also: *Midrash Rabba,* Exodus, *parsha* 33, chapter 1.

32. Rabbi Schneur Zalman of Liadi, *Tanya,* chapter 5.

Since the main body of the Torah was given over verbally, therefore, an essential part of Torah study involves reviewing and remembering.[33] The Talmud says,[34] "One who studies without reviewing is as one who has planted without reaping."[35] Reviewing and retaining the thoughts in memory are equal in value to the contemplating itself. A structured form of meditation is the continuous repetition of a Torah thought, engraving the knowledge into the memory.

Memory is comprised of three elements. The first step is the recording of the information, the mind then must retain that information, and finally be able to bring forth the information at will. When one is listening to a lecture or lesson and wishes to commit it to memory, it is vital that while recording the information, one should not attempt to ponder the issue. The listener should allow the mind to be like a tape recorder and simply record; for when the mind is engrossed in absorbing, it cannot simultaneously be involved with processing.[36] This

---

33. This was especially true prior to the documentation of the oral Torah. See: Rabbi Schneur Zalman of Liadi, *Hilchot Talmud Torah,* chapter 2, *halacha* 3. The Talmud teaches that when the Torah was taught for the very first time it was repeated four times (Talmud *Eruvin,* 54b). The simple reason for this repetition, was so that the studies should be remembered. The Midrash says that one's recall of Torah should be to the extent that when asked any question, one is able to replay without hesitation. See: Deuteronomy, chapter 6, verse 7; *Midrash Sifri,* cited by Rashi, ad loc.

34. Talmud *Sanhedrin,* 99a.

35. In Talmudic times the norm was for a study to be repeated one hundred times. See Talmud *Chagigah,* 9b; Rabbi Schneur Zalman of Liadi, *Tanya,* chapter 15.

36. In the laws of *kashrut* there is the law that says that (a utensil) "while being preoccupied ejecting from what is within cannot absorb (at the same time) anything." See: Talmud *Chullin,* 112b; Rashi, *VeOfot;* Rambam, *Hilchot Maachalot Asurot,* chapter 6, *halacha* 16; *Magid Mishnah,* ad loc; *Shulchan Aruch,* "Yoreh Deah," chapter 70, *halacha* 1. See also: *Shulchan Aruch,* "Orach Chaim," chapter 452, *halacha* 1, as explained by the *Aruch Hashulchan,* and the *Mishnah Berurah,* ad loc.

processing of the information can only occur later, after the lesson has been memorized.

Studies have demonstrated that memory can actually be improved upon. There are certain tricks a person can employ to increase the potential to memorize. The basic method is to identify and associate what one wishes to remember with something that is more familiar. For example, if a person is attempting to remember numbers, one should identify each number with a corresponding object or pattern that is familiar. The premise being that what is more common and familiar to the person easier to recall. One uses an object to remember a subject. The Talmud speaks of using signs while studying to assist memory,[37] in order for the subject to become ingrained in one's psyche.[38]

Memory can also be evoked through the senses, namely, by associating a thought with one of the five senses. While walking in the park on a rainy day, a new insight comes to mind. By recalling the mood of that moment, what one was seeing, hearing, smelling, and so on at the time of the thought, the thought may be easier to recapture. According to the Talmud, to help memorize one's studies, one should study with a tune.[39] By joining a thought with a familiar tune, the studies are better remembered. These types of meditations are specifically geared to enhance a person's memory.

---

37. Talmud *Eruvin,* 54b. See also: Talmud *Shabbat,* 104a; *Eruvin,* 21b; Rashi, *Agmerei.* This technique of using signs was utilized by the Talmudic sages throughout the Talmud. See: *Eruvin,* 54b; Rashi, *Simonim.*

38. Talmud *Eruvin,* 54b; *Moreinu Harav Shemuel Eliezer Eidels, Maharsah* (1555–1631), ad loc. "Only those who placed signs to their studies were able to remember their studies." Talmud, *Eruvin,* 53a.

39. See: Talmud, *Megillah,* 32a, as explained by the Tosefot, ad loc. See also: Rabbi Chaim Yoseph David Azulay, *D'Vash L'Phi* (Jerusalem: 1962), "*Marrechet Zayin,*" 7.

The Two Modes of Thinking

When we are faced with a difficult problem that needs to be solved how do we respond? An immediate reaction might be to ponder the subject matter, with all its intricacies, until a solution or answer comes to mind. One directs and channels the mind to focus firmly on the issue and dwell on it, with the least distraction possible. Yet, when a person operates in this intense modality of concentration, it may come at the expense of everyday mundane functions, such as eating, sleeping, and the like. By focusing entirely on a matter that needs to be resolved, one may lose concentration in other areas of life.

The art of focus may be what differentiates the genius from the average smart person. Perhaps the brilliance of a genius lies in his ability to be completely absorbed and focused on his quest. Yet, complete dedication and focus on one aspect of life, for instance developing musically, mathematically and so on, may cause neglect in other areas in one's development. As a result, a genius may not pay attention to his physical appearance or his social mannerisms. This type of behavior may prompt other people to consider him eccentric or weird.

In truth every human being has the potential to be a genius, and in a sense, everyone is a genius in what is important and matters to them most. The example given is of a layman who goes before a judge to argue a case. Although the judge is more learned and scholarly, nonetheless, at times, the layman may demonstrate great acumen, and argue with greater intelligence than the judge. The reason for this is that the case argued is a factual matter to him, while for the judge it is entirely hypothetical. The outcome of the case has much greater relevance to the layman than to the learned judge.[40]

---

40. The fourth Chabad rebbe, Rabbi Shmuel. See: *Hayom Yom,* The 9th of Elul.

Activating the genius within, by concentrating and focusing one's intellectual activity, may lead to a breakthrough, upon which entire new dimensions of thought and comprehension can occur. By stretching one's rational, conscious mind to its capacity, one transcends the everyday level of intellect, and calls forth deeper, unstructured thoughts—pure, intuitive, ingenious, nonlinguistic thoughts, that are not limited by logic or rationale.[41] On this level, thoughts may not be completely formulated in cognitive terms; however, they just seem to make sense. There appears to be a clarity that is beyond verbal description. And with it occurs a rush of excitement that overwhelms the person, and causes great joy and delight.[42] Legend has it that when Hiero II asked Archimedes to find a method to discern whether a crown was made of pure gold, or mixed with silver, the solution occurred to him as he began to lower himself into a bath. Archimedes realized that, that which is less dense when placed in water, displaces more water than an equal weight of something more dense, as in gold. Upon this realization, he rushed into the street without his pants, screaming "Eureka! Eureka!" ("I have found it! I have found it!") The rush of the new idea so overwhelms that at times it may eclipse all other considerations.

Additionally, while being in this state, one may feel fully energized. At times it appears as if the entire energy of the body is involved in the intellectual quest. When operating in this modality a person feels more alive, able and positive about himself and his world. This is another example of meditation, where the intense concentration becomes a full-body experience. The meditator feels an expansion and begins to operate on an elevated state of awareness.

---

41. The sixth Chabad rebbe, Rabbi Yoseph Yitzchak, *Sefer Hamaamorim 5701*, pp. 52–53; *Sefer Hamaamorim 5706*, p. 46.

42. Rabbi Yehudah's face would shine from happiness upon discovering a new insight of Torah. Jerusalem Talmud *Shabbat*, chapter 8, *halacha* 1.

The above is a particular modality of thinking, wherein one concentrates all his energies on a specific thought, and through intense concentration brings forth a solution. Yet, this is but one way through which innovation and invention may occur. There is also a phenomenon wherein innovative and inventive thoughts enter the mind, nonconsciously.[43] One may ponder a difficult issue for many days, and seeing no solution on the horizon, decide to give up on solving the problem entirely. Many days may pass, and the issue becomes all but forgotten, when all of a sudden, out of the blue, a solution appears. These are insights that tend to come suddenly and uncharacteristically, not in a study setting, but while relaxing in a bath, or taking a stroll, and the like. During these times of relaxation, following a concentrated focused intellectual endeavor, a flash of intuition occurs that brings clarity and resolution.

This is quite a common phenomenon. How many times in conversation have we attempted to remember someone's name, and try hard as we may, the name will not come to mind. You may even feel as if the name is on the tip of the tongue, but it simply cannot be verbalized. Hours may pass, and after you have completely forgotten the conversation, the name appears. When you tried to remember the name, you simply could not, and when you gave up on the issue, it somehow appeared. According to Kabbalah this occurs because a person's *co'ach hamaskil*—the source of intelligence, never ceases to function.[44] Although your conscious mind was previously scanning the memory to find the name and is now occupied with other thoughts, your subconscious mind is still working on finding that name.

---

43. The Chabad rebbe, Rabbi Yoseph Yitzchak, *Sefer Hamaamorim 5701,* pp. 52–53.

44. This only occurs following intense dedication and concentration of thought. See: The sixth Chabad rebbe, Rabbi Yoseph Yitzchak, *Sefer Hamaamorim 5700, "Ki Imcah,"* p. 14.

Many of the great discoveries were thought up while the inventor was in such states of awareness. Not while they were concentrating, but rather when they were relaxing. Countless scientists and inventors have said that their discoveries came to them seemingly out of nowhere. In the middle of doing something completely unrelated to their research, they were suddenly stricken by a bolt of light, a flash of insight, which illuminated the entire issue.

There is room to argue that the more relaxed the body and the mind are, the more one can be sensitive to his creative side. A state of relaxation causes a higher alertness in one's mental state. Epiphanies can occur when they are allowed through relaxation of the mind and body. Interestingly, there were many Chassidic masters who would pause for a moment or two while engrossed in intense contemplation, to sing a song.[45] They would use a melody as a meditative technique to relax the rational mind from its concentrated modality, and thereby become more intuitive.

Circulating in the mystical city of Safed in the sixteenth century was a meditative technique called *gerushin*—translated as exiles, or as divorcing. The 16th-century Kabbalist Rabbi Moshe Corodovero writes how he, with a group of his companions, would go out into the fields (exiling or divorcing themselves from society), with the sainted master Rabbi Shlomo Alkabatz. Once alone, they would become *involved* with the verses of Torah. This method entailed that they engaged in Torah study topically without going into depth, and through this type of meditation, new and previously unimaginable insights were achieved.[46] Today very little is known of this method. However,

---

45. A talk by the sixth Chabad rebbe, Rabbi Yoseph Yitzchak, *"Shabbat Parshat Noach,"* 5706 (1945).

46. Rabbi Moshe Corodovero writes that it is inconceivable for the person who was not there to believe the magnitude of the revelations that were there revealed. He calls these insights "gifts." See: Rabbi Moshe Corodovero,

it suggests a type of meditation that does not involve intense thinking, but rather, uses the verse as a mantra, to reach a higher state of awareness and understanding. Once they reached this expanded state, deeper and more innovative insights were revealed.

The cognitive structured type of meditation reached its zenith in the late 18th–early 19th century, with the development of the *Hitbonenut* method ormeditation. The goal of this style of meditation is for the conscious, rational mind to become enveloped in transcendence, and ultimately through the intellect, experience that which is beyond the intellect. This type of meditation will be explained further on.

Type C

There are also meditations that are transcendental and trance-like. The objective of these meditations is for the meditator to leave his ordinary state of mind and reach a higher, expanded state of awareness, perhaps even achieving a mystical experience. Usually, the path one takes to reach that place, is not through intellect, but through the emotions. The meditation is a nonintellectual one. The meditator does not ponder an issue with the intellect and then attain. Rather, he uses a meditation that is geared to touch another locus within, other than the intellect. For example, he may repeat a verse over and over again, he may listen to meditative music, dance meditatively, and so forth.[47]

Or Ne'erav, part 5, chapter 2, p. 40. He also writes that these new insights will be written about in a separate book. See: *Safer Gerushin* (Jerusalem: 1962). Rabbi Chaim Yoseph David Azulay writes that the book *Safer Gerushin* is called *Gerushin* because the meditator would exile himself for the sake of the *shechinah*. See: *Shem Hagdalim*, "*Marrechet Siforim*," *gimel* (48).

47. We find that the prophets would use music and dance as an introduction to reach prophecy. See: Chapter 1, footnote 21.

The objective and goal of these types of meditations is a panoscopic vision, which is something that is beyond the everyday. It is the ability to visualize more than the three dimensions, to experience a blur of the senses, extrasensory perception, to touch a place of timelessness and predict future events. The peak of the experience is to attain spiritual enlightenment, to experience a spiritual epiphany where the holy spirit rests upon the person. *Ruach hakodesh* being the lofty level that is one rung lower than actual prophecy.[48] Though prophecy in the Biblical sense ceased to exist thousands of years back,[49] the level of *ruach haKodesh* did not. It is still available to all who wish to attain it.[50]

Most of these Kabbalistic meditations, where the ultimate

---

48. *Ruach hakodesh* is a rung lower than prophecy. See: Rabbi Moshe ben Nachman, the Ramban, *Baba Batra,* 11b; Rabbi Meir Ben Gabbai, *Avodot Hakodesh,* part 4, chapter 22; Rabbi Yitzchak Aramah, *Akeidot Yitzchak,* "Parshat Bereishit," *shar* 6; Rabbi Moshe Chaim Luzzatto, *Derech Hashem,* part 3, chapter 3:6. *Ruach hakodesh* is not as clear as prophecy. The Talmud mentions a ten-step ladder that must be climbed before one can attempt to attain the level of *ruach hakodesh.* See: Talmud *Avodah Zarah,* 20b. See also: Mishnah *Sotah,* chapter 9, at the end; The Jerusalem Talmud, *Shekalim,* chapter 3, *halacha* 3; *Shabbat,* chapter 1, *halacha* 3. For different variations of what these ten are, see also: "*Tosfot Yom Tov*" at the end of *Sotah.*

49. Talmud *Sotah,* 48b; *Yuma,* 9b; *Sanhedrin,* 11a.

50. *Ruach hakodesh* was common in Talmudic times. See e.g.: Talmud *Eruvin,* 60b; Tosefot, ad loc; *Eruvin,* 64b; Jerusalem Talmud *Shevi'it,* chapter 9, *halacha* 1; *Sotah,* chapter 1, *halacha* 4; *Midrash Rabba,* Genesis, *parsha* 79, chapter 6. For the appearance of *ruach hakodesh* in the post-Talmudic era, see: Rabbi Yehudah Halevi, The Kuzari, *maamor* 5, chapter 12; Rabbi Avraham Ben David of Posqueres, the Raavad (1120–1198) on the Rambam, "*Hilchot Lulav,*" chapter 8, *halacha* 5; Raavad on the Rambam, *Hilchot Beit Habechirah,* chapter 6, *halacha* 14. See also: Rabbi Moshe Sofer, the Chatam Sofer, Responsa, "*Orach Chaim,*" chapter 208. The Kabbalist Rabbi Chaim Vital, writes that *ruach hakodesh* is a level that every human being can attain, even today. See: *Sharei Kedusha,* part 3, *shar* 6, in the beginning; part 3, *shar* 7. Rabbi Pinchas Eliyohu Ben Meir of Vilna, *Sefer Habrit,* part 2, *maamor* 11, chapter 3, p. 482. See also: Midrash *Tana Devei Eliyahu,* chapter 9.

goal is *ruach hakodesh,* or a similar type of revelation, require the meditator to have a comprehensive knowledge of the finer points of Kabbalah. They entail intricate details of Kabbalistic literature. The meditations for the most part involve pronouncing or imagining various *yichudim*—unifications of divine names. For most readers, it would seem inane and at best superfluous to talk about these *yichudim.* Therefore, although in the Kabbalah there is a fair amount of mention of these *yichudim,* for immediate purposes, only meditations that have practical application for everyone are recorded.

There is a method of trancelike meditation that was once famous, and is as applicable today as it was hundreds of years back. The author of the Shulchan Aruch—the code of Jewish law, Rabbi Yoseph Caro, a 16th-century scholar, was renowned as a man of law, and also known as a great mystic. Rabbi Yoseph would recite a Mishnah until he was able to connect with the soul of the Mishnah. When he would achieve a heightened state of awareness *a maggid—an* angelic energy associated with the Mishnah, would reveal illuminating insights into the Mishnah and life in general.[51]

An eyewitness to this occurrence tells how, together with his companions and Rabbi Yoseph Caro, he once resolved to stay awake the entire night of Shevuot to read Torah. First, he writes, they chanted portions from the Torah. When they concluded with the Torah, they began to study Mishnah. After a while, they began to hear the angelic voice of the Mishnah, revealing profound insights.[52] Reaching such a lofty level, where

---

51. He would communicate with the angelic force after reading several chapters from the Mishnah. See: Rabbi Yoseph Caro, *Magid Mesharim* (Jerusalem: Orah, 1960), pp. 4–5. Rabbi Chaim Vital also used this method. He speaks of inducing a state of meditation by reading a Mishnah three times. See: *Shivchei Rabbi Chaim Vital,* pp. 37–38.

52. In an introduction by Rabbi Shlomo Alkabatz (1505–1584) to *Magid Mesharim,* p. 18.

an angelic force appears, says a Chassidic Rebbe, is attainable to all of us.[53]

Type D

Prayer As Meditation.

There is a common misconception that prayer is exclusively a petition and a time to request sustenance. Prayer truly is that, but it is also much more. The Hebrew word for prayer is *tefilah*, which means to connect and join.[54] Prayer offers the opportunity for a finite man to connect with the infinite, to establish a soul-to-soul dialogue with the source of all reality. Intention plays a crucial role in prayer. There must be a general awareness and consciousness of the infinite throughout one's prayers. Without this awareness, prayers are likened to a body without a soul,[55] and in effect, prayer does not occur.[56] This general

---

53. Rabbi Moshe Chaim Ephraim of Sudylkov, *Degel Machanah Ephraim* (Jerusalem: Mir, 1995, "Parshat *Chukat*," p. 188b.

54. See: Genesis, chapter 30, verse 8, "*Targum Onkelot.*" See also: Rashi, "*Seforno,*" ad loc; Rabbi Mattisyohu Delecreta (Poland sixteenth century) in his commentary to *Shaarei Orah* (by Rabbi Yoseph Gikatalia) (New York: Moriah, 1985), *shar 2*, p. 63. Rabbi Schneur Zalman of Liadi: *Torah Or*, "*Parshat Terumah,*" p. 79d. The sixth Chabad rebbe, Rabbi Yoseph Yitzchak, *Sefer Hamaamorim 5709*, p. 79; Rabbi Menachem Mendel of Vitebsk, *Pri Ha'aretz,* "*Parshat Vayigash.*" See also: Rabbi Elimelech of Lizhensk, *Noam Elimelech,* "*Parshat Bereishit.*"

55. Rabbi Bachya Ibn Pakudah, *Chovot Halevavott,* "*Shar Cheshbon Hanefesh,*" chapter 3, part 9; *Safer Hayashar, shar* 13, p. 124.

56. See: Rambam, *Hilchot Tefilah,* chapter 4, *halacha* 15; *Shulchan Aruch Harav,* "*Orach Chaim,*" the end of chapter 101; Rabbi Yehudah Ha-Chassid, *Sefer Chassidim,* chapter 785. See also: Rambam, *Moreh Nevuchim,* part 3, chapter 51. Rabbi Chaim Brisker (1853–1918) explains that without the general intention that one is praying in the presence of God, it is as if one did

praying meditation should be on the divine presence, visualizing oneself standing in front of one's creator.[57] More specifically, with each part of prayer, another type of meditation is needed.

Prayer is analogous to the ladder in Jacob's dream, which stands on the ground and reaches up into the heavens. The ladder of prayer is comprised of four steps.[58] At the outset of the prayer one stands on the first rung, and through the course of the prayer one climbs the ladder of spiritual perfection, all the while communicating with the Source of life.

Kabbalah speaks of four general worlds.[59] The lowest world is our own physical universe, with its spiritual counterpart, the world of *asiyah*—completion. This is the world of action, the world the way we know it, with its physical dimensions of time and space. A higher, more refined universe is the world of yitzirah—formation. This is the world of pure emotions, the world the way it exists in a formatted state, but not yet completed. At this level there is still a sense of time, though not as apparent as in the world of *asiyah*. A higher universe is the world of *beriah*—creation, which is the world of intelligence, a mental-intellectual universe, where reality begins

---

not pray. See: *Chidushei Rabbi Chaim Halevi Al HaRambam,* "*Hilchot Tefilah,*" chapter 4, *halacha* 1, p. 2c.

57. The general meditation is based on the verse "I have placed God before me at all times," Psalms, chapter 16, verse 8. See: Talmud *Sanhedrin,* 22a; Talmud *Yuma,* 53b; Rashi, "*L'smoel*"; Rambam, *Hilchot Tefilah,* chapter 4, *halacha* 16; *Shulchan Aruch,* "*Orach Chaim,*" chapter 98, *halacha* 1. See also: Talmud *Berachot.*

58. Genesis, chapter 28, verse 12; See: *Zohar,* part 1, p. 266b; part 3, p. 306b; *Tikunei Zohar, tikkun* 45. See also: Rabbi Schneur Zalman of Liadi, *Likutei Torah,* "*Parshat Beshalach,*" p. 2b. Rabbi Yeshayah Halevi Horowitz, *Shenei Luchot Habrit, Shar HaShamaim,* p. 127.

59. These four worlds are alluded to in Isaiah, chapter 43, verse 7. The four letters of the name of God, the Tetragrammaton, allude to these four worlds. *Yod—atziluth,* the first *hei—Beriah, vov—yitzirah,* the final *hieasiyah.* See: Rabbi Chaim Vital, *Sharei Kedusha,* part 3, *shar* 1.

to emerge, yet its existence is without any shape or form. It is a world of transcendence and potentiality. The highest of the worlds is *atziluth*—emanation, nearness, a world that is close enough to its source to have no self-perceived existence on its own. It feels itself a mere extension of its Source.[60]

These four fields of consciousness are reflected in soul of man. There are four levels of one's soul.[61] The lowest is *nefesh*—soul. It is the physical life force, the realm of soul that animates the body and interfaces with the physical energy. It is manifested in the human capability to do action. It is a functional consciousness, which corresponds to the world of *asiyah*. A higher level is *ruach*—spirit. It is the emotional life force, the dimension of soul that gives rise to feelings and emotions. It is a feeling of consciousness, which is analogous to the world of *yitzirah*. The third level is *neshama*—breath, the power of intellect. It is a cognitive consciousness, which corresponds to the world of *beriah*, the realm of intelligence. The fourth is called *chayah*—living essence, man's power of will. It is a transcendent consciousness, corresponding to the world of *atziluth*.

---

60. The root of the word *atziluth* is *etzel*—near, for this is a world, a separate entity, which in a sense does not exist! However the world of *beriah* is the first world to exist as a separate reality. Thus the word *beriah* means cut off. See: Rabbi Moshe Cordovero, *Pardass Rimonim, shar* 16, chapter 1. See also: Rabbi Shabtai Sheftel Horowitz, *Shefa Tal* (Brooklyn: 1960), *shar 3,* chapter 1, pp. 47a–47b; Rabbi Menacham Azarya De Fano, *S'fas Emess* (Jerusalem), "*Erech Atziluth,*" p. 7a.

61. The Midrash enumerates five parts of the soul: *nefesh, ruach, neshama, chaiyah,* and *yiciddah*. *Midrash Rabbah* Genesis, *parsha* 14, chapter 9; *Midrash Rabbah,* Deuteronomy, *parsha* 2, chapter 37. See also: Talmud *Berachot,* 10a. The reason why only four are mentioned here, is because what is relevant to this discussion is the lower levels of soul (which is elevated and offered during the prayers), and these parts of the soul do not contain a counterpart for the level of *yiciddah*. See: the Lubavitcher Rebbe, *Likutei Sichot,* vol. 6, p. 107.

Traditionally the morning prayers are also divided into four segments. The four parts are *Birchot Hashachar*—morning blessings and recitation of the offerings; *Pisukei D'zimrah*—verses of praise; *Keriat Shema*—blessings and reading of the Shema; and the *Shemoneh Esrei*—eighteen benedictions. With each section of prayer, one attains a more refined state of consciousness; a higher level of soul is achieved and a more elevated world is revealed.[62]

The first segment of prayer is *Birchot Hashachar*, the morning blessings. These are comprised of two sections. In the first, a person offers thanks to the Creator for providing for all physical necessities, for giving strength to the weary, for dressing the naked, and so on. Then one recites the procedure of the offerings in the Holy Temple. The content of both these prayers are analogous to the lowest parts of one's soul, the power of action, functional consciousness. It also corresponds to the lowest level of worlds, the world of action. In the first part a person offers thanks and acknowledges the Creator for providing for all necessities, proclaiming that everything comes from a higher source—everything that is in this physical world of action and tangibility and therefore, by extension, all actions. The same is so with the second part of the prayer, the offerings. The concept is for man to take a physical entity, such as an animal,

---

62. See: Rabbi Chaim Vital, *Pri Eitz Chaim*, "Sharr Hatafila," in the beginning; "Shar HaKavanot"; *D'rushei Tefilat HaShachar, d'rush 1; Olat Tamid,* "Shar HaTefilah," p. 7a; Rabbi Yakov Yoseph of Polonnye, *Toldot Yakov Yoseph,* "Parshat Vayikra," p. 269. Rabbi Moshe Chaim Luzzatto, *Derech Hashem,* part 4, chapter 6:14; Rabbi Tzvi Elimelech of Dinav, *Derech Pikudecha,* p. 174. See also: The fifth Chabad rebbe, Rabbi Shalom Dovber, *Kuntres Ha'avadah,* in the beginning; *Beshoo Shehikdimu* 5672, part 1, p. 233; Rabbi Chaim of Volozhin, *Nefesh HaChaim,* shar 2, chapter 18. (For another way of dividing the prayers into four, see: the sixth Chabad rebbe, Rabbi Yoseph Yitzchak, *Sefer Hamaamorim—Kuntreisim,* vol. 2, p. 638. See also, Rabbi Klunimus Kalman, *Maor Vashemesh,* "Parshat Beshalach," p. 196.)

and transform it into holiness. This is achieved by having it be consumed in the Godly fire of the altar. This idea is also a declaration where man offers his world of actions, his *nefesh* as a vehicle to express the transcendent. This is the specific intention of the meditation that one should aspire to have while praying the first segment of the prayers. Having in mind a total transformation of all physicality, of the world at large, and of his world in particular, to the Spirit.

The second segment of the prayers, the second step on the ladder, is the world of *yitzirah* and the state of *ruach*—emotional consciousness. This part of prayer is called *Pisukei D'zimrah*, verses of praise. In this portion of prayer, one continuously praises the Creator for the miracles of creation and the wonders performed throughout the ages. This prayer arouses a person's emotions and feelings.[63] Praise can be a method a person uses to express his love and admiration. At this stage of prayer, all our feelings for the physical and materialistic are redirected and rechanneled to the Source of all life. The obstacles that stand on the path toward the infinite are by now put aside,[64] and the only emotions we experience are noble and transcendent.

Having dedicated all of one's emotions, one ascends the ladder of transcendence, the ladder of prayer. One enters the world of intelligence, the world of *beriah,* corresponding to the level of *neshama.* This sector of prayer is called *Keriat*

---

63. *Pisukei D'Zimrah* are songs that arouse one's emotions. Rabbi Schneur Zalman of Liadi, *Torah Or,* "*Parshat Beshalach,*" p. 62c.

64. The sixth Chabad rebbe, Rabbi Yoseph Yitzchak, *Sefer Hamaamorim—Kuntreisim,* vol. 2, p. 638. See also: Rabbi Meir Ben Gabbai, *Tola'at Yakov,* "*Sod Pisukei D'Zimrah,*" p. 21; Rabbi Yitzchak Abuhav, *Menorat HaMaor* (Jerusalem: 1999), *ner* 3, *klal* 3, chapter 3:3, p. 285. Rabbi Yeshayah Halevi Horowitz, *Shenei Luchot Habrit,* Torah Sh'Bektav, p. 169. *Shuvvim Tat,* p. 228.

Shema—blessings and reading of the Shema. During this segment of the prayer, one is seated,[65] contrary to the end of the
previous prayer where one was standing. The difference between standing and sitting is that standing indicates movement, excitement, emotions, while sitting shows that one is
calm, sedate, and collected. At this point in the prayer, one
takes all the previous excitement and inspiration experienced
during the prayer, all the previous emotions (which by now
have been transformed), and one begins reassessing from a different orientation. All the previous feelings are internalized
until they become a reality and not just a fleeting emotion. The
word *shemah* in Hebrew means hear, listen, understand.[66] One
takes all the inspirations experienced and listens to it. These
awesome feelings are not left in an emotional state. Often when
the initial excitement dies down so does the inspiration, but by
listening, hearing, and internalizing these emotions, one makes
them an indivisible part of one's experience, turning it over and
over, until it becomes part of his consciousness.

It is only following the reading of the *Shemah*, when one has
already channeled one's actions, emotions, and intelligence, that
one can enter God's, so to speak, private chamber.[67] One is
ready to pray the last and profoundest of prayers, the *Shemoneh
Esrei*.[68] During these prayers one's feet are together, indicating

---

65. It is preferable to sit during these prayers. See: *Tur,* "*Orach Chaim,*"
chapter 63. See also: *Midrash Rabbah,* Genesis, *parsha* 48, chapter 7.

66. Rabbi Schneur Zalman of Liadi, *Torah Or,* "*Parshat Bereishit,*" p. la.

67. The *kodesh hakodashim,* the holy of holies. Rabbi Yakov Emdin, *Sidur
Beit Yakov,* before *Shemoneh Esrei,* p. 66.

68. *Shemoneh Esrei* is the number eighteen in Hebrew, for when this prayer
was instituted by the "men of the great assembly" it had eighteen blessings.
See: Talmud *Megillah,* 17b. Later on, after the destruction of the second Temple,
during the period that Rabbi Gamliel was the *nassi* (leader of Israel), a nineteenth blessing was added. In the Talmud this prayer is referred to as simply
"the prayer."

that no further movement is needed, for by now one has reached the apex of the ladder.[69] The feet together also symbolizes a complete abandonment of one's sense of self as a separate, independent existence.[70]

Swaying during the prayers is for the most part encouraged.[71] Nonetheless during the *Shemoneh Esrei* the Kabbalists strongly discouraged it,[72] for in this state of prayer there is no room for self-expression.[73] One is completely nullified as a separate entity, and the notion of separateness ceases to exist. One enters the world of *atziluth,* the world of oneness. Upon

---

69. The Talmud teaches that one should pray this prayer with his feet together. Talmud *Berachot,* 10b. The Jerusalem Talmud offers a reason, and that is to resemble the angels and the priests in the holy Temple. Talmud, *Berachot,* chapter 1, *halacha* 1. See also: Rabbi Mordecai Jaffe (1530–1612), *Levush,* "*Orach Chaim,*" chapter 90:1.

70. Rabbi Shloma Ben Aderet, the Rashba (1235–1310), Talmud *Berachot,* 10b; Rabbeinu Bachya, Numbers, chapter 16, verse 22. See also: Rabbi Yoseph Caro, *Beit Yoseph,* "*Orach Chaim,*" chapter 95. There is also the reason to demonstrate that the right powers (the Godly inclinations) and the left powers (the evil inclinations) are both unified in service. Rabbi Moshe Metrani, *Beit Elokim,* "*Shar Hatefila*" (Jerusalem: Otzer Hasefarim, 1985), chapter 7, pp. 27–28; Rabbi Chaim Ben Betzalel (1515–1588), *Safer HaChaim,* "*Safer Selicha U'Mechila*" (Jerusalem: Machon Sharei Yoshar, 1996), chapter 8, p. 185.

71. See: *Zohar,* part 3, p. 218b. Rabbienu Yona of Gerondi, *Sharei Teshuvah,* "*Safer Hayirah,*" p. 166; Rabbi David Ben Yoseph, *Avudrham;* Rabbi Moshe Isserles, the Rama, *Shulchan Aruch,* "*Orach Chaim,*" chapter 48:2; Rabbi Yitzchak Abuhav, *Menorat HaMaor, ner* 3, *klal* 3, chapter 13:2, p. 309. See also: Rabbi Yehudah Halevi, the Kuzari, *maamor* 2, chapter 79–80. Rabbi Eliezer Ezcary, *Safer Cheraidim,* chapter 66:30, p. 234.

72. *Shulchan Aruch,* "*Orach Chaim,*" chapter 48; *Magen Avraham,* 4. See also: Rabbi Menachem Azaryah De Fano, *Asarah Maamorot, maamor* "*Aim Kal Chai,*" part 1, chapter 33; Rabbi Chaim Yoseph David Azulay, *Avodat Hakodesh,* "*Kesher Gudal,*" chapter 12:1. In the name of the Kabbalists.

73. See: Rabbi Yehudah Lowe, *Nesivoth Olam,* "*Nesiv Ha'Avadah,*" chapter 3.

reaching this level, one proclaims that even will, which is the nearest and closest thing to oneself, is now an extension of Godliness. At this stage, after transforming one's actions, emotions, intelligence, and will, all one desires and yearns is to be submerged entirely in the greater existence of the Infinite.[74]

These are the four basic divisions of the morning prayer, with their spiritual interpretations. It is understood that when one undertakes this spiritual journey of prayer, and joins with heart and intention, then the person will be radically changed for the better. The prayers will transform them. By having the appropriate intentions during the prayers, there is the potential to change a state of helplessness, hopelessness, and depression, to a state of liberation and empowerment. Whereas before praying one may feel their own *yeshut*—ego, self-centerness, and attachment to all things physical, at the conclusion of the prayers, one may feel transcendent and selfless. Prayer has a transformative potency that can change a person from being egotistical to Godly, from being in a limited confined state, to an elevated expansive one. Yet, a requisite for change is the realization of a problem. Consequently, it may be important that before beginning to pray, one should meditate on one's alienation and perhaps, one's spiritual incoherent state, and the powerfulness of God.[75] One should aspire to identify and unify with this power, through the meditation, that is prayer.

---

74. The Baal Shem Tov says it is a miracle that one remains alive following the prayers. See: *Tzavoas Horivash,* chapter 42; *Likutei Yekarim,* chapter 2; *Or Haemet,* p. 204; *Ba'al Shem Tov Al HaTorah,* "*Amud HaTefilah,*" pp. 116–117.

75. Rabbienu Yona on *Berachot,* 30b. See also: *Berachot,* 30b; Rashi, *Koived Rosh;* Rabbi Moshe Isserles, the Ramah, *Shulchan Aruch,* "*Orach Chaim,*" chapter 98, *halacha* 1; *Shulchan Aruch Harav,* "*Orach Chaim,*" chapter 98:1. Such meditations are especially important *before* one begins to pray; Rabbi Yakov Yehoshua Falk (1680–1756) *Pnei Yehoshua,* "*Berachot,*" chapter 5, in the beginning. See also: *Shulchan Aruch,* "*Orach Chaim,*" Rabbi Yisrael Meir Hakohen, *Mishnah Berurah,* chapter 98:1.

A Chassid once complained to his master that he had meditated so vigorously before beginning to pray that when the time came for him to actually pray, he had no more strength to meditate. The master answered him, "*Nu,* so what do you care if you have prayed, before praying. The essence of prayer is *deveikut*—adhesion, feeling and communicating with the infinite source of life, and you have already achieved that."[76]

A good example of a structured form of meditation are these set prayers. Besides the general consciousness of the Infinite's presence needed for prayer, one also uses the specific parts of prayer as a focus. Prayer is a rigidly structured style of meditation. Each part of prayer is designed to awaken another feeling, another state of awareness."[77]

Notwithstanding this, within the set daily prayers, room

---

76. Rabbi DovBer, the Maggid of Mezritch, says that *deveikut* in prayer is when one is so attached to the words of the prayer that he cannot let go of them, and thus utters each word meticulously. See: *Likutei Yekarim,* chapter 21, "*Or Haemet,*" p. 206.

77. There is also a more detailed meditation in prayer where each word of prayer is measured and counted. The Chassidei Ashkenaz—devotees of medieval Germany (who flourished from the twelfth century onward) would count the words of the *Shemoneh Esrie.* See: Rabbi Yakkov Ben Asher, *Tur,* "*Orach Chaim,*" chapter 113; *Baal HaTurim Al HoTorah,* Exodus, chapter 40, verse 33. The detailed type of meditation during prayer reached its zenith with the teachings of the AriZal. He taught that every word of prayer symbolizes the divine process. Those praying with this intention could spend hours in prayer. One can spend many minutes on each word of prayer. One such Kabbalistic school is the school Bet El in Jerusalem, which was founded in the early seventeen hundreds. Being that these meditations are complicated and necessitate a vast knowledge of the intricate details of Kabbalah, they are not mentioned. In the words of one of the codifiers of *halacha,* "If only we can have intention of the simple meaning of the words." Rabbi Yechiel Michel Epstein, *Aruch HaShulchan,* "*Orach Chaim,*" chapter 112:5. See also: *Shulchan Aruch,* "*Orach Chaim,*" chapter 98; *Magen Avraham,* in the name of the *Zohar.* However, the general division of the prayer into four segments, with their Kabbalistic interpretation and meditation is of greater relevance and can be attained to some degree by all.

was given in the middle of the *Shemoneh Esrei*, the loftiest of prayers, to beseech the Creator verbally for personal necessities.[78] What is more, there were even pious people who would express their own feelings in the middle of prayer, vocalizing their emotions in their own vernacular.[79] Today this is not commonly practiced however, for it is difficult to discern if the expression vocalized is an expression of soul or simply a vocalization of the ego.[80]

In truth, a sense of spontaneity and self-expression are vital elements in any prayer, formal or informal. It was only our lack of communication skills and our inability to express ourselves properly that a formal text of prayer was instituted by the men of the Great Assembly.[81] Today we do use this standard text, and complete spontaneity with God is left for the informal settings of prayer, the prayers that we utter throughout the day.

Kabbalists throughout the ages have advocated being open with our Maker. A person should train himself to be able to speak to God as a child speaks to his father and as one friend speaks to another.[82] Rabbi Nachaman of Breslov, who was one

---

78. In each segment of prayer one may beseech God for that which is relevant in that particular part of prayer, e.g., in the prayer for general health, one may ask for a specific case. However, in the prayer of *Shomeia Tefilah,* a person may ask for anything. See: Talmud *Avodah Zarah,* 8a; Rambam, *Hilchot Tefilah,* chapter 6, *halacha 3; Shulchan Aruch,* "Orach Chaim," chapter 119:1.

79. For the Halacha regarding this issue, *see: Aimrei Yosher,* part 2:109; Rabbi Chaim Eliezer (Shapira) of Munkatsch (1872-1937), *Nemukei Orach Chaim,* chapter 101 (2). See also: Rabbi Aaron Roth (1894-1944), *Shomer Emunim* (Jerusalem: Todot Aaron, 1964), vol. 2, p. 402b.

80. See the Lubavitcher Rebbe, *Igrot Kodesh,* vol. 6, p. 262.

81. Rambam, *Hilchot Tefilah,* chapter 1, *halacha* 2-4. See also: Rabbi Nachman of Breslov, *Sichot Haran,* chapter 229.

82. See: Rabbi Eliezer Ezcary, *Safer Cheraidim,* chapter 65; Rabbi Nachman of Breslov, *Likkutei Moharan,* part 2, chapter 95 and 99; *Likutei Aytzot,* "Hitbodedut," 20, p. 61. This costume was also encouraged by the masters of the *mussar* movement. See Chafetz Chaim, *Michtavei Chafetz*

of the great proponents of this style of prayer, taught that a person should set aside time each day to speak to his Creator. He recommends engaging in conversation with God in one's own language.[83] Through speech, one opens up new opportunities in life, and is able to persevere.[84] He speaks of going out into the open fields and meditating alone in solitude.[85]

Spontaneous communication with God paves the way for all future encounters. As in all close relationships, communication based on honesty, with oneself and the other person promotes greater closeness. As the ego is shed spiritual propinquity is enhanced and authenticity is increased. A degree of ease enters through such communication, until conversing with the Creator is similar to addressing our best friend, letting go of all pretenses and being completely ingenuous. Only when such openness is achieved can we truly be intimate with our Creator.

Type E

A primary reason for meditation is to relax mentally as well as physically. Through meditating one becomes more at ease with oneself, integrated and involved, and begins to feel less alienated,

---

Chaim, pp. 96–97, especially for the penitent. See: *Mishnah Berurah,* "Biur Halacha," chapter 571:2; Rabbi Eliyahu HaCohen, *Sheivet HaMusar,* chapter 20:39, p. 196. See also Rabbi Tzvi of Zhidachov. *Sur Meira V'asai Tov,* pp. 43 and 52.

83. Rabbi Nachman of Breslov, *Likkutei Moharan,* part 2, chapter 97. *Likutei Aytzot,* "Hitbodedut," 13, p. 59; *Sichot Haran,* chapter 229. Reb Nachman says that the spiritual levels he attained were a result of this type of prayer. See: *Shivchei HaRan,* 1:10, p. 5.

84. Rabbi Nachman of Breslov, *Sichot HaRan,* chapter 232.

85. Rabbi Nachman of Breslov, *Likkutei Moharan,* part 2, chapters 93–101; *Sefer HaMidot,* "Hitbodedut," p. 97; *Chayei Moharan,* "Ma'alat Hitbodedut," pp. 463–471; *Likutei Aytzot,* "Hitbodedut," pp. 56–62; *Sichot Haran,* chapters 227-234.

anxious and hostile. Additionally, the meditation can have a positive affect on the physical well being of the meditator, such as
reducing heart rate, blood pressure, and strengthening the
immune functions by lowering stress hormone levels. Meditation
can be an effective antidote in treating such stress-related
conditions as heart disease and migraines.

In Jewish thought the cultivation and nurturing of the
body, and making certain to be in good health is seen as a requisite and foundation for divine service.[86] Life is regarded as a
prime value, and saving a life supersedes all other Mitzvot.[87]
Man is also told that he is responsible for his own health, and
if he ails he must seek medical assistance.[88] Though the primary objective of Jewish meditation is not for health reasons,
mental or physical, rather to transform the meditator and bring
him closer to the Infinite. Nonetheless, anything that can con-
tribute to a person's well being is encouraged.

If through these types of meditations one's health will be
enhanced, then these meditations should be utilized. Yet, instead
of just focusing on trivialities to relax, focus on something of

---

86. The Talmud says that a person who afflicts pain to his body that he
cannot endure is considered sinning. *Tannit,* 11a; *Shulchan Aruch,* "*Orach
Chaim,*" chapter 571:1. See also: Rambam *Hilchot De'ot,* chapter 3, *halacha* 3;
chapter 4, *halacha* 1. Rambam *Shemonah Perakim,* chapter 4; *Kitzur Shulchan
Aruch,* chapter 32; Rabbi Moshe Chaim Luzzato, *Mesilat Yesharim, Hakdamah*
and chapter 26.

87. Talmud *Yuma,* 82a (except the three cardinal sins: adultery, idol worship, and murder).

88. Talmud *Baba Kamma,* 46b. The Talmud teaches that a wise person
should not reside in a city that does not employ a physician. Talmud *Sanhedrin,*
17b; Rambam, *Hilchot Deot,* chapter 4, *halacha* 23. Although the Ramban
Rabbi Moshe Ben Nachman, writes in his commentary on Leviticus, chapter 26,
verse 11 against seeking the aid of a physician. Nonetheless, the commentaries
explain that he is only talking of extremely righteous people, while everyone
else is obligated to seek the help of other mortal being. (See: Rabbi David Ben
Shmuel Halevi, known as the Taz, [1586–1667], *Shulchan Aruch,* "Yoreh
Deah," chapter 336:1.)

importance and use it as a meditation. The Talmud advises that if a person feels an impending headache or other physical ailment looming, he should study Torah, and thus prevent the sickness from taking hold.[89] In fact, with regard to mental stress or any other psychological illness, Torah can be the most fitting anodyne.[90]

Many sicknesses are actually caused by depression.[91] In some cases it is hard to know for certain what comes first, depression or sickness, mental ailment or physical ailment. What causes the other? Does depression arise from the body being weak and feeling run down, or does mental depression cause body illness? Which comes first is difficult to discern, and perhaps it works both ways. One thing for certain is that by becoming mentally sound and content, one may eliminate many illnesses. This is achievable through meditation, especially the *cheshbon hanefesh* type, where the meditator takes an inventory of his life situation, sees what needs perfecting, and what has already been achieved. He then observes his faults and his accomplishments. This type of meditation can be extremely helpful in creating the proper context in which joy can flourish and be made a part of one's reality.

A known Kabbalist speaks of the state following meditation, as having been awakened from one's sleep without any worries.[92] Additionally, meditating and the contemplation of

---

89. Talmud *Eruvin*, 54a. See also: *Midrash Rabba*, Deuteronomy, parsha 10, chapter 1. The Torah can only be used as preventive medicine. See: Maharsah on *Eruvin*, 54a, *Kesef Mishnah* on the Rambam, *Hilchot Akum*, chapter 11, *halacha* 12.

90. See: Proverbs, chapter 4, verse 22. See also: Rabbi Schneur Zalman of Liadi, *Torah Or*, "*Parshat Bereishit*," p. 8a. Rabbi Eliyahu ben Moshe Di Vidas, *Reshit Chachmah, shar HaTeshuvah*, chapter 5, p. 119a.

91. Rabbi Nachman of Breslov writes that all sickness is essentially caused from a lack of happiness. See: *Likutei Moharan*, part 2, chapter 24.

92. Rabbi Nachman of Breslov, *Sichot Haran*, chapter 228.

Torah can become a source of great joy.[93] The Torah offers the proper balance that is much needed in life, and thus through the study of Torah, the meditator may find a true measure of happiness he was always looking for.

---

93. See: Psalms, chapter 19, verse 9; Talmud *Erchin,* 11a; *Taanit,* 30a; Rambam, *"Hilchot Taanit,"* chapter 5, *halacha* 11. *Shulchan Aruch, "Orach Chaim,"* chapter 552:1.

CHAPTER
6

Meditation and the
Five Senses

Each one of us possesses five physical senses. These senses are activated automatically and are reflexive.[1] It is not by choice that we see, hear, smell, touch, and taste, and these senses are perpetually active. If one wishes not to see, hear, or smell, for example, one must actively do something to block that sense.

All of life's experiences are by nature apprehended by one or all of the five senses. When we look at something, we are only conscious of our optical sense, yet, simultaneously we may experience the vision with many of our other senses, albeit not consciously. The feelings one experiences in a museum, where there is a pleasant aroma and background music being played, is unparalleled to viewing an equally beautiful painting in a garage sale. When one is able to train oneself to marshal all of one's senses in an experience, taking notice of the effect on each of the senses during the experience, that experience will then be deeply enhanced.

Meditation works much the same way. Though meditation

---

1. See: Midrash *Tanchuma,* *"Parshat Chayei Sarah,"* chapter 12. See also: Talmud *Nedarim,* 32b.

is an experience of the mind or heart, it is of great benefit that all the senses be involved in the meditational experience. When one meditates one should make certain that the place and time of the meditation is delightful to the senses. (Though not overly welcoming, for then it may cause distraction.) By making sure of his, the meditative experience will take on a new dimension.

Every meditation has a point of focus, an anchor that grasps the meditator's attention to sharpen concentration. The focal Point may be a visual or a sound, and by joining the meditation with one of the senses, focusing one's attention on it, the meditator's concentration is retained. Indeed, the more advanced me is with meditation, the less one needs a physical point of focus. Once one has trained oneself to meditate, then, over time, here is less of a need for a physical object to hold the concentration.

In meditation one may also utilize the senses, not only as a tedium of focus to sustain the concentration, but as a method)f meditation itself. One may employ one of the five senses as a type of mantra. The word mantra is an adopted term from other traditions. The reason it is used here is because of the lack of an accurate Hebrew term for a repetitive act (repeating a phrase or word) as an exercise for meditation. Therefore, it is used solely as a literary device, because of its familiarity.

Auditory

A verbal mantra is the most frequently used, involving the auditory sense. It entails choosing a word or phrase, and repeating it over and over again, until it resonates in one's consciousness, so that the meditator is able to verbalize the mantra without the words actually registering in the conscious mind. Gradually, the word, or phrase, becomes the only concept in the mind, fully investing and filling the mind without allowing any other thoughts to occur.[2]

Eventually, after frequent repetition, the meditator becomes immune and oblivious to the tone of the mantra. (We do not consciously register sounds we are accustomed to hearing.) In he initial stages the mantra removes from the mind all other thoughts by filling it with its own content, and then, in the later stages, the meditator becomes insensitive to its sound as well, Ind the mind is completely clear for meditation. In this way, the recitation of the mantra serves as a prelude for the meditation.

This type of mantra meditation is found in the *Heikhalot* (a first-century mystical text), where it speaks of how through repeating various divine names, one gains entry to the mystical chambers above. The text presents a mystical name of God, and instructs the meditator to repeat the same name more than one hundred times.[3] The recitation of the various names is not intended as an end for itself, but rather, through the recitation, one opens doors to the inner chambers—the *heikhalot*. It is meant to bring the meditator into a state of awareness, by which one is able to travel through the upper chambers of reality.

---

2. Rabbi Yeshayah Halevi Horowitz, the Shalah Hakodesh, writes that if person is distracted by idle thoughts before praying, and he desires to rid himself of these inappropriate thoughts, he should repeat three times the verse of Psalms, chapter 51, verse 12: "Create in me a pure heart O God and renew within me an upright spirit." See: *Machtzit Hashekel* on *Shulchan Aruch, "Orach Chaim,"* chapter 98:1; Rabbi Yisrael Meir Hakohen (1838–1933), *Mishnah Berurah, Shulchan Aruch, "Orach Chaim,"* chapter 98:2. Perhaps the repetition of this verse (besides its innate spiritual powers) serves as a mantra and by repeating it over and over again, it fills the mind with its content while concurrently clearing the mind from all other extraneous thoughts. Incidentally, according to Rabbi Avraham Ben HaRambam, this verse is referring to internal isolation, which is a requisite for attaining prophecy. It is a plea by King David for prophecy. See: *Sefer Hamaspik Leovedei Hashem, "Erech Hitbodedut,"* p. 177.

3. *The Heikholot,* recently reprinted (New York: Gross Bros., 1966).

Mantras are classically used for relaxation. The sound of a mantra slowly becomes soothing and relaxing through its repetition. The Talmud tells of a certain sage who upon laying in bed, and being unable to fall asleep, would repeat the Shema continuously, until he would drift off.[4] This practice is actually advocated in Jewish law. If a person is suffering from insomnia, he should repeat the Shema to himself so that he can fall asleep ensuing the reading of the Shema.[5] Perhaps the repetition of the Shema serves as a type of mantra that causes the relaxation one seeds to fall asleep.

A meditator may also employ a mantra to relax the body in order to intensify the capacities of the mind. The premise being hat the more at ease the body is the less energy it needs, and the more energy is available for the mind. The more relaxed the body is, the more vibrant the mind becomes.

Incidentally, many find that choosing a mantra that has little to no meaning is more beneficial. By using a phrase that is not grounded in rational construct, the meditator makes certain that he does not become entangled in the meaning of the mantra, and stuck at the level of linguistic distinctions, without being able to rise to a deeper and more profound state.

An excellent medium for relaxation is the sound of flowing water.[6] Sitting next to a stream of water can work wonders as a soothing agent. The sound of the water can alleviate a person's shattered nerves and place a person at ease. The Talmud teaches

---

4. Jerusalem Talmud *Berachot,* chapter 1, *halacha* 1.

5. *Shulchan Aruch,* "*Orach Chaim,*" chapter 239; Rabbi Moshe Isserles, the *Ramah,* ad loc. See also: *Shulchan Aruch,* "*Orach Chaim,*" chapter 61:10. (It is important to note that when one wishes to repeat the Shema, he must repeat the entire portion of Shema, not only the first verse. Rabbi Eliyahu of Vilna (1720-1797), *Biur HaGra* on *Shulchan Aruch,* "*Orach Chaim,*" chapter 51:10.)

6. The Talmud speaks of the sound of dripping water helping a person fall asleep. (Falling asleep is an extreme case of overrelaxation.) See: Talmud *Eruvin,* 104a; *Shulchan Aruch,* "*Orach Chaim,*" chapter 338; *Magen Avraham,* 1.

that an omen for success in study is to study in close proximity o
a body of water.[7] The continuous sound of rushing water can serve
as a type of auditory mantra. At first, the relaxing sound of he
water fills the mind, while simultaneously emptying it from ill distracting thoughts, then that sound as well subsides, and the meditator is left with an open mind to meditate.[8]

Listening to appropriate music is another good example of
using the auditory sense as a means to relaxation. Music can
serve as a mantra type of meditation, calming the meditator
and enabling him to relax. The transformative power of music
is such hat it takes a nervous, tense, and disconcerted individual, and places him in a state of ease and tranquility.[9]

Music has the power to impel a complete shift of consciousness. At its best, it can cause a radical altering of a person's
consciousness, from the mundane to the sublime.[10] A prophet
would make use of this awesome medium. The prophet would
listen to music in order to induce a meditative state. The music
would cause a transformation from the prophet's normal state of
consciousness to an expanded state needed to prophesy.[11]
Playing or vocalizing a repetitive melody turns the tune into a

---

7. Talmud *Keritot,* 6a; *Horiot,* 12a.

8. See: Rambam, *Hilchot A'Kum,* chapter 11, *halacha* 6, with regards to
repetitive sounds and altered states of consciousness.

9. Listening to music can remove a person's worries. See: Talmud
Berachot, 57b. As explained in commentary by Rabbi Shemuel Eliezer Eidels,
the Maharsah, *Shelosha Moshivin.* See also: Rabb Shem Tov Ben Yoseph Ibn
Falaquera, *Safer Hamevakesh,* p. 12. Additionally, music can cure a person's shattered nerves. See: Samuel 1, chapter 17. Rabbi David Kimchi, the *Radak,* ad
loc; Rambam, *Shemonah Perakim,* chapter 5. See also: Rabbi Shem Tov Ben
Yoseph Ibn Falaquera, *Safer Hamevakesh,* p. 86; Rabbi Moshe Yichiel Elimelech
of Levertov, *Safer Shemirat HaDa'at,* "Aimrei Tal," *ma'amar Nigun,* pp. 5–7.

10. See: Rabbi Shem Tov Ben Yoseph Ibn Falaquera, *Safer Hamevakesh,*
p. 86.

11. Rambam, *Hilchot Yesodei HaTorah,* chapter 7, *halacha* 4. See also:
Rabbi Yitzchak Aramah, *Akeidot Yitzchak,* "Parshat Shemot," chapter 35.

mantra and brings the prophet to a higher and expanded state of consciousness.

Vision

Another type of mantra would be to use a visual device, to contemplate and concentrate on an object for a fixed period of time, allowing it to fill the mind completely.[12] Once again this type of mantra meditation is unstructured. One uses the mantra only as a launching pad, a starting point to reach a higher state of awareness. Rather than the concentration of the object being the goal of the meditation itself, like contemplating a painting for a long period time to have a better understanding of the painting, one uses the visual to first fill the mind with its content, while concurrently emptying it and erasing from it all other thoughts, ultimately giving the person the clarity to meditate.

Through silencing the normative information processor of the brain, emptying and clearing the mind of mundane thoughts, the meditator can become more sensitive and receptive to an expanded awareness. The prophetic experience is a good example of using a visual to empty the mind completely, thus allowing it to be open to higher experiences and receiving the divine influx. At times, by meditating on the two cherubim (angelic images) situated on top of the holy ark, the prophet would enter a prophetic state.[13] The object of his contemplation became his center of focus, while everything else seemed to vanish, and slowly he entered the higher expanded state needed for prophecy.

Using a visual mantra must be done with caution, for it can

---

12. The Rambam writes of a visual type of meditation, which ancient idol worshipers would use to induce an altered state. See Rambam, *Hilchot A'Kum,* chapter 11, *halacha* 6.

13. Rabbi Dan Yitzchak Abarbenal, Samuel 1, chapter 3, verse 3.

be spiritually risky. On the one hand, the meditator must view he visual object as an important article that must fill and suffuse the mind completely. Yet, he must make certain not to make the object an object of devotion. He must realize that the visual is only a means to reach beyond it, and is not an end for itself.

There was once a custom in many communities to write the four-letter name of God on a sheet of paper, and place the card with God's name in the prayer books. If during prayers one would feel the need to arouse intention and focus, then one would look at these cards and be reminded of God.[14] In this manner the visual was used to enhance the concentration.

There are various Chassidic masters who speak of using methods of visualization during prayer. They speak of picturing oneself standing in the holy temple praying.[15] This visualization an serve to enhance one's focus and enable one to concentrate more intensively on the prayers.

Visual meditation can also be done with an image in mind, an imaginary visualization. The Code of Jewish Law begins with the verse of Psalms[16] "I have placed God before me at all times."[17] Though this directive is meant metaphorically, implying that one is to feel the presence of the Creator at all times, there are some commentaries who interpret this literally.[18] This

---

14. See: Rabbi Eliyahu HaCohen, *Sheivet HaMusar*, chapter 31:21, p. 438; Rabbi Yisrael Meir Hakohen, *Orach Chaim*, chapter 1; *Mishnah Berurah*, 4. Rabbi Chaim Mardechai Morgolit, *Shari Teshuvah*, 3; *Orach Chaim*, Chapter 1.

15. See: Rabbi Elimelech of Lizhensk, *Noam Elimelech*, "Parshat Lech Lecha," p. 19. Rabbi Klunimus Kalmish (Shapiro), the rebbe of Peasetzna, *Hachsharat Ha'Avreichim* (Jerusalem: 1966), p. 32. See also: the sixth Chabad rebbe, Rabbi Yoseph Yitzchak, *Igrot Kodesh*, vol. 8, p. 200.

16. Psalms, chapter 16, verse 8.

17. The Ramah, *Shulchan Aruch*, "Orach Chaim," chapter 1.

18. Rabbi Yehudah Ashkanazi (Germany eighteenth century), *Be'er Heitiv* on *Shulchan Aruch*, "Orach Chaim," 1:3.

means that a person should envision and place the letters of the name of God in his mind, at all times.[19]

One of the celebrated Kabbalists of sixteenth-century Safed, Rabbi Eliezer Ezcary writes of a technique that involves meditating on the divine energy of the *shechinah* hovering overhead and imagining this all-encompassing, loving light pervading the immediate space until the meditator envisions himself dwelling in the heart of this light.[20]

This type of visualization can be performed with any concept in mind. The Zohar speaks of gazing at a flame.[21] The simpler the image, the easier it is to remember and visualize. For this reason many find that using the letters of the Hebrew alphabet as a visual is the lease complicated of visuals. Each letter of the alphabet, Kabbalah teaches, has a unique energy and spiritual life force. The letters are the building blocks of

---

19. See: Rabbi Yitzchak of Acco, *Meirat Einayim*, "*Parshat Ekev*," 11–22; Rabbi Yoseph Caro, *Maggid Mesharim*, "*Parshat Vayikra*," the end; Rabbi Chaim Vital, *Shar Ruach Hakodesh*, *derush* 1; *Sharrei Kedusha*, part 3, *shar* 4. Rabbi Aharon of Modena. *Ma'ava Yavak*. M'amor 1. Chapter 15.

Rabbi Chaim Yoseph David Azulay writes that one should envision the lame of God before going to sleep. *Avodat Hakodesh*, "*Tziparon Shamir*," chapter 8:121. There are those who assert that this visualization enhances a person's memory. See: *Or Tzadikim*, chapter 22. The Chassidic master, Rabbi Elimelech of Lizhensk, writes that the visualization of the name of God can assist to eradicate unwanted thoughts. See: "*The Tzetal Katan*," printed in the beginning of *Noam Elimelech*.

There is also the idea of visualizing and placing on a sheet of paper the various manifestations of the divine chariot. See for example, the Siddur by Rabbi Shalom Sharrei (1702–1777). There is the notion of *Yichudim*— unifications, where the meditater manipulates the various names of God and unifies two or more names together. This is also a complex and highly spiritual undertaking, and thus requires adequate spiritual preparations. See Rabbi Chaim Vital, *Sharei Kedusha*, part 1.

20. Rabbi Eliezer Ezcary, *Safer Cheraidim*, chapter 65.

21. See *Zohar*, part 1, p. 50b.

creation,[22] and the shape of each letter is deliberately designed and meant to convey a message.[23] The advantages of using the alphabet as a visual is twofold, each letter is a simple configuration of lines, semicircles, and so on, and therefore a visual that s easy to remember and envision, and since each letter is)rimming with meaning, it engages the meditator's interest and imagination for longer periods of time.

Before employing a Hebrew letter as a visual, it is advantageous to the meditation to comprehend the spiritual meaning of the shape and pattern of the letter, so that it can become deeply imprinted upon one's memory. For example, using the first letter of the Hebrew alphabet, the aleph (א), as a meditation, one takes notice of its physical structure, observing the various lines of which the letter is comprised. Deconstructing the letter, one begins to detect that the letter is actually a composite of three parts. There are two points, one above and one below, and in between these two points is a slanted bar that separates and simultaneously unites the two.[24] These three parts represent God, who is the point above, man, who is the point below, and he line in between alludes to the trait of humility that is the link that connects man with his Creator.[25] The lower point, man, is

---

22. *Sefer Yetzirah.* See also: Rabbi Schneur Zalman of Liadi, *Tanya, shar* "HaYichud VaEmunah," chapter 11; the Lubavitcher rebbe, *Sefer Hamaamorim Meluket,* vol. 1, p. 216.

23. Talmud *Shabbat,* 104a. See: Rabbi Avraham Azulay, *Chesed LeAvraham,* part 2, chapter 11; Rabbi Chaim Yoseph David Azulay, *Midbar Kadmot,* "Marrechet Alef," p. 6.

24. *Zohar,* part 1, p. 26b; *Zohar,* part 3, p. 223b. Rabbi Moshe Corodovero, *Pardess Rimonim, shar* 27, chapter 4.

25. See: the Lubavitcher rebbe, *Likutei Sichot,* vol. 2, p. 616. See also: *Hayom Yom,* the eighth day of Addar, the fifth Chabad rebbe, Rabbi Shalom DovBer, *Sefer Hamaamorim 5652-5653,* p. 167. The sixth Chabad rebbe, Rabbi Yoseph Yitzchak, *Sefer Hamaamorim 5708,* p. 219.

in an inverted position in relation to the point above, God, for what is above is reflected here below; man was created in God's image.[26]

Once a solid comprehension of the letter's meaning is achieved, one may find that writing the letter on a sheet of paper Ind gazing at it for an extended period of time, renders it easier :o bring it to memory whenever one desires to use it as a visual. The actual visualization of letters is like any other visual method. One begins by shaping the letter in one's mind, and then the image is held for a prolonged duration of time, allowing the letter to fill the mind completely, while blocking out all other thoughts.

Picture the letter as an object, imagining it to be an exquisite red rose in a field of grass. Imagine a fire erupting and consuming all that surrounds the rose. Begin to imagine the fire lying and becoming a thick black cloud, behold amidst the darkness a vibrant red rose standing alone. Further imagine these dark clouds dissipating and becoming white clouds, which then gradually emerge as transparent and translucent. Now all that exists is a red rose.

The advantage of this method of visualization, where one imagines a fire consuming the encircling images of the visual, is that it portrays what the objective of mantra meditation is all about. It is to clear the mind of all extraneous thoughts other than the mantra, and ultimately to clear it from the mantra itself. When the clouds disperse all that remains is the image, and then ultimately nothing.

At times one may find that by joining two types of mantras, reciting a verbal mantra while employing a visual one, concentration can be heightened further. For example, if one is using a letter as a visual, one may also chant the name of the letter. By

---

26. Genesis, chapter 1, verse 26. See: Rabbi Chaim Vital, *Sharei Kedushah,* chapter 3, *shar* 2; Rabbi Yoseph Yavetz, *Avot,* chapter 4, Mishnah 2.

involving more than one sense in the meditation, the experience becomes more real.

Tactility

There was a mystical school whose primary method of reaching higher meditative states was through the use of written words as a mantra. Instead of using a verbal or visual mantra, they would write a word repeatedly over and over again, in various styles and configurations. This technique was introduced and made popular by the 13th-century Kabbalist Rabbi Avraham Abulafia. He suggested that one write down a word and then attempt to Liter the order of the letters, and to permutate and cycle the letters of the word every which way possible. Combining and separating the letters, composing entire motifs of letters, grouping them and then joining them with other groups, and so forth. This is [one until one reaches new and higher states of consciousness.[27]
This type of meditation is called *chachmat hatziruf—the* art of

---

27. Though Rabbi Avraham Abulafia was a prolific writer and wrote over thirty books, most of his works were never published. Perhaps this is because his teachings were under sharp criticism from leading Torah personalities (even) in his own generation. One of his greatest opponents was Rabbi Shlomo Ben Adderet (1235–1310). See: *Teshuvat HaRashba*, part 1, *teshuvah* 548. See also: Rabbi Yehudah Chayit (1462–1529) in his commentary on *Ma'arechet Elokut* (Jerusalem: Mokor Chaim, 1963), "Hakdamah," p. 3b; Rabbi Yoseph Shlomo Delmedigo, known as The Yashar of Candia (1591–1656), *Metzaref LeChachmah*, p. 12. However, many great Kabbalists throughout the ages do, in fact, quote Rabbi Avraham's works. See: Rabbi Moshe Corodovero in his commentary on the *Zohar, Or Yakar,* "Shir Hashirim," quoted in Gershom G. Scholem, *Kitvey Yad BeKabbalah*, p. 232); Rabbi Shlomo Alkabatz (1505–1584), *Brit Halevi (Lvov:* 1863), p. 13c; Rabbi David Ben Zimra (1470–1572), *Magen David,* in the beginning of *Ot Zayin* and *Ot Tet, Teshuvhat HaRadbaz,* part 5, chapter 35; Rabbi Naphtali Hirtz Bacharach seventeenth century), *Emek HaMelech,* 9c. Rabbi Chaim Yoseph David Azulay, in his monumental work that catalogs all Hebraic works, *Shem*

combining letters.[28] While the permutation of the letters was being done, specific head motions, as well as breathing exercises, were performed.[29]

The concept of *tziruf*—combining letters—is analogous to harmonious musical composition. The various instruments have different sounds that when played in harmony shape into an orchestration while still allowing the listener to recognize the individual instruments and to appreciate how they come together. The same can be said in regards to letter combinations.

HaGedolim writes Rabbi Avraham's books are today commonly accepted. See: *Shem HaGedolim*, "*Marrecht Sefarim*," *chet*, 76.

28. An ancient Kabbalistic text, *Sharei Tzadek* (Jerusalem: Shar HaShamaim, 1989), speaks of transcending the body through *tziruf* meditation and then seeing one's own body image speaking and revealing future events. See: *Shoshan Sodot* (Koretz: 1784), p. 69b, attributed to Rabbi Moshe Ben Yakov of Kiev (1449–1518). (See: Rabbi Chaim Yoseph David Azulay, *Shem Hagdalim, Marrechet Siforim*," *Shin*, 43.) See also: Rabbi Tzodok HaKohen of Lublin, *Dover Tzedek*, p. 96a.

The Kabbalist Rabbi Yoseph Gikatalia writes that one who enters into the depths of (knowledge of) *tziruf* of letters, the depth of wisdom will be clarified and so will the wonders of creation. See: Rabbi Yoseph Gikatalia, *Shaarei Orah, shar* 5, p. 136. It is said that the Kabbalist Rabbi Yitzchak of Acco would, through the manipulation of the Hebrew letters *(chachmat hatziruf)*, communicate with angels.

Rabbi Chaim Yoseph David Azulay writes that he had seen manuscripts from both Rabbi Yoseph Tzayach and Rabbi Chaim Vital, where they write of this type of meditation. See: *Midbar Kadmot* (Jerusalem: 1962), *Marrechet Chet*, p. 21. Rabbi Avraham Azulay writes that this type of study can be very dangerous spiritually. See: *Chesed LeAvraham*, part 2, chapter 11.

It is believed that the sages of the Talmud were proficient in the knowledge of *tziruf*. See: *Safer Haplia* (An ancient Kabbalistic text attributed to the first-century saint Rabbi Nechuniah Ben HaKana) (Israel: Books Export), part 1, p. 17a. The Talmud mentions the knowledge of *tziruf* with regard to *Betzalel*, the architect of the Tabernacle. See: *Berachot*, 55a.

29. See: Rabbi Avraham Abulafia, *Chayay Olam HaBah*, pp. 150–151. Rabbi Moshe Corodovero, *Pardess Rimonim, shar* 21, chapter 1. See also: Gershom G. Scholem, *Major Trends In Jewish Mysticism* (New York: Schoken Books, 1961), p. 382, footnote 67.

Each letter has its own sound and tone, and in harmony the sounds combine and sing like a melody.[30]

Another method used to achieve a meditative state is the use of one's kinetic energy. The meditator uses his body as a vehicle o reach transcendence through rhythmic dancing and continuous body movement. The Talmud speaks of the great men of Israel who would dance on the holiday of Sukkot in the Temple throughout the night. These festivities were called the *Simchat Beit Hashoeivah*—the joy of the house of drawing. For it was here, at the height of the dancing, that these sages received and drew forth *ruach hakodesh,* divine inspiration.[31]

Dancing can be transformative, and when used correctly it has the power to prompt the shift of consciousness needed to experience that which is beyond the normal appearance. There are many Chassidic masters who employed dancing as a means to attain *hitpashtut ha'gashmiyut*—a divestment of the physical. By enlisting the body and dancing a holy dance, the dancer's body is metamorphosed into a spiritual entity, and the physicality of the body is transcended. The body, instead of being a concealment and camouflaging the soul, now becomes a medium or expression of the soul. Slowly, by dancing for extended periods of time and not heeding the weariness to one's body, the lancer frees and liberates himself from the materiality of the body, which is ego, and reaches soul. Attaining this noble condition of *hitpashtut ha'gashmiyut,* is a requisite for, and closely associated with, the prophetic experience.[32]

The Torah speaks of King David dancing fervently in the

---

30. *Safer Haplia* (1784) f. 52d–53a. See also: Rabbi Avraham Abulafia, *Chayay Olam HaBah,* p. 63.

31. The Jerusalem Talmud *Succah,* chapter 5, *halacha* 1; *Midrash Rabba,* Ruth, the end of *parsha* 4. See also: Talmud *Succah,* 50b, *Tosefot, Chad Tani.*

32. See: *Zohar,* part 2, p. 116b; Rabbi Yakkov Ben Asher, *Tur,* "*Orach Chaim,*" chapter 98; Rabbi Yoseph Caro, *Shulchan Aruch,* "*Orach Chaim,*" chapter 98. See also: Rabbi Schneur Zalman of Liadi, *Tanya, Kuntres Acharon,*

presence of God, while girded in a linen tunic.[33] In those times, dressing in linen cloths indicated that the wearer had reached an elevated state worthy of receiving prophecy.[34] When David found himself at the outskirts of the city, where it was quiet and serene, he recognized the area as appropriate for *hitbodedut*—isolation, and he danced to become attuned to prophecies.[35]

With the emergence of the Chassidic movement, the art of lancing was elevated to the highest pedestal. Chassidic masters recognized that everything in this physical world is a manifestation of a higher spiritual reality,[36] and that man is the quintessential reflection of this truth,[37] encompassing and containing within himself all the energies of creation. Consequently, every motion of the body has a ripple effect, not only on the weather in China, as science informs us, but as the Kabbalists assert, on the entire structure of creation, the physical as well as the spiritual. In Chassidic circles there are various dances, some of which are actually called after the names of God. For example, the *Sheim HaVaYa* dance, the Tetragramatton dance, and so forth. By dancing in a certain formation, the Chassid is acting out, on a physical plane, this lofty name. And by doing so, he is making the concept real and creating a unification with that name. When one dances with this in mind, the act becomes most noble and elevated.

---

essay 4; The sixth Chabad rebbe, Rabbi Yoseph Yitzchak. See: *Sefer Ha'Maamorim, "Bosi L'Gani,"* vol. 1, p. 8.

33. Samuel 2, chapter 6, verse 14.

34. Rambam, *Hilchot Klei HaMikdash*, chapter 10, *halacha* 13.

35. The Lubavitcher rebbe, *Likutei Sichot,* Vol. 1, pp. 228–229. Additionally, David danced to attain happiness, which is a prerequisite to prophesies. See: Rabbi Yakov Yoseph of Polonnye, *Toldot Yakov Yoseph, "Parshat Re'eh,"* p. 645.

36. See: Chapter 11, footnote 2.

37. See: Rabbi Moshe Cordovero, *Shiur Komah,* "Torah," chapter 4, p. 21; Rabbi Chaim Vital, *Sharei Kedushah,* chapter 3, *shar* 2; Rabbi Yoseph Yavetz, *Avot,* chapter 4, Mishnah 2; Rabbi Pinchas Eliyohu Ben Meir of Vilna, *Sefer Habrit,* part 2, *maamor* 1, chapter 10.

Modern Chassidim are known for their spontaneity and freedom of expression. They especially display their emotions through singing and dancing, and this is most pronounced during their prayers.[38] The Chassidim of the 18th-century master, Rabbi Abraham of Kalisk would perform somersaults while praying. Their prayers were accompanied by such a rush of emotions, and the energy so intense, that they were not able to contain it, and the prayers required physical expression. The outlet they employed was to swirl in somersaults. It is not common for one's prayers to be so intense, and for the most Dart, body movement is not an expression, rather a means to attain feelings. One uses body to reach soul. As a Chassidic master writes, if one desires to set his soul aflame, he should do so through body motion, for motion generates warmth.[39]

Olfactory

According to the Talmud, the sense of smell is unique among all the other senses in that smell is delightful for the soul.[40] In the garden of Eden all of the human senses were utilized in transgressing, save the sense of smell. "And the woman saw . . . and she took . . . and he ate . . . they heard."[41] Accordingly, the sense of smell is to a degree the most refined and spiritual of all five senses. It is the sense most enjoyed by the soul.[42]

---

38. Rabbi Yakov Emdin (writing in the early years of the Chassidic movement) said that he *heard* that there is a new group of Chassidim, who do various strange body movements during their prayers. See: *Matpachat Sefarim* (Jerusalem: Orach Tzadikim, 1995), chapter 9:47, p. 114.

39. Rabbi Nachman of Breslov, *Likutei Moharan,* part 1, chapter 156. See also: Rabbi Yisrael Baal Shem Tov, *Tzavoas Harivash,* chapter 68.

40. Talmud *Berachot,* 43b.

41. Genesis, chapter 3, verses 6 and 8.

42. Rabbi Tzvi Elimelech of Dinav (1785–1841), *Bnei Yissochar* (Bnei Brak: Heichel HaSefer), "*Maamorei Chodesh Adar,*" *maamor* 1, pp. 95a–95b.

Scent touches a place in the soul that is beyond manifestation in the body. For this reason, when fainting occurs and the connection of soul and body is severed, sniffing a powerful Fragrance awakens the person to consciousness.[43] Consequently, using the olfactory sense can work as an anchor in an overwhelming experience.

Aroma plays an important part, consciously or subconsciously, in the way we feel. A pleasant smell arouses pleasant Feelings, and vice versa. Strolling through a fragrant garden lifts our spirits, while passing an unpleasant odor disturbs us.

In Jewish thought there is no explicit mention of the sense of smell as a technique for meditation.[44] Yet we do find that in the holy temple, which was the source and location for all spiritual activities, special consideration was taken to make certain that the smell within the temple was pleasant. One of ;he services of the temple was the *ketoret,* the burning of the incense. The reason why incense was offered was to eradicate the unpleasant smells emanating from the animal offerings.[45] In our time, in the miniature temple, as the Talmud refers to a place of

---

See also: Rabbi Shmuel of Sochatchov (1856–1926), *Sheim Me'Shmuel,* "*Hagada Shel Pesach*" (Jerusalem: 1987), pp. 32–33.

43. The fifth Chabad rebbe, Rabbi Shalom DovBer, *Sefer Hamaamorim 5657,* p. 163. See: The Lubavitcher rebbe, *Sefer Hamaamorim Meluket,* vol. 2, 216, footnote 52, for additional sources.

44. In various ancient cults the aroma did in fact play an important role in achieving ecstasy. See: Rambam, *Hilchot A'Kum,* chapter 6, *halacha* 1–2; Rabbi Yoseph Albo, *Safer Haikkarim, maamor* 3, chapter 8.

45. See: Rambam, *Moreh Nevuchim,* part 3, chapter 45. (Though see: Rabbein Bachya, Exodus, chapter 30, verse 1.) According to the *Zohar* the *ketoret* was offered to eradicate spiritual unpleasantness. See: *Zohar Chadash,* "*Shir HaShirim,*" on the verse *Mishceini.* See also: *Zohar,* part 2, p. 118b. It can be argued that the Rambam is alluding to the spiritual smells as well as to the physical. See: The Lubavitcher rebbe, *Likutei Sichot,* vol. 14, p. 129. See also: Rabbi Mendel of Kotsk (1787–1859), *Emet VaEmunah* (Jerusalem: 1972), p. 25.

worship,[46] one must make certain that the odor is pleasing, to the extent that one is not permitted to pray if there is an unpleasant smell in his proximity.[47] As in prayer, where undivided concentration is needed and any distracting smells can disturb concentration, the same is true with meditation. When one meditates, one should see to it that there are no unpleasant smells in the vicinity.[48]

There were Chassidic masters who would actually use their sense of smell to assist in their concentration and mindfulness throughout the day, and especially to assist in their awareness during prayer. The Holy Seer of Lublin was one such master. Once, when he was asked by his opponents how he could sniff tobacco in the middle of talking to his Creator, he answered with a parable:

> There was once a king who was chronically depressed. Nothing could cheer him, and so he roamed his kingdom searching for relief from his dark state of mind. One day, while strolling the countryside he heard the sound of music being played by an old musician strumming on his fiddle, which had seen better days and better playing. However, this music roused such joy within the king that he immediately took the man to the palace, where he had him play for him constantly. It was obvious to the people in the king's court that this musician was incapable of carrying a true note

---

46. Talmud *Megillah*, 29a.

47. There is a lengthy discussion in the Talmud with regard to prayer in the proximity of unpleasant odors, when is it permitted to pray and when it is not. See: Talmud *Berachot*, pp. 24–26. See also: *Shulchan Aruch,* "*Orach Chaim,*" chapters 76–87 and chapters 90, 92, 97, 103. Furthermore, there were Talmudic sages who would not pray in a place that possessed a distinct smell (not necessarily from human wastes), which may cause distraction in their concentration. See: Talmud *Eruvin,* 65a. See: Rambam, *Hilchot Tefilah,* chapter 4, *halacha* 9. See: *Shulchan Aruch,* "*Orach Chaim,*" chapter 98:2.

48. Rabbi Bachya Ibn Pakudah, *Chovot Halevavot,* "*Shar Cheshbon Hanefesh,*" chapter 3, part 9.

and the music sounded awful, yet the king was euphoric over this music and chose this musician to play for him. So, too, when I was created, God endowed me with a nose that craves *tabbak,* yet God loves me despite this and I have been chosen to play God's tunes.[49]

The Holy Seer of Lublin snuffed *tabbak* to ground and intensify his thoughtfulness, as was the custom of other Chassidic masters, who would snuff tobacco, smoke a pipe, and so on, to ground their concentration. His response, however, was geared to someone who could not fathom how sniffing from a snuffbox could be of spiritual assistance. Additionally, by offering this metaphor, as opposed to explaining that he used his sense of smell to enhance awareness, he spoke of himself in humble terms. Instead of speaking of how he desired a greater attention span, and that sniffing a snuffbox helped him attain his goals, the metaphor offered a humble explanation to his seemingly puzzling actions.

Gustatory

There is always one taste or another in our mouth; the question is only which. Having an unpleasant taste in the mouth may cause distraction and can disturb meditation, while having a pleasant flavor may also cause distraction. Perhaps the best would be to have a neutral taste in the mouth.

Generally, food, as mentioned earlier, can be used to anchor a person during an experience of transcendence. If, through the meditation, the meditator feels that he is losing his homeostasis he may want to eat something, so that he can be drawn back into earthbound reality. Conversely, the lack of food may also cause

---

49. See: Eliezer Shtainman, *Be'er HaChassidut,* "*Al Admurei Poilin*" (Israel: Mochon Kemach), p. 44.

a transcendent feeling, of becoming lighter and light-headed. Therefore, many Kabbalists recommended that in order to attain a mystical transcendental experience, one needs to refrain from eating.[50] Through fasting, they would enter expanded states of awareness and loftier states of consciousness.

A gift of love and harmony was brought to this world in the year 1698, when the great master, the Baal Shem Tov was born. He taught that it was time for man to make peace with himself, his physical body, as well as peace with the physical world at large; enough of the duality and struggle. Let the body join the soul in serving its Creator.[51] It was time to relinquish the ways of physical mortification and begin working with the body. Fasting became a practice of the past.[52] The teachings of this inspired master opened up new paths to finding God, through celebrating life rather than through abstinence. One was now able and empowered to find God by reveling the beauty of creation, rather than to continue grappling with darkness. (Though, as mentioned, meditating on a full stomach is not a good idea, either. It is best to make time to meditate when one is not too hungry, nor too full.)

In this chapter we have discovered the applications of the Five senses to our meditation and how by engaging and con-

---

50. See e.g.: Rabbi Chaim Vital, *Shar HaGilgulim,* "Hakdamah," 38.

51. Rabbi Yisrael Ba'al Shem Tov, *Kesser Shem Tov,* chapter 231; *Hosofot,* p. 92; *Hayom Yom,* twenty-eighth of Sh'vat. See also: Rambam, *Hilchot De'ot,* chapter 4, *halacha* 1. Rambam, *Shemonah Perakim,* chapter 4; *Kitzur Shulchan Aruch,* chapter 32; Rabbi Moshe Chaim Luzzato, *Mesilat Yesharim,* "Hakdamah" and chapter 26.

52. The Talmud teaches that a person who is not able to fast because of weakness and fasts nonetheless is considered a sinner. *Tannit,* 11b. See also: *Shulchan Aruch,* "Orach Chaim," chapter 571:1. The ruling is that in today's day and age we are all considered weak and unable to fast, and thus we should not fast. See: Rabbi Schneur Zalman of Liadi, *Tanya,* "Iggeret Ha Tshuvah," chapter 3.

sciously including the senses in our meditation, the meditative session can be greatly enhanced.

Prior to meditation sound can be used to soothe and relax us into a state of meditativeness. Sound used repetitively can also assist in emptying the mind of all extraneous thoughts. As the meditation begins we use the senses to anchor and give focus to the meditation. Finally, in advanced meditation, senses such as taste and smell can ground the meditator so that he is not overtaken by the experience.

CHAPTER
7

The Four
Who Entered the Orchard:
The Spiritual Trappings of
Advanced Meditations

Numerous styles and methods of meditation were explored in the previous chapters, yet it seems that apart from a few high-profile individuals and the handful of meditational groups, there are very few practitioners of Jewish meditation. This seems quite puzzling, seeing as meditation is very much a Jewish tradition, practiced historically and cross-culturally. This begs the question, why? Why is it that in the large majority of Jewish circles meditation is looked upon as alien and with a degree of apprehension?

When speaking of meditation it must be stressed that meditational practice ranges from the obscure, transcendent variety to the more widely practiced and acknowledged meditation. There are extreme types of meditations that are practiced clandestinely, and even then only rarely and by members of secretive societies. There is great caution taken with these meditations as to who can meditate, being that these meditations are generally transcendental in nature, nonintellectual and aimed at having a mystical or perhaps even a revelational experience. And then there are meditations that are widely practiced. The reason that they are not widely known is that they are not commonly referred to as meditation. *Cheshbon hanefesh,* Torah contemplation, intentional structured, and spontaneous prayer, and so on, are all meditations though they are known by other names.

There is a tale in the Talmud that may shed light on the issue. The story allows us to better understand why some types of meditations are for the most part shunned, and why some are practiced, but only in secrecy, and why there are meditations that are indeed ubiquitously and overtly practiced. The Talmud tells of four sages who entered the mystical orchard.[1] Ben Azzai gazed and died. Ben Zoma gazed and was stricken (i.e., he went insane).[2] Acher—the other (née Elisha Ben Abuyah) gazed and cut off his plantings, that is, he transmogrified into a heretic.[3] Rabbi Akiva entered and exited in peace.[4] The orchard represents higher spiritual realms.[5] By reciting various mystical names, these four were able to ascend.[6] This was not a physical ascension, but rather, it appeared to them as if they had ascended. In actuality, they gazed and saw heaven within the inner depths of their souls.[7]

Within this dramatic tale lie the clues to some of the dilemmas one may encounter by undergoing a mystical experi-

1. Talmud *Chagigah*, 14b.
2. Rashi, ad loc.
3. Talmud *Chagigah,* 15a. Since the orchard represents their experience, thus the Talmud uses the term cutting off the plantings with regard to heresy. Rashi, *Acher.*
4. In the Talmud it says that Rabbi Akiva *exited* in peace. Talmud *Chagigah,* 14b. However, in the Jerusalem Talmud it says, he *entered* and *exited* in peace. *Chagigah,* chapter 2, *halacha* 1.
5. Orchard is a metaphor for heaven. Talmud *Chagigah,* 14b; Rashi, *Nicnesu LePardes* and Tosefot, *Nicnesu LePardes.* Others explain the orchard as a place similar to Gan Eden. See the commentary Rabbeinu Chananel ben Chushiel (990–1055) ad loc. The orchard is the inner chambers of the worlds above. See: Rabbi Nathan ben Yechiel (1035–1106), *HaAruch* (Israel: Sifrei Kodesh Y Greenvald). *Erech Even,* p. 6, in the name of Rabbi Hai Goan (938–1038). See also: *Ha'Ktov* on *Eyin Yakov,* 11; *Otzar HaGaonim,* ad loc; Rabbi Yehudah Halevi, The Kuzari, *maamor 3,* chapter 65.
6. Ibid.
7. Talmud *Chagigah,* 14b; Tosefot, *Nicnesu LePardes;* Rabbeinu Chananel ben Chushiel, ad loc. See also: Rabbi Nathan ben Yechiel, *HaAruch,* "Erech Even," p. 6, in the name of Rabbi Hai Goan.

ence without the proper preparation and balance in life,[8] as well as the subsequent attitude that biased the establishment against "unstructured" meditations.

Before this tale can be deciphered, it is important to note that erroneous parallels can be drawn between what these great saints experienced and what most people experience.[9] The truth is that for most, these experiences are inauthentic and purely imaginative, while the authentic experience is one where there is actual spiritual movement inward and thus upward.[10] There are different ways to travel the road in life's journey. There are those that make the journey on foot, actually encountering each bump and turn in the road, while there are others who merely imagine the road—playing out the journey in their minds—yet never actually packing their bags. At the end of the road there stands only one man—the one who arrived on foot. Meditation and indeed life, is a journey that entails persistence, focus, discipline, and the courage to keep on trying in the face of failure.

In the Talmudic tale Ben Azzai is said to have gazed and died. In mystical terms this phenomenon is called *ratzu beli shuve*—withdrawal without return. His intent for the experience was to reach a level of transcendence. When he was finally able to enter that world of transcendence, he remained there and ceased to exist in his bodily form.[11]

---

8. See: The fifth Chabad rebbe, Rabbi Shalom DovBer, *Sefer Hamaamorim 5646-5650*, p. 259, the footnotes, with regard to Rabbi Akiva.

9. See: Rabbi Chaim Vital, *Sharrei Kedusha*, "Hakdamah," p. 2.

10. See: Rabbi Aharon of Starossele (1776–1828), in the name of his rebbe, Rabbi Schneur Zalman of Liadi, *Sharei Hayichud V'Haemunah*, in the *Hakdamah*, where he writes that in today's day and age, the study of the esoteric is similar to a servant who is granted permission to observe the king's jewels from behind the walls of the fortress.

11. Ben Azzai gazed at the great illuminating light and thus joined and became one with the infinite. See: Rabbi Moshe Ben Yakov of Kiev, *Shoshan Sodot*, p. 57b. *Ratzu Beli Shuve* is a common term used on Ben Azzai. See: The fifth Chabad rebbe, Rabbi Shalom DovBer, *Sefer Hamaamorim 5646-5650*, p. 259.

A transcendent experience is one where the meditator rises above himself, so to speak, goes beyond his conventional modality, beyond the human sensory perceptions of time and space, and enters a realm of timelessness. The intensity of the experience may be so overwhelming that he may literally lose himself and cease to exist corporeally,[12] or be so enchanted by the experience that he may want to intentionally and deliberately lay his body to rest, and in effect commit suicide.[13]

Death via a kiss of God is regarded as a most elevated level.[14] It occurs when a person's soul leaves the body in a state of spiritual ecstasy and with pleasure. There is no pain, and death is seen as a transformation from body to its original state

---

When Ben Azzai would teach Torah a heavenly fire would encircle him. See: *Midrash Rabbah*, Leviticus, *parsha* 16, chapter 4. Generally, Ben Azzai seemed to be mystically inclined. In fact, he never received his Rabbinical ordination, which requires extensive knowledge of practical Torah law. *Avot*, chapter 4, mishnah 1, as interpreted by Rabbi Ovadiah Yarei Bertinoro (c.1440–1516). However, this does not suggest that he lacked in any which way in the knowledge of Jewish law. See: Talmud *Baba Batra*, 158b.

12. Rabbi Chaim Ibn Attar explains that this is what occurred with the two sons of Aharon Nadab and Abihu who died in spiritual ecstasy. See: *Or HaChaim*, Exodus, *"Parshat Acharei Mot,"* chapter 16, verse 1. See also: Rabbi Nachum of Chernobyl, *Meor Einayim, "Parshat Pinchas,"* p. 109; The Lubavitcher Rebbe, *Likutei Sichot*, vol. 3, pp. 987–993.

13. A master of advanced transcendental meditations (especially meditative, magical Kabbalah) was Rabbi Yoseph Della Reina (1418–1472). Legend has it that he attempted to utilize his powers to bring the redemption, and in the process he became spiritually injured. Some say he committed suicide, while others say that he became an apostate or went mad. Many Kabbalists took his actions as a warning for advanced transcendental types of meditations (especially meditative, magical Kabbalah). See: Rabbi Moshe Corodovero, *Pardess Rimonim, shar* 21, chapter 1; Rabbi Chaim Vital, *Sharei Kedusha*, part 3, *shar* 6. See also: Rabbi Pinchas Eliyohu Ben Meir of Vilna, *Sefer Habrit*, part 2, *maamor* 12, chapter 1, p. 481.

14. Talmud *Berachot*, 8a; *Moed Katan*, 28a; *Baba Batra*, 17a; *Midrash Rabba*, Deuteronomy, *parsha* 11, chapter 10.

of soul.[15] This type of death is regarded with reverence when one attains it at the end of one's life. Only when the time to inhabit a body is concluded, and the soul is ready to journey to the other side, and then, one transcends the physical body in a state of ecstasy, is it deemed worthy of esteem. However, one who rushes the process and aspires to transcend the body while there is still time and energy left to perfect the world, regarded as transgressing against life itself, and not someone to be emulated.[16]

Ben Azzai lived the life of a loner, without a wife, children, or family,[17] exchanging the realities of this life for a life of transcendence and holiness. In his own words (explaining why

---

15. The highest level of *d'eveikut* is when a person ascends to heaven without any physical pain, through a "kiss of God." See: Rambam, *Moreh Nevuchim,* part 3, at the end of chapter 51; Rabbienu Bachya, *Kad Kemach; Kisvei Rabbeinu Bachya* (Jerusalem: Mossad Harav Kook, 1995), *"Ahavah,"* p. 35; *Ma'arechet Elokut,* chapter 8; Rabbi Yehudah Chayit on *Ma'arechet Elokut,* chapter 8, pp 95b–96a; Rabbi Menachem Azaryah De Fano, *Maamor Hanefesh,* part 6, chapter 7; Rabbi Yehudah Ben Yitzchak Abarbanel (????–1535), *Vikuach Al Ahavah* (Israel: 1968), p. 41a; Rabbi Chaim Ibn Attar, *Or HaChaim,* Exodus, *"Parshat Acharei Mot,"* chapter 16, verse 1. See also: Rabbi Menachem Reconti Parshat Vayechi, *Levush Malchut,* vol. 7, p. 37b–38a)

16. The Rambam writes that when people of stature new that their time was coming to move on, they would meditate with intense concentration, until they would become one with the infinite. They allowed their souls to be drawn from their bodies in a state of ecstasy and bliss. Rambam, *Moreh Nevuchim,* part 3, at the end of chapter 51. Rabbi Chaim Ibn Attar writes that death through a kiss of God is an elevated level only when it comes from God. However, when it comes through man's own actions, through man's own initiative, it is a sin. *Or HaChaim,* Exodus, *"Parshat Acharei Mot,"* chapter 16, verse 1.

17. Ben Azzai professed the merit of marriage and the harshness of not getting married (marriage being the ultimate expression of involvement in this world) on a physical level as well as on a mental level. See: Talmud *Yevamot,* 63b. Nonetheless, he himself never married. See: Talmud *Yevamot,* 63b; *Sotah, 4b;* Rambam, *Hilchot Eishut,* chapter 15, *halacha* 3. According to other opinions, he was once married only later to get divorced. Talmud, *Sotah,*

he did not marry): "What can I do if my soul yearns to contemplate Torah?"[18] His ambitions were to transcend the physical mundane reality. Ultimately, he reached his goal. When he entered the orchard he gazed and died. He died in a state of spiritual ecstasy, with the kiss of God.[19]

Of Ben Zoma it is said that he gazed and was stricken, he became insane. From the little known about Ben Zoma we are told that he was very wealthy,[20] and that he was an intuitive person,[21] with the ability to articulate a thought quite well.[22] It also seems that he was very much inclined to abstract thinking. At times he was more focused on the sublime than on the mundane.[23] Perhaps it was his lack of focus and his disinvolvement in the physical that caused him to lose his mind. When he saw more than what is usually seen, he became so overwhelmed that he permanently surrendered his sanity.[24]

An authentic mystical experience involves settling the conscious mind, and opening oneself to higher knowledge. The well-balanced person is equipped for the experience, while one who suffers imbalances is not. A person with the proper equilibrium can be a skilled surfer and know how to ride the

---

4b. There are those opinions that say that even if he did marry, his marriage was never consummated. See: Talmud *Ketubot*, 63a; Tosefot, *Bartei*.

18. Talmud *Yevamot*, 63b.

19. See: Rabbi Yechiel Ben Shemuel of Pisa (c.1493–c.1566), *Minchath Kenaoth* (Jerusalem: Makor Publishing, 1970), p. 104.

20. Talmud *Berachot*, 58a.

21. The Talmud says that one who sees Ben Zoma in a dream should await *chochmah*—intuitive knowledge. Talmud *Berachot*, 57b. See however, Rabbi Yitzchak Aizik of Komarna, *Aimrei Kodesh, Mosar Chagigah*, p. 88.

22. Ben Zoma was known for his great ability to articulate ideas. See: Talmud *Sotah*, 49a.

23. See: Midrash Rabbah, Genesis, *parsha 2*, chapter 4. See also: Talmud *Chagigah*, 15a.

24. Ben Zoma entered the orchard without intellectual balance. See: Rabbi Moshe Ben Yakov of Kiev, *Shoshan Sodot*, p. 57b.

current; he learns to master the waves, while the inexperienced, unbalanced person thrashes about.

Entering expanded states of consciousness without being properly prepared and balanced, may cause one to be so overwhelmed that he may lose himself in the experience. One may become stuck in another realm, having difficulty reestablishing his connection to physical reality (especially a person who has a history of mental instability).

The experience may become blinding rather than illuminating. Ben Zoma was one such person. It was said of him that he had gazed at the sun too intently.[25] The sunlight is a generous commodity, warming everything that is cold, illuminating darkness, and causing delightful sunny days. When the sun shines upon the earth, the world feels blessed, and everything within it seems just right. Yet, when one attempts to look directly at the sun, not only does one not gain enhanced perception and clarity, but everything that once looked so beautiful begins to look hazy and opaque. The only way to look at the sun is through shades, which have a dual purpose. They temper the intense brightness of the sun, while still allowing a limited radiance to pass through. The same can be said of the mystical experience. In properly readying oneself by grounding oneself in this reality, the experience becomes illuminating and revealing.

Acher gazed and cut off his plantings. He became a heretic. Following his experience in the orchard, he proclaimed that there are two authorities in this universe.[26] One is the force of light, and the other is the force of darkness. Two separate energies sustain this world; one is the domain of good, and the other is the domain of evil.[27] The (angelic) images he saw in the

---

25. Rabbi Shimon Ben Tzemach Duran, *Magen Avot,* part 2, chapter 2, p. 18a.

26. Talmud *Chagigah,* 15a. See also: Rabbeinu Chananel ben Chushiel, quoted by Rabbi Hai Goan in *Ha'Ktov* on *Eyin Yakov, Chagigah,* p. 14b, 11.

27. The basic tenet of the ancient Zoroastrian cult.

orchard impressed him so much that he believed them to have an independent existence from that of the Creator.

At first glance, it appears that the many images of the universe, the multitude of powers and energies, are unrelated to each other. Each entity, each energy, seems to exist independently and autonomously. A person who possesses a totality of vision can see that they are in fact, all parts of one all-encompassing picture. All the seemingly independent images and forces are actually branches of one tree and they are all holographic. Everything in truth is but a manifestation of the Infinite. The problem occurs when one lacks such vision. Being too close to the picture, overly engrossed in the physical world and its trappings, the image becomes pixelated and one is unable to see it as a whole. The consequence of this vision is the cutting of the plantings, where each individual branch is perceived as a separate entity unrelated to the next. The root of idol worship is taking a part for the whole, seeing one part, one power, and believing it to be the all.

Entering the orchard, on is mystical journey, Acher observed all the various entities of the universe and thought of them as separate existences.[28] In deep meditation on the heavenly imagery, he mistook each power as a sovereign energy separated from the divine chariot.[29] Ache; being an empiricist, was convinced and affirmed only by that which is seen.[30] There

---

28. Rabbi Shimon Ben Tzemach Duran, *Magen Avot,* part 2, chapter 2, p. 14b and 18b.

29. See: *Ma'arecht Elokut,* attributed to Rabbi Todros HaLevi Abulafia (1220–1298), chapter 9. The author there attests that in an advanced stage of transcendental meditation, the meditator may perceive the heavenly imagery as sovereign powers.

30. Rabbi Yoseph Shlomo Delmedigo, known as The Yashar of Candia, *Safer Eilam,* p. 91. See also: Rabbi Shimon Ben Tzemach Duran, *Magen Avot,* part 2, chapter 2, p. 18b.

According to the Rambam, however, Acher aspired to comprehend ideas that were beyond his intellectual capabilities, thus, his imagination over-

was no room left for him to exercise his associative abilities. Images, angels, powers were all taken to exist the way they appeared to him, with each energy as a separate independent entity.

The reason that Acher, as opposed to his companions, felt this separateness, was because his feelings were a reflection of his life, which was one of internal rift and dichotomy. Acher was torn between what is sacred and what is profane. In fact, he was never entirely dedicated to either of them. While being a man of faith, he would listen to profane music, and while flaunting his proclamation that he was a nonbeliever, he still continued to teach Torah.[31] There was never a time when he was comprehensively involved and integrated in one lifestyle. He suffered from a sort of spiritual schizophrenia

Rabbi Akiva was the only sage who was able to enter and exit the mystical orchard without being scarred. Being a man of remarkable spiritual stature, Rabbi Akiva was able to take that journey and return whole. He was able to live in both realities, the physical, mundane and the lofty, spiritual, simultaneously.[32]

Rabbi Akiva was a towering intellectual figure who pos-

---

whelmed his intellect. See: Rambam, *Moreh Nevuchim,* part 1, chapter 32; Rabbi Yehudah Halevi writes that once he attained such an elevated level of spirituality, he thought to himself: if the entire purpose of mitzvot is to empower man to reach this exalted state, and he has already attained it, why then is there the need for actual mitzvot? See: *The Kuzari, maamor* 3, chapter 65.

31. From the Talmud we see that even when Acher—Elisha Ben Avuyah—was a man of faith and was a great Torah scholar, he had an affinity for heretical ideas. See: Talmud *Chagigah,* 15b. His entire life was split between the sacred and the profane. See: *Tosefot Yeshenim* on Talmud *Yuma,* 87a. Even after he proclaimed himself as an nonbeliever he continued to teach Torah. See: Talmud *Chagigah,* 15a–15b. Following his death this dichotomy continued. The Talmud says that when he died he was neither allowed to go to *Gan Eden* because of his sins, but neither was he able to go to *Gehenim,* for all the Torah he learned. Talmud *Chagigah,* 15b.

32. Rabbi Yehudah Halevi, *The Kuzari, maamor* 3, chapter 65.

sessed a commanding knowledge of both segments of the Torah, the revealed law[33] as well as the concealed mystical.[34] But being who he was[35] and knowing what he had accomplished[36] did not color his attitude toward other human beings. It did not cause him to feel, in any which way, superior to others. During his lifetime he accumulated great wealth,[37] yet he was always sensitive to the poor. His hand was considered "the hand of the poor," for he was the one who distributed monies to the poor.[38] It was only he, of the four sages, who had the proper balance in life. Grounded as an empathetic human being, while highly mystical and spiritually elevated, he alone was able to enter and exit in peace and remain complete.[39]

By way of this story we are made aware of some of the problems that can arise when transcendence is sought. A meditation that is designed to elevate the meditator to a state that is beyond the regular rational consciousness has the possibility of producing any one of these three counterintuitive results. The deleterious experiences that occurred to three of the

---

33. See: Talmud *Gittin,* 67a; *Avot DeRabbi Nathan,* chapter 18:1; *Menachot,* 29b. His supremacy of law was such, that if there was a disagreement between Rabbi Akiva and any of his contemporaries, the law follows the opinion of Rabbi Akiva. See: e.g., Talmud *Sanhedrin,* 86a.

34. As evident from this story.

35. Rabbi Akiva reached such an elevated state that Moses thought that the Torah should be given to Rabbi Akiva in his stead. See: Talmud *Menachot,* 29b.

36. Rabbi Akiva only began to study Torah at the age of forty; until then he was an ignoramus. See: *Avot DeRabbi Nathan,* chapter 6:2; Midrash Rabbah, Genesis, *parsha* 100, chapter 10. See also Talmud *Nedarim,* 50a; *Ktubot,* 62b.

37. Talmud *Nedarim,* 50a–50b; *Avot DeRabbi Nathan,* chapter 6:2. Jerusalem Talmud, *Ma'aser Sheni,* chapter 5, *halacha* 4; Talmud *Kiddushin,* 27a; Rashi, *DeYad.*

38. The fifth Chabad rebbe, Rabbi Shalom DovBer, *Sefer Hamaamorim 5646–5650,* p. 259.

39. The fifth Chabad rebbe, Rabbi Shalom DovBer, *Sefer Hamaamorim 5646–5650,* p. 259.

sages can also occur to any meditator to a greater or lesser degree.

A meditator can undergo an experience similar to that of Ben Azzai, where the meditation can provoke a permanent transcendence of the physical. One may experience an ecstasy of such proportions that one may reach a level of *ratzu beli shuve,* a withdrawal without return. This danger looms to a greater extent when the meditation focuses on nothingness. In the advanced stages of such types of meditations, there is the risk that the meditator can become swallowed up within the nothingness of the meditation. The danger of death can be literal, as in the case of Ben Azzai, who aspired to comprehend and envision what is beyond a human's capacity. He attempted to realize that which is beyond the physical, the spiritual nothingness, which resulted in his being consumed by the nothingness.[40] However, death can also be experienced metaphorically. Having been there, and having experienced transcendence, the meditator may never want to return to the so-called pettiness of life. He may become stoic, lifeless, and uninvolved with life. Living out life because he has not yet been killed in an accident.

The meditator can also be affected as Ben Zoma was and become insane. One may have a transcendental, mystical, or even a prophetic type of experience, and then have trouble rebounding into reality. One may become so overwhelmed and enthralled by the experience, that he loses focus on everything else in life.

The 16th-century master, Rabbi Chaim Vital, one of the leading interpreters of Kabbalah, writes that once when he was meditating he became overwhelmed with emotion. His entire body began trembling terribly; his head became heavy; his mind began to drift. At once, he decided to conclude meditating. The

---

40. Rabbi Shimon Ben Tzemach Duran, *Magen Avot,* part 2, chapter 2, p. 18a.

following day, his master, the AriZal, Rabbi Yizchak Luria rebuked him: "Did I not warn you? Had it not been for the fact that you are a reincarnation of Rabbi Akiva, who had entered and exited in peace, you may have gone insane as Ben Zoma, with no cure at hand!"[41]

Insanity is a mental condition where one cannot make rational decisions. A person who is insane has his capacities for rational thinking obscured. Extreme denial and self-deception are manifestations of such a state. A common feeling that can occur to people who experienced transcendental experiences is foolish self-pride—having a distorted belief in oneself, losing all proportion of situations, and fostering a clouded view of life.[42]

---

41. Rabbi Chaim Vital, *Shar HaGilgulim, Hakdamah* 38. Rabbi Avraham Abulafia writes that a person who may feel bewildered and lost by meditations should not be taught these secrets. Rabbi Avraham Abulafia, *Or HaSechel,* part 1, p. 11.

42. A dangerous trapping in such type of transcendental meditations is a feeling of possessing supernatural powers. An example of this may be Rabbi Shlomo Molcho. Molcho was first known as Diogo Pires (a Marrano who was baptized) who was the scribe of the king of Portugal King John III. Upon meeting David Reuveni, he circumcised himself and fled to Solinica and was from then on was known as Shlomo Molcho. He went on to become a Kabbalist and was able, through meditation, to communicate with a *maggid*—an angelic force. (This method he later taught to Rabbi Yoseph Caro, who himself communicated with a *maggid*. See chapter 5.) In the 1532, Molcho sought an audience with the king of Spain, Charles V. The king was not very impressed and handed him over to the Inquisition, who in turn put him to death. Many Kabbalists take this to be a warning for advanced transcendence types of meditations (especially meditative, magical Kabbalah) where you may feel like a Superman, who can overcome any obstacle. See: Rabbi Chaim Vital, *Sharei Kedusha,* part 3, *shar* 6. Although it must be stressed that Rabbi Shlomo Molcho's death is viewed as a heroic act of self-sacrifice and sanctification of God's name. Rabbi Eliezer Ezcary calls Molcho a *kadosh*—one who was killed sanctifying God's name. See: *Safer Cheredim,* chapter 63. The great legalist and mystic, Rabbi Yoseph Caro, wished that he would die the same way as Rabbi Shlomo Molcho, sanctifying God's name. *See: Maggid Mesharim, "Parshat Ttzaveh,"* in the beginning, and *"Parshat Beshalach."*

This is particularly the case with regard to people who suffer from emotional instability to begin with. Bringing emotional instability to a peak experience can exacerbate an existing condition. By having such a supreme high, the meditator could begin having illusions of fantastic grandeur and permanently lose his mental balance and perspective.

In our youth we are all troubled by the monumental questions of life. Who is the Creator of life? What am I doing here? Is there any purpose to my existence? and so on. As we grow older, we exchange these questions for a whole new set of questions. How can I make money? Where is the best place to shop? and so on. Yet, there are a few who throughout their lives keep asking the original important questions. They are seekers, and some turn to meditation for answers. However, a caveat for those who think that by simply reaching heightened states of awareness answers will be found: In actuality, as a prerequisite to finding truth one may need to relinquish one's preconceived and habitual way of thinking.

There are questions, and there are questions. Some are sourced in intellect, and thus need to be satisfied with the rational, while there are those that emanate from the heart— soul questions—for which the answers lie beyond the equation of one plus one. Transcendental meditations are a way to reach that "place." Yet, in order to reach it, one must abandon rational intellect and operate from a higher state. Hence, rationalists may experience some difficulties at these levels.[43] Herein lurks the danger of insanity. There is a measure of uncertainty anytime one is told to surrender one's rational modality of thinking. The risk is in the return. Can the meditator reorganize and reconnect to normative thinking and behavior? These moments of tran-

---

43. When entering the inner/upper chambers, one must transcend rational intellect and operate on a transcendent state of consciousness. Therefore, intellectuals may have difficulties at these levels. Rabbi Tzodok of Lublin, *Likutei Maamorim* (Bnei Brak: Yehadut, 1973), p. 206.

scendence serve as a positive bolt of energy, yet at no time is it recommended to abandon one's rational capacity permanently.

This type of insanity, caused by a distorted perception of spirituality, can occur especially in advanced states of transcendental meditation. Upon reaching higher and expanded states of awareness, the images of the mind become more vivid and alive and the inexperienced meditator may not know how to interpret these visions. One may regard the images as a prophetic or revelational experience, when in fact they may be mere fantasies. Instead of regarding these images and visions on an aesthetic level, one may observe them as a prophetic experience. It is understandably tempting to believe in these visions as authentic prophecies, rather than just fantastic imagery.

What is more, at times, fooling oneself and acting out a vision can be harmful. Not every mystical experience is positive. There is something that is called diabolical mysticism, where instead of the experience being a compelling agent for life, it turns out to be a negative force, and the complete antithesis of life.[44] Therefore, it is only a trained and sensitive meditator who knows when his experiences are in fact positive and meaningful to him, and when they are stumbling blocks for further growth.

Foolish arrogance, which is closely related to insanity, is another phenomenon that can be evoked by being in a transcendental state of consciousness. It is common for a person who reaches these levels of comprehension, which are beyond normal consciousness, to experience arrogance, conceit, and feelings of superiority over other people, especially to those who have not yet reached these levels. Operating on this expanded state, where the parameters, definitions, and the confines of the physical universe cease to exist, one may begin to feel that all definitions are trivial. What society defines as normative behavior is to him

---

44. William James, *The Varities of Religious Experience* (Penguin Classics, 1985), "Lecture on Mysticism," p. 426.

just fictive thinking. For example, he may question the normality of dancing with one's feet and clapping with the hands, and invert it to dancing on the hands and clapping with the feet. Obviously, a person who thinks such thoughts is bordering on insanity. There are indeed rules in physics and etiquette, whether one agrees with them or not, that enables people to live as a coherent harmonious society. The meditator may go even further, thinking that not only does he transcend societal definitions, but even the definitions and parameters established by the Creator. He may begin to believe as Acher did, that there is more than one force.[45]

Operating on a higher state of consciousness the meditator may feel that he is experiencing the tree of life, which is beyond the concept of duality, beyond the definitions established by the tree of knowledge. For it was only after Adam and Eve had eaten from the tree of knowledge, that they knew good from bad. Prior to that, they existed in a state of *Gan Eden*—paradise, a profound state of unity and oneness, without the awareness of separateness.

History is replete with individuals who believed (erroneously) that on their level of spirituality everything was permitted. Their argument is that, indeed, most people operate within the confines of time-space. They exist in a world of separation, definitions, and borders. For example, you-me, right-wrong, black-white, and so on. They need clear-cut dividers that define for them what exists and what is permitted and prohibited. However, for those who have mastered and transcended all limitations and separateness, and are living and operating on a higher plane than most people, everything seems to be permitted

---

45. Nietzsche, who wrote of the *ubermensch*—the superman, also wrote of being beyond Good and evil. Interestingly, another title to one of his works is *Thus Spoke Zarathustra*. Zarathustra was the founder of the Zoroastrian religion, which was the cult Acher later believed in. See this chapter, footnote 26.

and capable of being sanctified.[46] A heretic is one who feels that all the so-called limitations that were set as part of reality have no relevance to his exalted state of being.

It was only Rabbi Akiva who was able to enter and exit in peace. Being a true master, he realized that the objective was not to meld with the light and not return to physicality, as Ben Azzai did, or mentally, as Ben Zoma did. Nor was it to feel personal release or ecstasy. But rather to go there and return here, with the proper wisdom to serve in the here and now.

The dangers of death, stoicism, insanity, heresy, confusion, and so on, can be mitigated to a certain extent, when the meditation is done in the presence of another person, for this reason the Baal Shem Tov admonished the meditator not to meditate alone.[47] Nonetheless, this caveat is not absolute, and the dangers remain. The proof is in the story, where four entered, but four did not emerge safely.

Now we begin to understand why transcendental meditation, where the objective is to reach above oneself and beyond the limitations of time and definitions, never became mainstream. For how many Rabbi Akivas are there? There are not many who have such balance. This is not to imply that if one desires to become a Rabbi Akiva he cannot, for we can even be like Moses, if we only desire it.[48] The reality is, however, that not many people are willing to live their lives with such discipline, dedication, and commitment. Most people are not

---

46. Rabbi Eliyahu BenAmozegh (1823–1900) writes that in the world of imagination everything appears to be permitted. See: *Be'Shevilei Mussar* (Israel: Mossad Harav Kook, 1966), pp. 60–61. See also: Gershom G. Scholem, *Major trends in Jewish Mysticism*, Eighth Lecture, "Sabbatianism and Mystical Heresy." See also: Aldous Huxley, *The Perennial Philosophy*, chapter xxv, "Spiritual Exercises."

47. See: chapter 4, footnote 23.

48. Rambam, *Hilchot Teshuvah*, chapter 5, *halacha* 2. See also: *Tana Devei Eliyahu*, chapter 25.

even willing to attempt to reach such spiritual heights. (And if a person has in fact reached these levels, he will know for himself that he can meditate. Additionally, his teacher, or teachers, will inform him of his advances, and when he is ready for such meditations.)

Another area of spiritual danger lies in the mantra type of meditation. A primary tool for transcendental meditation is using a visual or audible mantra. The meditator allows the mantra to empty the mind and leave it a fitting receiver for the mystical experience. Many people have erred by misusing a visual for contemplation. By extensively fixating on an object, and allowing its image to fill the mind, the image may become an end to itself. Slowly, one forgets that the object of their contemplation was meant to be a means to an end. The object becomes real, and then alive, and finally an object of religious devotion.[49]

These so-called dangers exist to a greater degree when one is contemplating the heavenly spheres. Simply looking at the aesthetics of a sunrise, observing how the heavens demonstrate the mastery of the Creator,[50] can lead one to sun worship. Maimonides writes that the source of all idol worship was the original reverence man showed toward creation. From admiration it became adoration and worship.[51] For this reason, whenever Jewish law demands one to contemplate a visual, one is also instructed to make certain that mere contemplation should not become devotion. For example, there is a mitzvah to bless the moon each month. Yet caution is taken that the moon should not become an object of devotion. The code of law instructs that

---

49. Aldous Huxley writes of people who take the object of their meditation as an objective reality and serve it as an idol. *The Perennial Philosophy,* chapter xxv.

50. Psalms, chapter 8, verse 4.

51. See Rambam, *Hilchot Avodei Zora,* chapter 1, *halacha* 1. See also: Rabbi Nisan Ben Reuven, *Derashot HaRan,* derush 9, p. 155.

when one blesses the moon, one should look at the moon once before the blessings, and no more.[52] Perhaps, contemplating the moon, when saying a prayer, may lead people to think of the moon as an object worthy of deification and worship.[53]

52. *Rabbi* Yeshayah Halevi Horowitz, *Shenei Luchot Habrit, Shar Ha'otyot,* p. 344. See also: *Magen Avraham, Shulchan Aruch,* "*Orach Chaim,*" chapter 426:8, and the *Be'er Heitiv,* 6, ad loc.

53. Thus, there are various customs with regard to blessing the moon, which were instituted so that the mistake should not be made by the onlookers that one is worshiping the moon. See: *Safer Ta'amei HaMinhagim* (Israel: Eshkol, 1982), p. 204.

CHAPTER
8

The Spirituality of the Torah
as It Relates to Meditation

Heaven and Earth. The two realities we live with. While some ignore heaven and live merely on earth, there are others who see heaven as the sole reality. Judaism stresses the balance between heaven and earth, spirituality and materialism, and ultimately the fusion between finite man and the Infinite Creator. Understanding the contrast between other perceptions of spirituality and that of Judaism is perhaps the key to unlocking the deeper reason that the mystical, transcendental meditation never wholly merged with the Jewish experience and why it was, and to some degree still is the less practiced method.

Every spiritual discipline asserts that it is a map to the road leading to a better, more meaningful, more transcendent life. If it is followed correctly, they say, one will become more spiritually oriented. And most of them agree that spirituality is synonymous with the word God, for God is the ultimate spirit, being incorporeal. Therefore, if one desires to come closer to the Spirit, one must first detach and rid oneself of all things physical and live a more spiritual life. The premise being that the spiritual is closer to God than the physical. Heaven is closer to God than earth. Consequently, only by transcending the limitations of a human being can man touch the divine. A saint is one who lives

in self-abnegation, hidden away somewhere on a remote moun-
taintop, living as a recluse.

Judaism teaches that God transcends all. God is beyond
the physical and is the creator of the dimensional, as well as the
creator of the dimensionless. Spirituality is but a creation, as is
the physical, and consequently, spirituality is no closer to God
than is the physical. Just as living a materialistic lifestyle is
devoid of Godliness, living a life of spirituality can also be void
and empty of Godliness. The word God and the word spiritual
imply two distinct concepts. God is the *creator,* and the spiritual
is *a creation.* Therefore, if a human being desires to come close
to God, he can do so by doing mitzvot, for mitzvot are transcendent deeds, and when one performed, one connects with
God.[1] By doing a mitzvah one becomes Godly, which is beyond
being spiritual.[2]

God, who is the creator of both the physical and spiritual,
chose the physical as the vehicle through which man connects
with the ultimate spirit. Therefore, mitzvoth are grounded in
the reality of the here and now, in the minute details of everyday life. The objective of Torah is not in the heavens per se, but
rather, to teach man how to create heaven here on earth. The
challenge and task is to be human, not angelic, and to create a
dwelling place for Godliness within this world.[3] Essentially, the

---

1. The root of the word *mitzvah* is *tzaysa,* which means connection. By
doing a mitzvah man connects with the infinite. See: Rabbi Schneur Zalman of
Liadi, *Likutei Torah,* "*Parshat Bechukotai,*" p. 45c; Rabbi Avraham Yeshoshua
Heschel, *Ohev Yisroel,* "*Parshat Vayera,*" p. 14. See also: Rabbi Eliezer Ezcary,
Safer Cheredim, chapter 70.

2. See: Rabbi Yehudah Loew, *Tifferet Yisrael,* chapter 9.

3. The world was created out of God's desire to have a dwelling place on
this earth. See: *Midrash Tanchumah,* "*Parshat Nosa,*" chapter 16. In the Kabbalah
there are many reasons given why there was a creation of the physical. For
example, so that humans as independent creatures can serve God. (*Zohar,* part
2, p. 44b.) That man can recognize God's greatness. (Rabbi Chaim Vital, *Eitz
Chaim,* "*Shar HaKelalim,*" in the beginning.) Nonetheless, all agree that

reason the soul descends is not for its own spiritual aggrandizement and to gain life experiences (albeit, that indeed occurs), but to elevate and transform the physicality of the universe into something more spiritual and transcendent.[4] The purpose lies in the domain of the physical, which by its nature is separate, unconscious, and inert, elevating it and refining it through the performance of mitzvot.[5]

Since the purpose occurs in the world of actuality, the intentions of the mitzvot are to some degree, not as important as the actual deed. For example, a person walking down a street loses a bundle of money and a poor person finds it and uses it to feed himself. Even if the man had no idea that the money fell from his pocket, it is nonetheless considered a mitzvah.[6] Ultimately, Torah is expressed in deeds, not in faith, in actions and not in feelings, in body and not in soul. The main point is to actually align ourself with its purpose and directives.

Having set this premise, one can begin to understand why any experience that attempts to supersede the rational, conventional modality of thinking is looked upon with suspicion. A Jewish experience entails involvement and integration. Transcendental types of meditations, where the objective is to release and set free one's rational, three-dimensional consciousness, is viewed with trepidation. Jewish mysticism aspires to take the rational mind on the mystical journey, working with the mind, and through it, to arrive at a place that is beyond it.

Normally, the objective is to work within one's limitations, as opposed to ignoring and attempting to transcend them.

---

the ultimate purpose for the creation of this physical world is to make a dwelling place for God. See: The Lubavitcher Rebbe, Likutei Sichot, vol. 6, p. 21.

4. Rabbi Avraham Azulay, *Chesed LeAvraham*, part 4, chapter 4.

5. Rabbi Schneur Zalman of Liadi, *Tanya*, chapter 37.

6. *Sifri*, Deuteronomy, chapter 24, verse 19; cited by Rashi, ad loc. See: Rabbi Yoseph Engel, *Athvan Deoraitha, klaal* 23.

Judaism however, does acknowledge the mystical experience that goes beyond human comprehension, but it is viewed as a reward for the soul. A transcendental experience is seen as a glimpse into the reward the soul will receive on a higher plane, following the body's demise.[7] Yet, being that "God does not withhold the rewards of any living creature."[8] Thus the soul, here on earth is also spiritually rewarded.[9] But what it sees is only a glimpse, for only after the soul is free from the trappings of the physical body, can it truly experience its rewards. A Chassidic master writes that through transcendental meditation one can reach a world where all is good and one can be completely consumed in a world of infinite light. This is a state of awareness where one can hear the speech of the animals and trees, and experience their souls ascending their bodies. Nevertheless, all these lofty levels pale in comparison to the spiritual delights the soul experiences prior to descending into this world.[10]

The preeminent transcendental and mystical experience attainable to man is that of prophecy. Yet, interestingly, the greatest prophet of all times, Moses,[11] the most unique and

---

7. Rabbi Chaim of Volozhin (1749–1821) writes in the introduction to the commentary by Rabbi Eliyohu of Vilna (1720–1797) to the book *Sifra DeZeniuta* that the revelation the soul experiences without the conscious mind laboring to attain (i.e., in sleep) is a glimpse of the rewards in a future world. See: *Sifra DeZeniuta* (Jerusalem), *Hakdamah*, p. 5.

8. A Talmudic dictum mentioned in the Talmud numerous times, e.g., Talmud *Baba Kamma*, 38b; *Nazir*, 23b; *Pesachim*, 118a.

9. See: The Lubavitcher Rebbe, *Likutei Sichot*, vol. 15, p. 247.

10. The sixth Chabad rebbe, Rabbi Yoseph Yitzchak, *Likutei Diburim*, vol. 1–2, pp. 272–273.

11. "Never again has there arisen in Israel a prophet like Moshe (Deuteronomy, chapter 34, verse 10). According to the Rambam the belief that Moshe was the greatest prophet of all time is the seventh principle of faith. See also: Rambam, *Hilchot Yesodei Ha Torah*, chapter 7, *halacha 6*; Rabbi Nisan ben Reuven, *Derashot HaRan*, *derush* 8, p. 127; Rabbi Chasdai Cresces, *Or Hashem, maamor 2, klall 4*, chapter 3; Rabbi Yoseph Albo, *Safer Haikkarim, maamor 3*, chapters 10–11 and chapter 17. Rabbi Moshe Metrani, *Beit Elokim,*

chosen one among all the prophets,[12] is not remembered as Moses the Prophet, but rather, as Moshe *Rabbeinu*—Moses the Teacher. What he had attained spiritually through prophetic consciousness is not as important as the fact that he was a masterly skillful teacher, who inspired a generation and shifted the world's perspective toward monotheism.

At one time, according to the Talmud, there were literally millions of prophets,[13] though only a minute few are actually remembered, and their prophetic visions documented. That is because, while these anonymous prophets achieved impressive spiritual heights, their knowledge and insights are of no relevance today.[14] The point of prophecy is not the vision, nor is it the high one attains, but what one does with the inspiration.[15]

"Shar Hayesodot," chapter 21, p. 233; Rabbi Meir Ben Gabbai, *Avodat Hakodesh,* part 4, chapter 23.

12. See: *Midrash Rabba,* Genesis, *parsha* 76, chapter 1.

13. See: Talmud, *Megillah,* 14a. The Midrash says that in one period of time there were over six hundred thousand prophets. See *Midrash Rabba,* Lamentations, the end of chapter 4. Furthermore, there is the opinion in Midrash that in that particular time there were over one million prophets. *Midrash Rabba,* Ruth, on chapter 1, verse 2; *Midrash Rabba,* Song of Songs, on chapter 4, verse 11. (Interestingly, according to this Midrash, for every male prophet there was a female prophetess.) In addition, this number (mentioned in the Talmud and Midrash) does not include all the "sons of prophets" that the Torah mentions. See: e.g., Kings 1, chapter 20, verse 35; Kings 2, chapter 2, verse 2. These were young prophets in training. See: Rabbi Moshe Chaim Luzzatto, *Derech Hashem,* part 3, chapter 3:2. Thus, the number of people aspiring to the prophetic experience increases astronomically. These "sons of prophets" were dressed distinctively in special garb signifying that they were worthy of prophesy. See: Jerusalem Talmud *Sanhedrin,* chapter 10, *halacha* 2; Rambam, *Hilchot Kli HaMikdash,* chapter 10, *halacha* 13.

14. See: Talmud *Megillah,* 14a; *Midrash Rabba,* Ruth, on chapter 1, verse 2; *Midrash Rabba,* Song of Songs, on chapter 4, verse 11.

15. In Hebrew, a prophet is called *a navie,* which means a spokesman. (Exodus, chapter 7, verse 1.) A person who speaks words of inspiration and rebuke to the masses. See: Rashi, Exodus, chapter 7, verse 1; Rashbam, Genesis, chapter 20, verse 7; Rabbi Nisan ben Reuven, *Derashot HaRan, derush* 3, p. 38.

Prophecy is not about experiencing clairvoyance and seeing the future, but rather, it is in the business of perfecting the world, and assisting man in reaching that objective.[16] Inspiring people to *teshuvah*.[17] A selfish prophetic experience, where the objective is to gain spiritual insight and understanding[18] is analogous to holding a candle on a cold winter night; it is warming for the one holding it (and for no one else), and it is only warming while it is still burning. Therefore, these prophetic visions were never recorded, for there was no message for coming generations. Hence, the Talmudic dictum, "A wise person [a teacher] is greater than the prophet,"[19] for his teachings live on to eternity.

The Torah tells of a gentleman named Baruch, who was the principal student of the master prophet Jeremiah. Having attained a spiritual state of consciousness worthy of the prophetic experience, and not having received it, he lamented to his master, "Why have I not found serenity?[20] Where is the prophecy?" God replied through Jeremiah, "My home is being destroyed and you are looking for greatness."[21] The prophetic experience he was so eagerly anticipating was a quest for personal greatness. He desired prophecy, the mystical transcendental experience par

---

See also: *derush 5*, p. 63. Rabbi Yonathan Eibeschuvetz, *Yarot D'vash*, part 1, p. 22a. Rabbi Meir Ben Gabbai writes that prophecy can only be attained if the prophetic vision will have an effect on the masses *Avodot Hakodesh*, part 4, chapter 25.

16. Rabbi *Yoseph Albo, Safer Haikkarim, maamor 3*, chapter 8, chapter 12.

17. See: Rabbi Eliyahu ben Moshe Di Vidas, *Reshit Chachmah*, "*Shar HaTeshuvah*," chapter 1. See also: Rambam, *Hilchot Teshuvah*, chapter 7, *halacha* 5. The miracles the prophet performs are not to exhibit his spiritual strength, but rather to inspire people to return to God. See: Rabbi Moshe Metrani, *Beit Elokim, "Shar Hayesodot,"* chapter 19, p. 229.

18. Rambam, *Hilchot Yesodei Ha Torah*, chapter 7, *halacha* 7. See also: Rabbi Moshe Metrani, *Beit Elokim, "Shar Hayesodot,"* chapter 19.

19. Talmud *Baba Batra*, 12a.

20. Jeremiah, chapter 45, verse 3.

21. Ibid.

excellence; however, God answered: There is much to be done. Why sit around and wait for personal aggrandizement when the world is being destroyed? Go do something about it and cease being selfish.

When the nation of Israel deviated, God spoke to Moses: "Go descend, for your nation . . . has become sinful."[22] The Talmud interprets the descent as a spiritual demotion.[23] There was no room for Moses to continue in his ascent while the people he was sent to inspire languished. There was a symbiotic relationship between the leader and his people, and when they spiritually plummeted so did he.

From all the above it is clear that in Judaism, the profoundest mystical prophetic experience is one that can be rechanneled into physical reality. The prophet who is able to take the mystical journey, later to return, and cause a practical, tangible difference, is regarded in the highest esteem. It is the master prophets, the ones whose lives and words inspired generations, whose teachings galvanized entire new paradigms, whose names are enshrined in the memory of mankind forever. But this does not mean that a mystical experience that is purely in the realm of spirit, without having any practical applications (notwithstanding the prophet's spiritual aggrandizement), is looked upon with disdain. It also serves a purpose, and it too has its place in spirituality, primarily as a reward. And, in fact, there were such prophets, too. The difference, however, is that they sought personal gain, while the masters were on an egoless quest to serve mankind. It is this selflessness that makes all the difference. It is what differentiates the masters from the rest.

Mention was made earlier of a type of meditation called *chesbon hanefesh*—an accounting of the soul, with the objective of self-betterment. This is done through studying and meditat-

---

22. Exodus, chapter 32, verse 7.
23. Talmud *Berachot,* 32a; Exodus, chapter 32, verse 7; Rashi, ad loc.

ing on a devotional work of ethics. The meditator carefully examines the negative traits discussed in the text, and then scrutinizes himself, and seeks out these traits within himself. There is, however, an obstacle in the way of self-evaluation, and that is one's ego, the thick protecting veil that obscures the true self. By meditating and achieving a metatranscendent state, the meditator can become an objective observer which is needed for proper self-evaluation. From this transcendent vantage point, the meditator can deconstruct the patterns and negative traits that dominate his life, and aspire to improve them.

Being that this type of meditation involves transcendence, it can be as perilous and risky as the other transcendent meditations. To attain genuine objectivity of one's spiritual status, without becoming transcendent, an observer of one's life, an unbiased outsider, besides oneself is recommended. Acquire a friend, the talmudic sages advise.[24] We are told to find a close and trusted confidant who understands our personality, so that he can cast light on the areas that may need refinement.[25] Find yourself a friend, the Midrash says, so that he can teach you the secrets of your behavior.[26] At times, only another person, an objective, unprejudiced individual, can observe what is really going on within us, whether self-deception is occurring, and to advise us on what needs rectification and which areas need reinforcement.[27] In the words of a thirteenth-century philoso-

---

24. *Avot,* chapter 1, Mishnah 6.

25. See: The flowing commentaries on *Avot,* chapter 1, Mishnah 6; Rambam, *Pirush HaMishnayot;* Rabbi Menachem Ben Shlomo, *Meiri;* Rabbi Yom Tov Lipman Heller (1579–1654), *Tosefot Yom Tov;* Rabbi Shemuel De Uzeda (1540–1605), *Midrash Shemuel.* See also: Rabbienu Yona of Gerondi, *Iggeret HaTeshuvah* (Israel: Eshkol, 1978), "Day Six," p. 211; Rabbi Asher Ben Yechiel, known as the Rosh; *Orchat Chaim,* "Day two," p. 157; Rabbi Eliyahu HaCohen, *Sheivet HaMusar,* chapter 40:24, p. 577.

26. *Tana Deve Eliyahu Zuta,* chapter 16. See also: *Sifri, Parshat Nitzavim,* p. 304.

27. See: *Safer Or HaMussar* (a compilation of discourses by the masters

pher, "A man without friends is as the left side without its right."[28]

Throughout history, many great sages, individuals who were deemed to have reached elevated states of spirituality, had their own trusted friends from whom they took advice regarding their spiritual status. The 18th-century master, Rabbi Eliyahu of Vilna is an example of one such saint. The Vilna Gaon, as he was known, would listen to admonishment offered to him by Rabbi Yakov Kranzt, The Maggid of Dubno.

This type of introspective conduct is not limited to individuals alone; it can be extended to entire communities as well. Years back, communities throughout Europe would welcome a traveling preacher, a *maggid,* who would inspire and arouse them. A pious *maggid* would go from town to town and observe what was lacking in each community, and then inform the townspeople what he thought needed perfecting. In Chassidic circles it is the rebbe, or the *mashpiah*—the spiritual guide— who takes this role.[29]

This form of evaluation is ubiquitously practiced, while the method of attaining a metatranscendent state through meditation, where one, so to speak, hovers above oneself is not. The reason for this is, as discussed earlier, the attendant spiritual, and at times, even physical dangers associated with that path, especially for the untrained and untutored meditator.

Another technique to achieve transcendence is to take a

---

of the *mussar* movement), part 2 (Bnei Brak: 1966), article by Rabbi Simcha Zissel Ziv of Kelm, p. 146. See also: *T'nuat HaMsusar,* Vol. 1, p. 297.

28. Rabbi Yedaya Ha'Penini (????–1305), *Mivchar Ha'Pninim* (Jerusalem: Vagshal, 1995), "*Shar HaChaveirim,*" p. 68. See also: Rabbi Eliyahu HaCohen, *Sheivet HaMusar,* chapter 29:72, p. 417; chapter 40:24, p. 577. The Talmud says friends or death. Talmud *Taanit,* 23a. See: Rabbi Yeshayah Halevi Horowitz, *Shenei Luchot Habrit, Shar Ha'otyot Shar Chet,* p. 295.

29. Today, in non-Chassidic circles, they are called *mussar zogers*— preachers of ethics. These are individuals who are traditionally supervisors of a yeshivah.

passage of a Mishnah and repeat it, until the meditator connects with the soul, the *maggid* of the Mishnah, the angelic energy associated with the Mishnah, through which greater insights are revealed. Inner dimensions of the Torah, and future events are unveiled during such transcendent experiences.

In addition to the three previously mentioned undesired effects that can occur in all types of trancelike meditations, there are other difficulties that can occur in this particular style of meditation. Whenever an experience entails external entities, souls, angels, energies, and such, there is the uncertainty that the so-called external forces are but a figment of one's own imagination. At a heightened and altered state of consciousness, it is difficult to discern what is real and what is imaginary and self-delusional. Furthermore, even if one has the spiritual acumen to discern the authentic entities from the false ones, it is still difficult to know for certain that it is a holy, positively charged energy, and not the contrary.

Angels were uttered into being at the beginning of creation, and continuously ever since. The angels that are being created are manifestations of a human's deeds, or misdeeds. With each good deed one creates and releases a positive energy into the ether, while conversely, negative force is created through every negative action.[30] The angels—*maggidim*, which reveal insights, are created by the meditator himself. Therefore, the truth or falsehood, the positivity or negativity of the revelation, depends on the spiritual stature of the meditator. If the angel was created in purity and nobility, then it reveals only truth, but if the angel was created with mixed feelings and ulterior motives, then the angelic force created contains elements of truth and falsehood.

---

30. "He who does a good deed acquires for himself an advisory." *Avot,* chapter 4, Mishnah 11, as interpreted by Rabbi Ovadiah Yarei Bertinora, ad loc. See also: Rabbi Moshe Corodovero, *Tomer Devorah,* chapter 1, p. 2; Rabbi Yeshayah Halevi Horowitz, *Shenei Luchot Habrit, Torah Sh'Bektav,* p. 142; Rabbi Klunimus Kalman, *Maor Vashemesh, "Parshat Yitro,"* p. 232.

Consequently, the good parts speak truth, while the impure segments reveal falsehood.[31]

What is more, the relative authenticity of the revelation is not entirely in the hands of the meditator. In addition to the meditator's spiritual status, what is also crucially relevant to the experience is the time and location of the experience.[32] Not-withstanding that the meditator's actions may have been most noble and the *maggidim* created as a result are pure and immaculate, just being in the diaspora, poses another obstacle to the authenticity of the experience. The *maggidim* one experiences on unholy soil are a mixture of good and holy, positively charged energies, and evil, negative energies.[33]

Some of the great masters, in spite of knowing that the angelic forces they would have communicated with would have

---

31. Rabbi Chaim Vital, *Sharei Kedusha*, part 3, *shar* 7; *Shemone Sheorim,* "*Shar Ruach Hakodesh,*" Derush 1, p. 10. Rabbi Avraham Azulay, *Chesed LeAvraham*, part 3, chapter 19, p. 57; Rabbi Chaim Yoseph David Azulay, *Midbar Kadmot, marrechet mem*, p. 37b; Rabbi Pinchas Eliyohu Ben Meir of Vilna, *Sefer Habrit*, part 2, *maamor* 11, chapter 4, p. 483. See also: Rabbi Tzodok HaKohen of Lublin, *Dover Tzedek*, p. 81a.

32. See: Chapter 4, footnote 4. The world is comprised of three dimensions: souls, space, and time.

33. See: Rabbi Chaim of Volozhin in his introduction to the commentary by Rabbi Eliyohu of Vilna to the book *Sifra DeZeniuta, Hakdamah,* p. 5. Interestingly, there are many who assert that prophecy (the pinnacle of a transcendental revelation experience) cannot be experienced outside the land of Israel. See: Midrash *Mechilta on Shemot, parsha* 12, chapter 1; *Tanchuma,* "*Parshat Bo,*" chapter 5; *Sifri on Devarim,* 18:15; Rabbi Saddiah Goan, *Emunot VeDeyot, maamor* 3, chapter 5; Rabbi Yehudah HaLevi, *The Kuzari, maamor* 2, chapter 14; Rabbi Moshe Ben Nachman, the Ramban, Deuteronomy, "*Parshat Shoftim,*" chapter 18, verse 15. Rabbi Shlomo Ben Adderet, *Teshuvaht HaRahsba,* teshuvah 548. There are a number of levels in divine revelations, and indeed the lower levels can be felt even outside the Holy Land. See: Rabbi Yakov of Marve'ge, *Responsa from Heaven* (Jerusalem: Mossad Harav Kook, 1957) in the introduction by Rabbi Reuven Margaliut, for many sources on this issue. See also: Rabbi Pinchas Eliyahu Ben Meir of Vilna, *Safer Habrit,* part 2, *maamor 9,* chapter 3.

been pure, scorned such revelations.[34] These revelations, which
are beyond the normal human capabilities of comprehension
and understanding, come from above, as opposed to revelations
from within; thus, they are viewed as being *nahama dekisufa*—
shameful bread.[35] Bread, or for that matter anything else, that
is received via another person's benevolence, causes shame for
the recipient. Bread that is earned is received with honor and
nobility, even if the amount earned is less than the amount
given. The Talmud states, "A person would rather possess a dol-
lar earned, than nine dollars granted."[36]

The same is true with Torah. The wisdom of the Torah was
transmitted to man[37] along with the task of developing, ex-
pounding, and by extension, expanding its primal ideas. Using
intellectual capabilities, man is told to be a *mechadesh,* one who
unveils and initiates new insights of Torah.[38] For this reason,
many sages throughout the ages felt no desire to receive insights

---

34. Rabbi Chaim of Volozhin writes this with regard to his teacher, in his
introduction to the commentary by Rabbi Eliyohu of Vilna on the book *Sifra
DeZeniuta, Hakdamah,* p. 4.

35. Jerusalem Talmud, *Orlah,* chapter 1, *halacha* 3; Talmud *Kedushin,*
36b; Tosefot; Rabbi Yoseph Caro, *Magid Mesharim,* "*Parshat Bereishit,*" p. 10;
Rabbi Schneur Zalman of Liadi, *Likutei Torah, Parshat Tzav,* p. 7d. Rabbi Moshe
Chaim Luzzatto, *Da'at Tevunoth,* in the beginning, "*KaLaCh Pischei Chochmah,*"
number 4.

36. Talmud Baba Metzia, 38a.

37. Being that the Torah was given over to man, the angels descend to
listen to the Torah studied by man. See: Midrash Rabbah, "*Shir HaShirim,*"
chapter 8, verse 13.

38. There is actually an *obligation for* a person to reveal new insights of
Torah. See: *Zohar,* part 1, p. 12b. Rabbi Moshe ben Nachman, Ramban, *Kisvei
HaRamban* (Jerusalem: Mossad Harav Kook, 1982), *HaEmunah VeHabitachon,*
p. 364. *Ramban Hakdamah Mildhemet Hashem,* Rabbi Schneur Zalman of Liadi,
Hilchot Talmud Torah, chapter 2:2; *Iggeret HaKodesh,* chapter 26; *Torah Or,*
"*Parshat Mikketz,*" p. 38c. See also: Rabbi Chaim of Volozhin, *Nefesh
HaChaim, shar 4,* chapter 12. (Thus, the question of the Rashash, Rabbi
Shmuel Shetrashun, on the Talmud *Megillah,* 3a is answered.) These *new*
insights of Torah that are revealed, are based on the general precepts

or breakthroughs of Torah, by way of revelation, from a *maggid,* or the like.[39] In fact, attaining Torah knowledge through revelation is contrary to the premise that the "Torah is not in heaven."[40] In fact, with regard to practical Torah law, an opinion that is based on a revelation is nonvalid. A scholar's ruling of Torah law must be rooted in his intellect, not based on a revelation.[41]

When the celebrated sage, Rabbi Schneur Zalman of Liadi, beheld the tremendous erudition that his grandson Menacham Mendel displayed for Torah study, he wished to bless him with the gift that the entire Torah should come to him instinctively, without effort or toil. The young scholar declined, saying that he desired to achieve mastery of Torah through his own arduous pursuit. He wished to reap the intellectual fruits of his labor, without being infused with its knowledge as a gift. Such is the way of Torah. The little one earns through one's own effort is of greater value than the largest and loftiest gifts that are bestowed.

---

of Torah that were given at Sinai. See: Midrash Rabbah, Exodus, *parsha* 41, chapter 6; Rabbi Yeshayah Halevi Horowitz, "*Shalah HaKodesh,*" introduction to *Beit Chachmah.* Every new innovation of Torah was (in a concealed manner) given at Sinai. See: Jerusalem Talmud, *Peah,* chapter 2, *halacha* 4, Midrash Rabbah, Exodus, *parsha* 47, chapter 1. See also: Talmud Megillah,19b; Midrash Rabbah, Leviticus, *parsha* 22, chapter 1; *Midrash Tanchuma, "Parshat Yitro,"* chapter 12.

39. Rabbi Chaim of Volozhin in his introduction to the commentary by Rabbi Eliyohu of Vilna on the book *Sifra DeZeniuta, Hakdamah,* pp. 4–5.

40. Deuteronomy, chapter 30, verse 12.

41. One does not head attention to a revelation in matters of law. See: Talmud *Baba Metzia,* 59b; *Temurah,* 16a. See also: *Berachot,* 52a; *Eruvin,* 7a; *Pesachim,* 114a; *Chullin,* 44a; *Yevamot,* 14a; *Tanya,* "*Iggeret HaKodesh,*" chapter 26. This principle extends to a prophet as well. A prophet who rules based on a prophetic vision is considered a false prophet. Rambam, *Hilchot Yesodei Ha Torah,* chapter 9, *halacha* 4. Rambam, *Hakdamah LePirush HaMishnayot.* Though, in a case where there is uncertainty in a factual matter, one is permitted to rely on a revelation that reveals the fact. See: Talmud *Makkot,* 23b. See: Rabbi Chaim Yoseph David Azulay, *Ayin Zocher, Marrechet Alef (15).*

These reservations regarding transcendental meditations leaves the uninitiated and untrained meditator with meditations that are grounded in the intellect and normative pursuits, such as prayer, Torah contemplation, *cheshbon hanefesh,* and the like. These are the primary types of Jewish meditation, which were and are, widely practiced. However, the experience of the meditations that are rooted in one's intellect are not always limited to a cognitive experience. At times, through the intellect, one is capable of reaching beyond the intellect. A good example of such a meditation is the *Hitbonenut* method, where one uses one's rational, conventional mode of thinking, as a stepping stone to reach transcendence. The rational mind is utilized as a tool to transcend its own limitations. One uses the capacity of intellect to go beyond it, as will be explained in the following chapter.

CHAPTER
9
Intellectual Analytical Meditation

It was a monumental wedding, a joining of two illustrious families. The grandchildren of Rabbi Levi Yitzchak of Berdichov and Rabbi Schneur Zalman of Liadi, the great luminaries of Chassidism, were about to be wed. Just as the families prepared to walk down the aisle to the *chupa,* a heated debate ensued. The intense discussion centered around a narrow passageway leading to the *chupa* through which only one person could pass at a time. The question was who would precede whom. Rabbi Schneur Zalman offered that Rabbi Levi Yitzchak, who was much older, should have the honor of going first, while Rabbi Levi Yizchak insisted that Rabbi Schneur Zalman go first, being that he was more learned. As the argument continued with no resolve in sight, Rabbi Levi Yitzchak declared, "Let us just go through the wall." Hearing this, Rabbi Schneur Zalman disagreed and suggested that rather than destroying something, an expansion (of the passageway) would accomplish the same.

Rabbi Schneur Zalman was alluding to Rabbi Levi Yitzchak's philosophy of life. There is a belief that invoking metaphysical practices (such as walking through walls) is intrinsic to living a more spiritual life. Rabbi Schneur Zalman on the other hand taught that one should aspire to work within the normative parameters and broaden the doors. The doors of perception can and therefore need to be widened to their maximum. Spirituality is gained within and through the dimensional, broadening and expanding the human intellect so it too can become a fitting vehicle in comprehending that which is beyond it.

Reb Schneur Zalman was the founder of the ChaBaD mystical school of thought. The ChaBaD style of meditation is referred to as *hitbonenut*—contemplation, the root of which is in the word *binah*—understanding. *Hitbonenut* is practiced by taking a mystical thought and pondering it and thinking it through thoroughly. While there are meditations that are geared toward emptying the mind of all thought, *hitbonenut* meditation attempts to fill the mind with thoughts that are deliberately chosen.

Generally speaking, we are all meditators on one level or another. Thoughts are continuously occurring, and we are always thinking or fixating on something or another. The question is, to what degree do we have hegemony over our thoughts? Do we consciously choose what to think about, or do these thoughts simply occur to us? And when we finally choose to think and meditate, what is it that we choose? Do the thoughts and meditations originate from the false sense of self, the ego, or do they come from the authentic self, which is transcendent? Are they generated by a paradigm of insufficiency and need or do they reflect a context of sufficiency and benevolence? Are the thoughts in the service of survival or the expression of the Ultimate Spirit? The primary goal of *hitbonenut* meditation is to replace mundane thoughts with transcendent spiritual thoughts. An example of this would be the meditation "There is nothing besides the Oneness," contemplating its practical relevance, realizing that all physical pleasures pursued are in reality illusionary and devoid of genuine substance and that all that truly exist? is Oneness.

This type of contemplation evolves in stages. At first one

maintains a thought until it becomes fastened in the mind. Then one feels the energy of the topic that one has been contemplating, the inner energy or life source of the subject, until he is able to feel the transcendent quality of the subject.[1] This way, our mundane consciousness (or unconsciousness) is sensitized into apprehending, experiencing, and feeling the Infinite's light sustaining and giving life to all existence.

Within each of us there exists two modalities of thinking. One is to assess reality through the prism of the selfish egotistical consciousness, the instinctual part of the soul.[2] The soul whose capacity is to perceive reality as separateness and otherness, a condition in which we are all to some extent mired. While the other is to perceive reality through the eyes of the Godly part of the soul, a transcendent perspective, where one sees reality in its true oneness.

---

1. The sixth Chabad rebbe, Rabbi Yoseph Yitzchak, *Igrot Kodesh*, vol. 3, pp. 525–526. See also: *HaYom Yom*, twentieth of Tammuz.

2. Traditionally, these two souls are called the *yetzer tov* and *yetzer ha-ra*, the good and the bad inclinations. (See, e.g., Talmud *Berachot*, 61a; *Sukkah*, 52b.) The good inclination aspires to do good while the bad inclination aspires to sustain and secure its own existence. The Midrash says the verse "and lo it was good" (Genesis, chapter 1, verse 31) refers to the good inclination, while, "And lo it was very good" refers to the evil inclination. For were it not for that inclination, a person would not build a home, marry, have children, do business, and so on. See: *Midrash Rabba*, Genesis, *parsha 9*, chapter 7. The nature of this inclination is not necessarily evil and harmful; rather, egotistical and selfish. Thus, since selfishness can lead to evil, this inclination is called evil and it is man who makes it evil. See: Midrash *Tanchuma*, "*Parshat Bereishit*," chapter 7. See also: Rabbi Yisrael Salanter, *Igeret HaMussar*, reprinted in the end of *Mesilat Yesharim* (Israel: Eshkol, 1978), pp. 160–161. In the Kabbalah a soul is called the *animal soul*. See, e.g., Rabbi Meir Eben Aldavia, *Shivilei Emunah* (Jerusalem: 1990), *nosiv 3*, p. 107; *nosiv 6*, p. 306. Rabbi Schneur Zalman of Liadi, *Tanya*, chapter 9. See also: Rabbi Chaim Vital, *Arba Meot Shekel Kesef* (Jerusalem: 1971), pp. 72b–73. Rabbi Eliyohu of Vilna on the book *Sifra DeZeniuta*, chapter 4, p. 29a.

Both of these states of soul are comprehensive. They encompass intelligence, emotions, and the ability to actualize thoughts and feelings. Consequently, they each function and accomplish things differently. The instinctual soul, being a creation as any other creation, operates within the laws of nature, within the confines and parameters of the time-space continuum. Its thought process is restrained to sequential and dimensional thinking. One plus one is two, two plus two is four, and so on. It is this modality that processes all information, gathering snippets of data. The Godly part, however, is a part of God and is not a creation, but an extension of the creator.[3] It operates and functions on a transcendent level. Its mode of thinking, understanding, and processing information is differ-

---

3. The verse says, "and He blew into his nostrils a breadth of life" (Genesis, chapter 2, verse 7). The commentaries explain that he who blows, blows from his innermost essence. Hence, man's soul originates from the inner essence of God. See: Ramban on Genesis, chapter 2, verse 7; *Kisvei HaRamban, Derashot. Toraht Hashem Temimah* (Jerusalem: Mossad Harav Kook, 1982), p. 159; Rabbi Shabtai Sheftel Horowitz (1565–1619) writes that a Jew possesses a soul that is part of God; *Shefa Tal* (Brooklyn: 1960), *Hakdamah*, p, 1a. See also: Rabbi Moshe Corodovero, *Pardess Rimonim, shar* 32, chapter 1; *Or Ne'erav,* part 1, chapter 3, p. 8. *Shiur Komah, "VaYifach,"* p. 109. Rabbi Avraham Azulay, *Chesed LeAvraham,* part 2, chapter 44; Rabbi Yoseph Yavatz, *Avot,* chapter 1, Mishnah 17; chapter 3, Mishnah 19; Rabbi Menachem Azaryah De Fano, *Maamor HaNefesh,* part 3, chapter 8; Rabbi Yeshayah Halevi Horowitz, *Shenei Luchot Habrit,* Torah Sh'Bektav, Or Chadash, p. 23; Rabbi Nephatali Hirtz Bacharach (seventeenth century), *Emek HaMalech* (Jerusalem: Rokeach), *Shar TiKunei Teshuvah,* chapter 1, p. 15c; Rabbi Schneur Zalman of Liadi, *Tanya,* chapter 2; Rabbi Menacham Mendel of Vitebsk, *Pri HaAretz, "Parshat Vayeshev,"* p. 30; Rabbi Pinchas of Karitz, *Aimrei Pinchos,* p. 33. Rabbi Moshe Chaim Luzzatto, *Da'at Tevunoth,* the beginning; Rabbi Yonathan Eibeschuvetz, *Yarot D'vash,* part 1, p. 8b; Rabbi Nachum of Chernobyl, *Meor Einayim, "Parshat Yitro,"* p. 71; Rabbi Tzodok HaKohen of Lublin, *Dover Tzedek,* p. 2a. Rabbi Ze'ev of Zhitomir, *Or HaMeir,* Parshat Kedoshim, p. 310. See also: Rabbi Chaim of Volozhin, *Nefesh HaChaim, shar* 1, chapter 15.

ent, and to a degree it is beyond the linear and conventional ways of thinking. It is not restricted by dimensional and rational thoughts; it has the ability to contemplate transcendent form-less thoughts.[4]

The aspiration and primary ambition of *hitbonenut* medi-tation is that the rational mind become transcendent, that the mundane intelligence be released from its confined way of per-ceiving, to become a vehicle capable of comprehending that which is beyond it.[5] The finite, rational modality of thinking should be transformed, so that it too can grasp that which is beyond dimensions,[6] and comprehend a mystical thought that is lodged in infinity.[7] Ultimately, the objective is that the trans-

---

4. The sixth Chabad rebbe, Rabbi Yoseph Yitzchak, *Sefer Hamaamorim 5709*, pp. 53–54.

5. The fifth Chabad rebbe, Rabbi Shalom DovBer, *Sefer Hasichoss,* "*Toras Sholom,*" p. 113. See also: The Lubavitcher rebbe, *Kuntras Inyano Shel Toraht HaChassidut,* printed in the back of *Sefer Ha'erchin Chabad* (New York: Kehot, 1970), chapter 1.

6. See, e.g., The sixth Chabad rebbe, Rabbi Yoseph Yitzchak, *Sefer HaSichot 5696,* p. 3. The Lubavitcher rebbe, *Sichot Kodesh 1958,* the nineteenth of Kislev, chapter 23.

7. Though one connects with the infinite's wisdom through studying the revealed parts of the Torah, and this connection is no restricted to Kabbalistic thoughts. As it says, "God and the Torah are one." (*Zohar,* part 73a. See also: Rambam, *Hilchot Yesodei Ha Torah,* chapter 2, *halacha* 10.) Thus, when one studies Torah he is intimately connected with God. And precisely for this reason the Torah is equated to food (see: Proverbs, 9:5), for the Torah as food is internally consumed. As King David said, "And Your Torah is within my innermost parts" (Psalms, chapter 40, verse 9). Hence, in any Torah study one becomes internally connected with God. (See: Rabbi Schneur Zalman of Liadi, *Tanya,* chapter 5.) Thus, why is mystical thought signaled out? Isn't it also possible to connect and feel the infinite in the revealed parts of Torah? There is, however, a difference between the two dimensions of Torah and the difference lies with the one who is studying. The Talmud speaks of the Torah becoming poisonous to the student) (Talmud *Yuma,* 72b). Being that the revealed parts of Torah are concerned with the seemingly mundane issues, laws governing our day-to-day life, it is conceivable for a person to study Torah and

formation be all comprehensive, suffusing the meditator so thoroughly, that his entire being, intellect, emotions, and actions, are permeated with the meditation. At its peak level, the meditator metamorphoses entirely into a transcendent human being, free of negativity and filled with positive expansion, allowing for integration, empathy and inner peace.

Having explained the objective of *hitbonenut* meditation, we now turn to its actualization.

Intellect resides in the chambers of privacy.[8] Therefore, *hitbodedut*—isolation—is a sine qua non for intellectual meditation. It has a greater effect when it is done alone. This explains why most philosophers are by nature introverts who enjoy being in isolation.[9] Furthermore, it is not sufficient to have external isolation in order to blank out distractions. The meditator must also experience internal isolation, a suspension of the stimulation of the senses, where all activity and functioning are

---

forget that it is the Creator's Torah that he is studying. Forget the Giver of the Torah. (See: Talmud *Nedarim*, 81a. The commentary by the Ran, *Dovar Zeh*, Rabbi Yoel Sirkes (1561–1604), *Beit Chadash; Shulchan Aruch*, "*Orach Chaim*," chapter 47. See also: Rabbi Yehudah Loew, *Tifferet Yisrael*, the author's introduction.) Thus, though the revealed segments of Torah are in reality as the mystical parts, nonetheless, there remains a difference by the person who is studying it.

8. See: The sixth Chabad rebbe, Rabbi Yoseph Yitzchak, *Sefer Hamaamorim 5699*, p. 183.

9. It is for this reason that our forefathers, the sons of Jacob and Moses were all shepherds, so that they would have the time to be alone in the fields and meditate. See: Rabbi Avraham ben HaRambam, *Hamaspik Leovedei Hashem*, "*Hitbodetut*." Rabbi Shimon Ben Tzemach Duran, *Magen Avot*, part 2, chapter 2, p. 16a; Rabbi Shlomo Ephraim Lunshitz (c. 1550–1619), *Kli Yakar*, Genesis, chapter 4, verse 3. By meditating alone in the fields, they would make themselves ready to receive prophecies. See: Rabbein Bachya on Genesis, "*Parshat Vayigash*," chapter 47, verse 32 and Exodus, "*Parshat Shemot*," chapter 3, verse 1.

minimized and kept unmanifested.[10] This quieting down is then extended to one's mind as one prepares for the meditation.[11]

Also consequential to the success of a meditation is the mood of the meditator. There are times, when a person contemplates his sense of alienation and estrangement and still remains arrogant and conceited. And there are times when even the slightest thought of remorse awakens the greatest feelings of contrition.[12] There is *mochin de'gadlut*—consciousness of maturity—and there is *mochin de'katnut*—consciousness of immaturity. One can experience expanded consciousness, or one can experience constricted consciousness. On a simple level, it is the difference between what we call having a good day, where one feels empowered, energetic, and able, and having a bad day, where one feels lethargic, heavy, and incompetent. In a constricted mood of consciousness, one may feel as if his power of intellect is reduced to that of a young child.[13] These states of consciousness should be taken into consideration before one

---

10. The sixth Chabad rebbe, Rabbi Yoseph Yitzchak, *Sefer Hamaamorim, "Kuntreisim,"* vol. 2, p. 300. See also: Rabbi Avraham ben HaRambam, *Hamaspik Leovedei Hashem, "Erech Hitbodetut,"* in the beginning. Rabbi Levi Ben Gershon, *Melchemet Hashem, maamor* 2, chapter 6, p. 19.

11. The sixth Chabad rebbe, Rabbi Yoseph Yitzchak, *Sefer Hamaamorim, "Kuntreisim,"* vol. 2, p. 300.

12. Rabbi Schneur Zalman of Liadi, *Maamorei Admur Hazoken, "Inyonim,"* p. 130.

13. Rabbi Schneur Zalman of Liadi, *Maamorei Admur Hazoken, "Inyonim,"* p. 201. The Baal Shem Tov teaches that even while experiencing constricted consciousness, it is possible to reach great spiritual heights. See: *Tzavoas Horivash,* chapter 67. Rabbi Schneur Zalman of Liadi says that constricted state of consciousness is similar to a sleeping state. See: *Torah Or, "Parshat Mikketz,"* p. 35c. Parenthetically, in a sleeping state one is more in touch in a sense with himself, his subconscious, than in an awake state. Additionally, one of the objectives of meditation is to become in touch with oneself. Thus, it can be argued that in a constricted state of consciousness, where one behaves as a child, one is also more in touch with himself. Children act without inhibitions; they express themselves and actualize their feelings.

meditates. Gauging one's mood enables one to maximize the effect of the meditation by preparing for it appropriately.

What needs to be taken into consideration as well, is the climate and environment one wishes to meditate in, for there are various meteorological conditions and environments that are particularly conducive for meditation.[14]

Following the preparatory steps needed to meditate, one can then actually begin the meditation. In the *hitbonenut* meditation itself there are various levels and degrees attainable. The primary technique in *hitbonenut* meditation is to meditate on a mystical thought, so that one can arouse and intensify one's feelings toward the Infinite.

Each of us oscillates between the polarities of the intellect and the emotions. Intellect is the capacity to apprehend external information, process it, and henceforth draw conclusions. Emotions are the feelings one has for someone or something else. Intellect gathers from the outside in, while emotions are felt inside out. For this reason knowledge can be acquired even when there are no other people around, as long as there exists information, while emotion depends on an audience.[15]

---

14. See: Rabbi Shalom DovBer, the fifth Chabad rebbe, *Sefer Hamaamorim 5669*, p. 42.

15. Emotions are only displayed adequately when there are other people who can embrace the emotions. Additionally, emotions generally are aroused because of and in the presence of other people. Even at times when one may feel that he has emotions bundled up within him desiring to be expressed. (As the Torah says with regard to Abraham who sat at the door of his tent in the heat of the day [Genesis, 18:1] sitting and waiting in the heat of the day to invite the passersby, to share with them his hospitality [Rahsi, ad loc]. Abraham was a man of kindness, a man of *chesed*. [*Safer HaBahir*, chapter 191. See: Rabbi Moshe Corodovero, *Pardess Rimonim, shar* 22, chapter 4.] Thus, naturally he desired and needed to express his love.) Nonetheless, even these emotions that seem to arise from within, are also essentially for other people. For if it weren't for other beings in this world, one would not feel the need to

These two qualities seem even further from each other than the distinction mentioned. Intellect is cold and detached, while emotions are involved and passionate. The Kabbalah links intellect to water, which is naturally cool,[16] and emotion to fire, which burns with a passion.[17] Therefore, intellectuals are frequently calm and collected by nature, or by second nature, through training and behavior,[18] while emotional people brim with energy and vitality.[19] And yet, though they seem to be diametrically opposed qualities, there exists a direct link between the two. Intellect is the parent of emotion.[20] What one thinks will affect the way one feels.[21] It is, however, not

---

share a feeling. See: Rabbi Shalom DovBer, the fifth Chabad rebbe, *Sefer Hamaamorim 5669*, p. 169.

16. Water is by nature cold. See: Rambam, *Hilchot Yesodei HaTorah*, chapter 4, *halacha* 2; Rabbi Meir Eben Aldavia, *Shivilei Emunah, nosiv* 2 (Jerusalem edition: 1990), part 1, p. 62. See also: Proverbs, chapter 25, verse 25.

17. Rabbi Yoseph Yitzchak, the sixth Chabad rebbe, *Sefer Hamaamorim 5701*, p. 127.

18. Habit becomes (second) nature. See: Rabbi Meir Eben Aldavia, *Shevilei Emunah, nosiv* 4, part 2; Rabbi Menachem Azaryah De Fano, *Responsa*, chapter 36; Rabbi Schneur Zalman of Liadi, *Tanya*, chapter 14, 15, and 44. See: Rabbi Eliyahu HaCohen, *Sheivet HaMusar*, chapter 20:46, p. 299. See also: Rabbi Eliyahu ben Moshe Di Vidas, *Reshit Chachmah*, "*Shar HaTeshuvah*," chapter 5, p. 118.

19. Rabbi Yoseph Yitzchak, the sixth Chabad rebbe, *Sefer Hamaamorim 5701*, pp. 126–127. Thus, the Mishnah states: A man of wisdom the older he gets the smarter he becomes. *(Kanim, chapter 3, Mishnah 6.)* For the older one is the more weakened the physical body becomes, and thus one's intellectual levels are heightened. See: the following commentaries on this Mishnah: Rambam, Bartenurah, Tosfot Yom Tov.

20. Rabbi Schneur Zalman of Liadi, *Tanya*, chapter 3.

21. See: Rambam, *Hilchot Yesodei HaTorah*, chapter 2, *halacha* 2 and chapter 4, *halacha* 12. One's love is according to one's understanding. See Rambam, ibid; Rambam, *Moreh Nevuchim*, part 3, chapters 28 and 51. See also: Rabbi Yehudah Ha-Chassid, *Safer Chassidim*, chapter 14.

Furthermore, one has the potential to control what seems to be instinctive feelings. The Rambam writes of a person shifting his attention

sufficient to simply think casually about an issue, for in order to arouse emotions, one needs to concentrate intensely. A complete dedication and commitment to the meditation is necessary if one desires to awaken feelings.[22]

A good example of using meditation to arouse one's feelings is demonstrated with regard to the mitzvah of loving God. Many have wondered about this peculiar commandment. Love seems to be an emotion that either one feels or does not feel. Ostensibly, one cannot be coerced into loving someone, or something. Thus, it is puzzling that there is a mitzvah, a commandment to love.[23] Indeed, it is true that love cannot be forced upon someone. However, one can create the proper context in which love can grow, and that is precisely what the mitzvah requires. The mitzvah is the meditation. One is instructed to think and meditate on the possibilities that will arouse one's love for God.[24]

---

during battle and thus not experiencing fear. See: Rambam, *Hilchot Malachim,* chapter 7, *halacha* 15. See also: Rabbi Schneur Zalman of Liadi, *Likutei Torah,* "*Parshat Vaetchanan,*" p. 6d. The sixth Chabad rebbe, Rabbi Yoseph Yitzchak, *Sefer Hamaamorim 5703,* p. 78. The Lubavitcher rebbe, *Sefer Hamaamorim,* "*Meluket,*" vol. 2, p. 245.

22. Rabbi Schneur Zalman of Liadi, *Maamorei Admur Hazoken,* "*Inyonim,*" p. 127.

23. Rabbi Chasdai Cresces writes that there can only be a mitzvah where there is choice involved. See: *Or Hashem,* "*Hatza'ah,*" the beginning. See also: Rambam, *Shemonah Perakim,* chapter 2; Rabbi Dan Yitzchak Abarbanel, *Rosh Amanah* (Jerusalem: *1988),* chapter 4, p. 7; *Mifalot Elokim* (Jerusalem: Otzhar HaPaskim, 1993), *maamor* 1, chapter 3, pp. 18–19, and his commentary to Exodus, chapter 20:2.

24. See: Rabbi Dan Yitzchak Abarbenal, *Mifalot Elokim, maamor* 1, chapter 3, p. 19. In Chassidic thought this answer is offered in the name of the *maggid* of Mezhirech, Rabbi DovBer. See: Rabbi Issak Homeler (1780–1857), *Shnei HaMe'orot,* part *2,* chapter 2. See also: the sixth Chabad rebbe, Rabbi Yoseph Yitzchak, *Sefer Hamaamorim 5701,* p. 116. The Lubavitcher rebbe, *Sefer Hamaamorim,* "*Meluket,*" vol. 2, p. 245. Also see: Rabbi Avraham of

Friends, or even couples, argue and quarrel with one another over pettiness and often think of separating. A good solution at such times would be to think of all the positive traits in the other person. Meditating on the good aspects in the other person in the relationship may rekindle one's friendship, or even one's love for the other. This mechanism works the same way in man's relationship with his Creator. Our relationship with God is analogous to that of a marriage.[25] If one is lacking in love for God, then he should meditate on the goodness bestowed upon him, and his intellect will recruit his emotions.[26] Meditation causes a paradigm shift. It can prompt a redirecting of one's consciousness to the more positive aspects of life and thus rouse the emotions accordingly.

To awaken the appropriate emotions through meditation it is essential that one should meditate on a specific issue, rather than just a general idea. Focusing on the idea of "There is nothing else besides the Oneness"[27] can be useful as a general meditation, seeing how in every detail of creation, in every grain of sand, there exists a divine energy that animates and gives it life. Or one can turn the meditation into a more specified meditation; meditating on how the Creator's glory is manifested in the details of one's own experiences in life. When the meditation is on a general idea, the concepts remain abstract and aloof. However, when one meditates on the details of the concept, then the meditation has a stronger and more lasting effect.[28]

Stolin (1804–1883), *Yesod HaAvodah* (Jerusalem: 1979), part 2, chapter 6, p. 114; *Mechtevei Kodesh*, p. 76.

25. Man's relationship to God is equated to a marriage. See: Talmud *Taanit*, 26b. *Midrash Rabbah*, Exodus, *parsha* 15:31.

26. Rabbi Moshe Chaim Luzzatto, *Mesilat Yesharim*, chapter 21.

27. Deuteronomy, chapter 4, verse 35.

28. See: Rabbi Shalom DovBer, the fifth Chabad rebbe, *Kuntras HaTefilah*, chapter 2.

Following an intense session of meditative prayer, a Chassidic master asked his young disciple, "With what did you pray?" Assuming that his teacher was inquiring as to which meditation he had prayed with, he responded that he was meditating on the idea of "There is nothing besides the Oneness." Hearing this, the master rejoined that he himself had prayed with the bench that he was sitting on. The master was teaching his student that while it is indeed admirable to contemplate such noble concepts as "There is nothing besides the Oneness," what is also of importance is the bench one is sitting on. One must realize that everything is included in "There is nothing besides the Oneness," including the bench. There remains no detail in one's life that is not included in this lofty axiom. (Additionally, the master was teaching his young pupil that at times the very enormity of a concept can diffuse the power of the meditation, especially at the early stages of learning.)

Ultimately, the meditation needs to be turned inward. The meditator must become at one with the concepts he is contemplating, realizing that this principle of unity encompasses him as well, and that his life is a manifestation of God's desire. This is called *simat lev,* taking the ideas to heart. In the Torah it is written "You shall know this day, and take unto your heart."[29] It is not sufficient to know. The Torah requires that it be internalized—*simat lev*—taken to heart. In order for meditation to have its desired effects, the meditator must internalize the meditation.[30] The subject matter one is meditating should become integrated and personal.

---

29. Deuteronomy, chapter 4, verse 39.

30. Rabbi Yoseph Yitzchak, the sixth Chabad rebbe, *Sefer Hamaamorim 5700,* p. 165. The Rambam writes that studying alone is not sufficient to beget emotions; one also needs to pique and arouse his interest in the subject matter, to arouse his own emotions. See Rambam, *Moreh Nevuchim,* part 2, chapter 4; Rambam, *Shemonah Perakim,* chapter 2.

A story is told of a wealthy sage who owned a timber fac-
tory. Once, a fire erupted and destroyed his entire fortune. His
students, not knowing how to tell him the terrible news,
decided to ask him a theoretical question. "What if," they asked,
"a person lost his entire wealth; how would you console him?"
He immediately replied, "Surely I would remind that person
of the saying of the Talmud: 'Whatever God does, is for the
best.'"[31] Upon hearing this, they told him the news, and he
fainted. After being revived, the onlookers questioned him:
"Don't you, of all people, know that 'all that God does is for the
best'?" The sage humbly explained that up until this incident,
the concept was for him but a theory; now, all of a sudden, it
had factual implications, and for this he said, he was not
prepared.

Understanding and meditating on a universal concept,
without concretely relating it to one's own life, relegates it to
the abstract and the theoretical. Taking it to heart relates the
concept of the meditation to one's own circumstances.
Meditating on the abundant kindness bestowed on the general
population evokes vague and dispassionate feelings, while meditating on the kindness bestowed on one in particular elicits passionate and heart-felt emotions.[32]

The Kabbalah speaks of a passageway, a bridge that connects the mind to the heart.[33] This enables the heart to feel
what one's mind is thinking. It is through this passageway that
thoughts travel en route to becoming emotions. A cold, abstract

---

31. Talmud *Berachot*, 60b.

32. Rabbi Yoseph Yitzchak, the sixth Chabad rebbe, *Sefer Hamaamorim
5701*, pp. 116–117.

33. Rabbi Chaim Vital, *Likkutei Torah: Le'Ari Zal*, "*Parshat Vayeshev*." See
also: Rabbi Schneur Zalman of Liadi, *Torah Or*, p. 58b. Rabbi DovBer, the
second Chabad rebbe, *Biurei HaZohar*, p. 37c.

theory is transformed into a passionate, warm emotion by passing through this funnel.[34]

The physiognomy of the human body parallels that of the spiritual configuration of the soul. The neck is what physically separates one's head from one's heart. Spiritually, the neck represents the passageway through which intellect is channeled into emotions. A thought as it is being funneled through this passageway is neither pure intellect, nor is it yet transformed into an emotion. In this state the thought relinquishes its intellectual status, but has not yet become an emotion.[35]

When an individual goes through a traumatic experience and reacts as if nothing has occurred, then the experience has most likely not yet sunk in. The data is in the intermediate period between the gathering of the information and the time when it becomes fully processed and absorbed. The information is still lingering on in the passageway and has not yet trickled down into the heart. This occurs with all types of information. There is always a lapse between receiving information and the emotional absorption of that information. The only variable is how long this takes. Some information is processed immediately, while other data takes more time to absorb and to be registered emotionally. At times we smile walking down the street because of something we heard hours earlier, and it is only then that we feel its impact.[36]

There are times when this connection is impaired, or severed, so that one's ability to feel what one thinks is all but absent. This occurs when the passageway is cluttered, and it is a no go between the mind and heart. On a physical level, within

---

34. Rabbi Yoseph Yitzchak, the sixth Chabad rebbe, *Sefer Hamaamorim 5700,* p. 41.

35. Ibid.

36. See: Rabbi Yoseph Yitzchak, the sixth Chabad rebbe, *Sefer Hamaamorim 5700,* p. 47.

the neck of a human being there exist two passages, the esophagus, which is the food pipe, and the trachea, which is the windpipe. In the spiritual domain as well, these two passages can be stuffed and cluttered. Spiritual blockage of the food pipe occurs when one is filled to excess with physical nourishment, when one is so overly engrossed in consuming and absorbing physical pleasures that one neglects the spiritual. The windpipe, on the other hand, represents air and ambiance. When this pipe is clogged, it means that one is not in an appropriate environ-ment conducive to the arousal of noble emotions. When these connecting pipes are congested, the intellect has no avenue to penetrate the heart. The thoughts cannot evolve into emotions, and so they remain in the mind.[37]

In Kabbalistic terminology this phenomenon is called tim-*turn halev*—dullness of the heart. This is when one suffers from the inability to be responsive and to feel emotions. One may perceive with one's intellect how one should love, yet one's emotions remain silent. One is incapable of feeling or being spiritually moved. This spiritual numbness arises from and is a manifestation of one's ego, where all that one feels is one's own existence and need for survival. The preoccupation with coarse bodily experiences does not allow for genuine sensitivity to spirituality. In this state of spiritual numbness, the ego does not allow the light of comprehension to illuminate the emotions. The Zohar offers a solution how to rid oneself of this dullness. It offers the metaphor of a wooden beam that only when splintered catches fire. Similarly, a body needs to be readied to receive the light of the soul; it needs to be (metaphorically) crushed.[38] This means that, rather than augmenting the light,

---

37. Rabbi Yoseph Yitzchak, the sixth Chabad rebbe, *Sefer Hamaamorim 5703*, p. 21.

38. *Zohar*, part 3, p. 168a.

fanning the flame of contemplation, one must first remove the *timtum halev,* by subduing and humbling one's *yeshut*—one's sense of self and ego.[39] Since the root of the *timtum halev* is man's obsession with ego, the ego must be tamed so that the light of one's comprehension can permeate one's existence. "Where ego exists God cannot."[40] The notion of *yeshut* can only perpetuate itself in the illusion of separateness, while Godliness is unity and oneness.

Consequently, the primary goal in *hitbonenut* meditation is to be in control of what one thinks about, by filling the mind with thoughts that are deliberately chosen. Once a subject for meditation is chosen, a mystical thought, for example, then one can contemplate the issue and arouse one's feelings. In this way, the meditation of the mind becomes automatically a meditation of the heart, rousing one's feelings toward the Infinite.

To appreciate the concept of *hitbonenut* one must have an understanding of what the word *ChaBaD* means. *ChaBaD* is an acronym comprised of three words: *chochmah, binah,* and *da'at.* These are the three facets of comprehension through which intellectual thoughts fully develop and reach fruition.[41] *Chochmah* is wisdom, intuition, and conception. *Binah* is understanding and comprehension. *Da'at* is knowledge, perception, and

---

39. Rabbi Schneur Zalman of Liadi, *Tanya,* chapter 29.

40. Rabbi Schneur Zalman of Liadi, *Tanya,* chapter 6 and 22. The Talmud asserts that when a person feels his own presence God says, "He and I cannot simultaneously exist." Talmud *Sotah,* 5a; *Erchin,* 15b.

41. In order to build the *Mishkan,* the Tabernacle, the artisan needed to possess these three basic levels of intelligence, wisdom, understanding, and knowledge. See: Exodus, chapter 31, verse 3. The juxtaposition of these three types of intellect is found throughout the Torah. E.g., Proverbs, chapter 3, verses 5–7, chapter 8, verses 12–14 and chapter 30, verses 2–3. They are also found mentioned in the same verse, e.g., Exodus, chapter 31, verse 3; Proverbs, chapter 9, verse 10; Isaiah, chapter 11, verse 2.

intellectual awareness.[42] With these three faculties one deciphers and internalizes a thought.[43]

Chochmah, intelligence, is where kernels of thought begin

---

42. The translation of *chochmah* as wisdom, *binah* as understanding, and *da'at* as knowledge, is based on the King James translation of the verse in Exodus, chapter 31, verse 3, where the Torah recounts the qualifications that Betzalel had, so that he could build the tabernacle. "I have filled him with the spirit of God, with *chochmah,* with *tevunah, (binah)* and with *da'at."* The King James edition translates these three as wisdom, understanding, and knowledge. This translation of these three faculties are the accepted translation today. Though it must be stressed that the accuracy of this translation can be questioned. For *chochmah* is more than wisdom. *Webster's Dictionary* interprets wisdom as accumulated learning that contributes to greater insight. *Chochmah* is more than that. It is the abstract creative force, intuition, and so on. *Binah* is translated as understanding. *Webster's* defines the word *understand,* as to grasp the meaning and comprehend. This is indeed a more accurate translation, though *Binah* also has the potential to develop new *innovative* thoughts. *Da'at* is knowledge. *Webster's* explains knowledge as understanding gained by actual experience, range of information, clear perception of truth, something learned and kept in mind. *Da'at* is indeed clear perception and intellectual awareness, but it is not a range of information. The best way to describe *da'at* is identification.

43. The *Zohar* tells of three compartments in the physical brain. (See, e.g., *Zohar,* part 3, p. 136a, 146a, and 162a.) In each of these three compartments there is manifested one of these three intellects, *chochmah, binah,* and *da'at.* See: Rabbi Moshe Cordovero, *Pardas Rimonim, shar* 31, chapter 8. Rabbi Shem Tov Ben Shem Tov, *Sefer Ha'emunot, shar* 4, chapter 10; Rabbi Schneur Zalman of Liadi, *Torah Or,* "*Parshat Tetzaveh,*" p. 83d. Rabbi Shalom DovBer, the fifth Chabad rebbe, *Sefer Hamamorim 5678,* p. 146. Rabbi Yoseph Yitzchak, the sixth Chabad rebbe, *Sefer Hamaamorim 5710,* p. 257; *Sefer Hamaamorim 5704,* p. 163; *Sefer Hamaamorim: Kuntreisim,* vol. 1, p. 401; *Sefer Hamaamorim 5700,* p. 164. See also: Rabbi Avraham Eben Ezra, Exodus, chapter 31, verse 3; Rabbi Gershon Ben Shlomo, *Shar HaShamaim, maamor 9,* p. 52. Today, we know that there are various compartments in the brain that are associated with different types of intelligence. There are parts that are connected to memory, and there are parts connected to speech, and so on. Since the physical brain is the receptacle for intellect, it is therefore important to watch what one eats, for what one consumes will ultimately becomes part of the

to sprout. It is where new thoughts occur and begin to germinate. The word *chochmah* is comprised of two Hebrew words *choch* and *mah,* which means literally *the potential of what is.*[44] *Chochmah* is the potential of all further thought that arises. Yet at this level the thoughts remain elusive; one can still ask "What is it?" Thoughts the way they exist in *chochmah* consciousness are undefinable and incomprehensible. They cannot be explained in clear, logical terms, for they exist only in potentiality. It is the first flash of intuitive knowledge, the bare idea, that cannot yet be fully articulated in rational thought. Once the thought is brought into the domain of *binah,* the potential into the actual, one cogitates this seminal point into finer detail. *Binah* is the cognitive ability that absorbs the ambiguous seeds of *chochmah* and shapes it into transmissible form through the process of associative analysis.[45] The kernel of *chochmah* is nurtured into maturity through the power of *binah. Binah* gives the thought form and configuration.

With the power of *binah* one constructs the details that constitute the totality of the thought, in its length and breadth. Examining and pondering a thought in its length involves taking the thought from a purely abstract state and making it into something more readily understandable. Broadening a thought means to give the thought greater implications, dressing and giving the thought comprehensible and rational connotations.

Chochmah is likened to the male, who supplies the semen,

---

mind. Rabbi Yoseph Yitzchak, the sixth Chabad rebbe, *Sefer Hamaamorim: Kuntreisim,* vol. 2, p. 918.

44. *Zohar,* part 3, p. 28a, 34a, and 235b; *Tikunei Zohar,* the beginning of the introduction; *Tikunei Zohar, tikun* 65 and *tikun* 69; Rabbi Yehudah Chayit on *Ma'arechet Elokut,* chapter 4, p. 71b; Rabbi Moshe Cordovero, *Pardas Rimonim, shar* 23, chapter 8; Rabbi Menacham Azarya De Fano, *S'fas Emess,* "*Erech Chochmah,*" p. 18b. Rabbi Shabtai Sheftel Horowitz, *Shefa Tal, shar* 2, chapter 3, p. 40a; Rabbi Schneur Zalman of Liadi, *Tanya,* chapter 3.

45. Rabbi Yoseph Yitzchak, the sixth Chabad rebbe, *Sefer Hamaamorim: Kuntreisim,* vol. 2, p. 576; *Sefer Hamaamorim 5701,* p. 107.

the germ of the concept, and *binah* is likened to the female, who receives the germ and develops it in the womb into a fully grown, particularized creation.[46] In *binah* consciousness the kernel of *chochmah* incubates until it articulates into a comprehensible thought. *Chochmah* is the unchannelled creative force, which can only be brought into fruition when enclosed and channeled in the womb *of binah*.

In Kabbalah, *chochmah* is likened to a dot.[47] It occurs as a flash of insight. It appears in the form of a concentrated intuitive lightning bolt.[48] The thought flashes in front of one's eyes. It is as if one sees the thought and is certain of its existence but cannot yet explain it. *Chochmah* is the seminal idea before the details are formulated and externalized, while *binah* is where the abstract is made into rational sense. *Chochmah* is likened to seeing the thought, and *binah* is analogous to listening, that is, internalizing and making sense of it.[49]

---

46. This idea of the father giving the general concept and the mother providing the details, is manifested in a physical sense as well. In the Kabbalah it is written that a child genetically acquires from the father the general capacities of will and character, while a child receives from the mother the particular type of intelligence they will have. See: Rabbi Chaim Vital, *Shar HaGilgulim, Hakdamah* 10. (A close resemblance of this idea is also found in Western philosophy. See: Arthur Schopenhauer, *Essays And Aphorisms* (New York: Penguin Books, 1970), "On Affirmation and Denial of the Will To Live," p. 64.)

47. *Zohar*, part 1, p. 6a; *Tikunei Zohar, tikun* 5; Rabbi Schneur Zalman of Liadi, *Tanya*, "*Iggeret HaKodesh*," chapter 5; *Likutei Torah*, "*Parshat Re'eh*," p. 18b.

48. See: Rabbi Schneur Zalman of Liadi, *Torah Or*, p. 74b. Rabbi Yoseph Yitzchak, the sixth Chabad rebbe, *Sefer Hamaamorim 5703*, p. 54.

49. *Chochmah* is analogous to vision and *binah* to hearing. Rabbi Schneur Zalman of Liadi, *Torah Or*, "*Parshat Mishpatim*," p. 75a; *Maamorei Admur Hazoken*, "*Haktzorim*," p. 555. Rabbi DovBer, the second Chabad rebbe, *Shaarei Orah*, "*Shar HaChanuka*," p. 40; *Toraht Chaim*, "*Bereishit*," p. 48a; Rabbi Yoseph Yitzchak, the sixth Chabad rebbe, *Sefer Hamaamorim*

Binah is equated with fire.[50] The nature of fire is to deconstruct all that it consumes. In *binah* one deciphers and breaks
down all thoughts into finer detail.[51] *Chochmah,* on the other
hand, is equated with water.[52] In its primary state it is like an
undiluted fluid, which needs channeling in order to become a
comprehensible idea.[53] Concepts occur as images as opposed to
detailed patterns. Einstein once said that he rarely thought in
words; rather, his ideas first appeared to him as symbols and
images. Only later were they processed into comprehensible
thoughts and expressed in words.[54]

Maimonides writes that the mysteries and secrets of creation are never fully revealed to any man. It is only that at times
flashes of the truth illuminate the darkness momentarily. What
differentiates the prophet from the layman are these moments
of illumination and their frequency. The prophet, while walking
in darkness, experiences a sudden flash of light, of radiance,
which brightens his path. Only to Moses, the greatest of all
prophets, were these bolts of lightning continuous, transforming his darkness into constant light.[55] *Chochmah* is similar to this
illumination. At times one may feel as though he walks in

5701, p. 132; *Sefer Hamaamorim 5709,* pp. 59–60; Rabbi Yisroel, the *magid* of
Koznitz, *Avodat Yisroel,* "*Parsaht Bo,*" p. 95.

50. *Sefer yetzirah,* 1:12, Ravvad, *Otzar Hashem,* ad loc.

51. Rabbi Yoseph Yitzchak, the sixth Chabad rebbe, *Sefer Hamaamorim:
Kuntreisim,* vol. 1, p. 201.

52. See: Rabbi Chaim Vital, *Eitz Chaim, shar* 50; Rabbi Schneur Zalman
of Liadi, *Tanya,* chapter 3. See also: *Safer Habahir,* chapter 119; *Zohar,* part 1, p.
32b.

53. *Chochmah* is unchanneled water. See: Rabbi DovBer, the second
Chabad rebbe, *Derech Chaim,* "*Shar Hateshuvah,*" p. 61; Rabbi Yoseph Yitzchak,
the sixth Chabad rebbe, *Sefer Hamaamorim 5708,* p. 24.

54. *Chochmah* is the initial stage in thought, and it is where thoughts exist
prior to descending into words. See: Rabbi Yoseph Yitzchak, the sixth Chabad
rebbe, *Sefer Hamaamorim 5708,* p. 24.

55. See the Rambam in his *Hakdamah* (foreword) to his monumental
philosophical work, *Moreh Nevuchim,* p. 7. Rabbi Avraham Abulafia writes

darkness, at a loss for a solution to that which eludes him; a lightning strike of *chochmah* will then appear and illuminate his path.

The difference between *chochmah* and *binah,* can best be illustrated with a practical analogy. You have purchased a new gadget and are trying to figure out how to assemble it. You begin thinking to yourself about how to put it together. Reading the instructions confuses you even more. You become intensely concentrated, until your mind completely locks on the issue, but, hard as you try, you still remain clueless as to what has to be done. All of a sudden, as if out of the blue, a thought occurs to you that illuminates the matter. You feel as if you have figured it all out, and the issue has been resolved. You know how it should look, and somehow, how it should be done. And yet, when you try to explain it (even to yourself), you have difficulty. It is as if you see the solution as an image, without being able to articulate it in rational terminology. The linguistic distinctions have not yet been formulated. Such is the level of *chochmah* where one intuits thoughts, while at the level of *Binah* one understands.[56]

Who is *a chocham,* a wise person? the Talmud asks. It is one who learns from every mans.[57] Each person he meets becomes his

---

that generally wisdom comes to a person as an illuminating light. See: *Or HaSechel, Hakdamah,* pp. 2–3.

56. In the Talmud there is mention of an argument between two sages. In the course of their argument one sage is asked by his contemporary a question that seems to refute his opinion completely, and yet, this sage, to whom the question was addressed, did not change his mind. (See: Talmud *Beitza,* 6a.) The reason is that even though he was not able to explain his opinion rationally, in linguistic terms, nonetheless, he felt as if he knew with certainty that his opinion was correct. His level of understanding was at a level of *chochmah.* See: Rabbi Yoseph Yitzchak, the sixth Chabad rebbe, *Sefer Hamaamorim 5708,* p. 102.

57. *Avot,* chapter 4, Mishnah 1. See also: Exodus, chapter 31, verse 3; Rashi, ad loc.

teacher. A wise person is able to discern a lesson from every living being, even from someone who is immoral.[58] On the level of *chochmah* there are no distinctions, and a person is taught by all.

Rabbi Zusya of Hanipoli, the celebrated 18th-century Chassidic master, once said that he had learned many positive traits from a lowly thief. A thief is stealthy and only goes where he will not be noticed. He perseveres and is persistent. He moves with alacrity, and he is always anticipating and hopeful.[59] This great rebbe was able to find noble character traits, that command admiration within a mere thief. Other masters teach that a wise person, a *chocham,* should learn even from his evil inclination.[60] A *chocham* is one who is able to acquire wisdom from the obscurest of sources.

Elsewhere, the Talmud repeats the question: Who is wise? and answers, One who perceives the future.[61] *Chochmah* is the pure undivided mind, which in a sense transcends the limitations of sequential time. On this level, past, present, and future have not yet been separated as distinct time zones. Accordingly, "A wise person is one who can observe the end in the beginning."[62] A wise person's comprehension transcends time.

For this reason *chochmah* is associated and connected to

---

58. Rabbi Yaakov Yoseph of Polonnoye, *Toldot Yakov Yoseph,* "Parshat Pekudei,"* p. 260; *Sefer Baal Shem Tov Al Ha Torah,* "Parshat Ki Tetze" (Note 1).

59. See: The Lubavitcher Rebbe, *Hayom Yom,* the third of Iyar. See also: Rabbi Yisrael of Modzitz, *Divrei Yisrael,* Parshat Chayei Sara, p. 69. Rabbi Yakkov Yoseph of Ostro (1738–1791), *Safer Rav Yeivi,* Parshat Shelach, p. 151.

60. *Baal Shem Tov Al HaTorah,* "Parshat Bereishit," Rabbi Yakov Yoseph of Polonnye, *Toldot Yakov Yoseph,* "Parshat Pekudei,"* p. 260; *Ben Porat Yoseph,* p. 53, 169; *Tzafnat Paneach,* p. 83a; Rabbi Moshe Chaim Ephraim of Sudylkov, *Degel Machanah Ephraim,* "Parshat Vayishlach," p. 43.

61. Talmud *Tamid,* 32a.

62. Jerusalem Talmud *Sotah,* chapter 8, *halacha* 10.

memory.[63] Memory is stored in the mind in a nonverbal modality (a level of *chochmah*). It lies somewhere in one's subconscious, and it can be activated without cerebration, reflexively. Distinctions and sequential thinking, as for example, one plus one . . . exist only on the level of *binah*. In fact, the root of the Hebrew word *binah* is *bein*, which means in between.[64] Ideas, the way they exist in *binah*, are separate, and individually deciphered.[65] *Binah* is likened to fire that separates incidents and categorizes thought, while *chochmah* is likened to water; the nature of water is to connect. In *chochmah* the thoughts are seamless, interconnected, and exist as one.[66]

Memory is stored in the mind as a nonverbal entity, as a totality of thought or experience. Only when the memory is brought to a level of consciousness does it pass from its existence in the everything of *chochmah* and become a distinctive verbalized thought. Additionally, memories are analogous to the male gender, in that the past influences the future, while the future is likened to the female, for whatever will occur in the future is but an extension of its impregnation by the (male) past.

The Kabbalah teaches that all that exists in this physical realm is paralleled by its spiritual counterpart. Therefore, males are (generally) more inclined toward the characteristics of *chochmah*, while women are more inclined to *binah*.[67] Women

---

63. Rabbi Schneur Zalman of Liadi, *Likutei Torah*, "Shir HaShirim," p. 33a. See also: *Maamorei Admur Hazoken 5564*, p. 142; Rabbi DovBer, the second Chabad rebbe, *Toraht Chaim*, the sixth Chabad *rebbe* "Shemot," p. 33a.

64. Rabbi Avraham Eben Ezra, Exodus, chapter 31, verse 3.

65. Rabbi Shalom DovBer, the fifth Chabad rebbe, *Sefer Hamaamorim Ranat 5659*, p. 57.

66. Rabbi Shalom DovBer, the fifth Chabad rebbe, *Sefer Hamaamorim Ranat 5659*, p. 73.

67. A theory based on the Kabbalah that is found also in Western thought. See: Arthur Schopenhauer, *Essays And Aphorisms*, "On Women," pp. 80–88.

generally show a greater bend for comprehension than men.[68] Women and men approach thoughts differently. Faced with an issue that needs to be resolved, the male will immediately seek to find solutions, while the female will look to further articulate the problem into finer detail. One operates with *chochmah* consciousness, while the latter operates with *binah,* the power of articulation. A female desires to speak of her problems (and then perhaps find a solution, although the problem is actually reduced somewhat with the speaking of it), while the first instinct of the male is to resolve the issue, as fast as possible.

Within the human brain there are many compartments, each responsible for the various functions and dimensions of thinking. Generally, the brain is divided into the left and the right hemispheres. The left side controls the functions and movements of the right side of the body, while the right side of the brain controls the left side of the body. In addition to controlling the body they also differ in their intellectual functions. People who have injured the left side of their brain, through a stroke or an accident, suffer disabilities in the right side of the body and may lose the ability to speak. The left hemisphere of the brain controls speech, and it appears to specialize in detail analysis and the processing of external data in a sequential manner. The right hemisphere, in addition to controlling the left side of the body is the creative center of thought. It functions by taking whole and abstract notions and converting them into comprehensible ideas. The right hemisphere controls the intellectual capacity of processing spatial and

---

68. Talmud *Niddah,* 45b. *Midrash Rabbah* Genesis, *parsha* 18, chapter 1. It is interesting to note that, though men on the average are physically more imposing than women, they are 10 percent taller, 20 percent heavier, and 30 percent stronger (especially in their upper bodies). Nonetheless, women are generally more resistant to fatigue. Therefore, the longer a race between men and women (who are generally equally as fast), the more likely a woman will be victorious.

visual concepts, grasping shapes and pictures.[69] For example, people with an impaired right-brain lobe tend not to comprehend known sayings, such as "You are what you eat," a phrase that sounds meaningless if analyzed word for word. They tend to lack the ability to view ideas as a whole.

Chochmah wisdom is associated with the nonverbal right hemisphere of the brain. The kernel of the creative thought as it existed prior to descending into verbalization. The power of *binah* is associated with the speech center of the left hemisphere. To function at optimum capacity, both creatively and analytically, requires the coordination of both hemispheres. Studies have demonstrated that talented musicians, who play instruments, possess larger masses of nerve fibers that connect the brain's two hemispheres.[70] Being creative and being able to bring one's creativity into fruition is largely contingent on one's ability to operate with both hemispheres.

As the female is more connected with *binah* than the male, it is of interest to note, that women are by nature more skilled in languages than men. They have an easier time learning languages. They also like to talk more[71] and are much better communicators. When a difficult situation arises, the male desires to be left alone and to have his own space, while the female wishes to connect by talking about the problem. The Kabbalistic explanation for this phenomenon is that women contain more *binah* than men.[72] The power of articulation and speech are inherently more closely associated with the female

---

69. Studies done by Dr. Elmer Green.

70. Based on studies done by Dr. Gottfried Schlaug, instructor in neurology at Harvard University.

71. See: Talmud *Berachot,* 48b. According to the Talmud, there are ten measurements of speech given to mankind: nine were taken by women, and one was left for men. Talmud *Kiddushin,* 49b.

72. Rabbi DovBer, the second Chabad rebbe, *Derech Chaim,* "Shar HaTefilah," p. 121. Being that women possess more *binah* than men, and the source of *binah* is *keter* (a level beyond intellect), thus, they have more of

ender than the male. (Although men are more right-hemisphere
oriented and women more left, there are obviously no absolutes
in this matter.)

Each human being, male and female alike, has the
potential, and thus the opportunity, to harness and mobilize both
these intellectual capacities to meditate on the Creator's omnipresence. It is through their utilization that emotions are born.[73]

To ensure that the progeny of this union is healthy, a good
relationship needs to be fostered between the parental poles.
Respect, nurturing, and exercise are what cause / allow *chochmah*
and *binah* to birth creative, focused, and articulate thoughts and
feelings. *Chochmah* seeds the kernel of the insights, though lacking gravity and permanence, while *binah,* lacking in creativity,
nurtures and anchors the thoughts.

The Zohar speaks of *chochmah* and *binah* as two inseparable
friends.[74] Their friendship is so strong that, in fact, they merge,
and there is a measure of *binah* in *chochmah,* and a measure of
chochmah in *binah.*[75] The *chochmah* within *binah* protects the
original thought from dilution. The ruminations of *binah* can
cause one to lose focus and to stray from the initial premises.
And so *chochmah* maintains the integrity of the thought
process. *Binah,* on the other hand, grounds the intuitive
and the creative aspect of *chochmah* to settle in the mind.[76]
For one to have a comprehensible thought, harmony and unity

---

keter. Keter being the source of words, languages. See also: Rabbi Sholom
DovBer, the fifth Chabad rebbe, *Sefer Hamaamorim Ranat 5659,* pp. 3–9.

73. *Chochmah* is the father, the male. *Binah* is the mother, the female.
Zohar, part 3, p. 290a; Rabbi Moshe Cordovero, *Pardas Rimonim, shar* 8, chap-
ter 17; *shar* 9, chapter 5. Together they are the parents of emotions. See: Rabbi
Schneur Zalman of Liadi, *Tanya,* chapter 3.

74. *Zohar,* part 1, p. 123a.

75. *Sefer Yetzirah,* chapter 1, Mishnah 4.

76. Rabbi Sholom DovBer, the fifth Chabad rebbe, *Sefer Hamaamorim
5679,* p. 226. Rabbi Yoseph Yitzchak, the sixth Chabad rebbe, *Sefer
Hamaamorim 5702,* p. 16.

between the intellects is needed. Then the thoughts produced
are healthier and, in turn, the emotions that come forth are also
healthier and longer lasting.

Up until this point the modality of creative thinking discussed was inductive reasoning. This modality is termed in the
Kabbalah as *or yashar*—direct light. At first the conceptual
thought, then the details flowing from it, and supporting it.
The term *or yashar* suggests a straight and smooth course of
development. An epiphany arises, a light is opened, and the
issue at hand becomes illuminated. These intuitions and inven-
tions can arise in the mind while walking down the street, taking a bath, and so on, even when the mind is not actively
engaged in reverie. It just appears out of nowhere and sheds
light on an entire issue.

There is another modality termed *or chozer*—returning,
reflective light. It is a deductive approach to creative thinking,
where *binah* precedes *chochmah*. To use a previous example, one
is surrounded by parts and instructions to a new gadget that one
has acquired. By collating the information available one intuits
and infers until creativity is achieved and new insights are
gained. *Binah,* says the Talmud, is when one understands one
thing from the other.[77] As one's mind is engaged and one idea
forms the next, organizing a plan or theory, the power of innovation and intuition is activated and greater insights are
revealed. These innovative and creative thoughts are called
reflective lights, for the flash of insight sort of bounces off the
other ideas.

Binah, through *or chozer,* can entail more than just extract-
ing a model of thought from the original generic thought of
chochmah. Rather, it has the capability to build toward a more
inclusive thought, even greater than that which is encoded
within the level of *chochmah* itself (the seed becomes a tree).

---

77. Talmud *Chagigah,* 14a; Exodus, chapter 31, verse 3; Rashi, ad loc.

Through meditating one reaches higher and more creative levels of thought than one would attain by *chochmah* itself.[78]

The feeling one has when operating in the *or chozer* mode is similar to that of walking into a dark unfamiliar room. Entering the room, one begins to slowly stumble around, bumping into the furniture, learning where each article in the room is. Slowly, one begins to discover the formation of the room. When at last one finds the light switch and turns it on, everything one came to know in the darkness is suddenly illuminated with light. *Or chozer* is when there is a difficult problem that needs to be deciphered, and being that there is no resolve on the horizon, one feels as if they are stumbling in darkness and confusion. Slowly, with arduous labor, one begins to figure out something, and then finally an intellectual break-through occurs, and it all becomes illuminated.

The third letter of ChaBaD stands for *da'at*. Traditionally *da'at* is translated as knowledge.

The Torah uses the term *da'at* to connote the idea of attachment, connection, and union.[79] The word *da'at* means to internalize a thought, or concept, and create an association with the idea.[80] With *da'at* consciousness, the boundary that usually separates the knower from the known is eliminated.

Knowledge is commonly perceived as a function of the intellect associated with the mind, while in fact *da'at* is an act of identification. *Leda'at*—to know—means to experience an identification with. *Da'at* is the attachment of the mind to that

---

78. Rabbi Yoseph Yitzchak, the sixth Chabad rebbe, *Sefer Hamaamorim 5701*, pp. 52–53.

79. Genesis, chapter 4, verse 1.

80. *Tikunei Zohar, tikun* 69; Rabbi Moshe Corodovero, *Pardess Rimonim, shar* 23, chapter 4, "Da'at," Rabbi Chaim Vital, *Eitz Chaim, "Shar Haklipot,"* 2; Rabbi Schneur Zalman of Liadi, *Tanya*, chapter 3; *Tanya: Iggeret HaKodesh*, chapter 15; Rabbi Yehudah Chayit on *Ma'arechet Elokut*, chapter 4, p. 63a. See also: Rabbi Tzvi Elimelech of Dinav, *Agrah DePerkah*, chapter 132, p. 15a.

which it is contemplating. A thought becomes fully absorbed in *da'at*. There is no thorough and complete understanding *(binah)*, until the thought is brought down into *da'at*.[81]

Eating from the tree of knowledge caused an identification and attachment to evil. Prior to eating from the tree of knowledge, Adam and Eve intellectually understood that good and evil exist. Their understanding, however, remained abstract and external. By eating from the tree, they internalized evil. From then on, evil ceased existing as an external objective reality, and became an internal subjective interpretation. From then on mankind knew and identified with both good and evil. The good resides within us and so does the potential for evil.[82]

Earlier there was mention of the right and left hemispheres of the brain, and how they are connected with *chochmah*, and *binah*. *Da'at* also occupies a particular region in the brain. There is a large area toward the front of the brain on the right and left sides, which are called the frontal lobes. It has been observed that this area of the brain is responsible for judgment and planning, in other words, the function of *da at*.[83] Still, this could not occur without the requisites of *chochmah* and *binah*. There

---

81. "If there is no *da'at* there is no *binah*." *Avot*, chapter 3, Mishnah 17.

82. Rabbi Schneur Zalman of Liadi, *Torah Or*, *"Parshat Bereishit,"* pp. 5c–5d. The Rambam writes that before the sin they intellectually understood truth and falsehood; following the sin they knew good and evil intimately and internally. Rambam, *Moreh Nevuchim*, part 1, chapter 2.

83. The frontal lobes of the brain serve to identify an objective, project a goal based on that, and then forge a plan to reach that same goal. See: Elkhonon Goldberg. The *Executive Brain: Frontal Lobes and the Civilized Mind* (Oxford University Press, 2001). See also: Oliver Sacks, *The New York Review of Books* (April 26, 2001), pp. 46–48. The sources suggest that the intellect of *da'at* exists toward the rear of the brain. See: Rabbi DovBer, the second Chabad rebbe, *Toraht Chaim*, *"Shemot,"* p. 395b; Rabbi Shalom DovBer, the fifth Chabad rebbe, *Sefer Hamamorim 5678*, p. 146. Nonetheless, they also indicate that *da'at* is connected to the front of the brain.

cannot cannot be *da'at,* where one internalizes thoughts, if there are no thoughts.[84]

Da'at is seen as a bridge between the mind and the heart. Through its function of internalization it causes the concepts of the mind to enter the heart and then to translate into action. For this reason *da'at* is associated with the spinal cord,[85] which serves as a conduit for the messages of the brain to travel to the body, and the messages of the body, to reach the brain. The Kabbalah calls *da'at* the key to all emotions.[86] For through *da'at,* a person's intellectual comprehension does not remain in the domain of the theoretical, but rather, it has a practical relevance in the way he behaves. The divide that exists between the heart and the mind is magnified in an individual who lacks in the faculty of *da'at.* The Talmud speaks of such a dichotomy when it says that there are thieves, who in the midst of stealing, cry out to the Almighty for assistance.[87] They understand intellectually that there is a God, who is worthy of being prayed to, and that it is forbidden to steal; yet, their understanding lacks the element of *da'at,* which is internalization. They behave immorally, though they understand it to be wrong. There is a disconnect between their minds and their heart, their thoughts and their feelings.

A child may score high on an IQ exam. He may have the ability to understand concepts that even adults have trouble comprehending. Yet even child prodigies are not deemed

---

84. "*Da'at* can only exist if *binah* does." *Avot,* chapter 3, Mishnah 17.

85. Rabbi Moshe Cordovero, *Pardas Rimonim, shar* 31, chapter 8 (also see: *shar* 23, chapter 8).

86. *Zohar,* part 2, p. 177a. See also: Rabbi Menacham Mendel, the Tzemach Tzedek, the third Chabad rebbe, *Derech Mitzvosecho, "Ha'amanot Elokut,"* chapter 2.

87. Talmud *Berachot,* 63a; the version of the *Ayin Yaakov;* Rabbi Menacham Mendel, the Tzemach Tzedek, the third Chabad rebbe, *Derech Mitzvosecho, "Ha'amanot Elokut,"* chapter 2. See also: Rabbi Shalom DovBer, the fifth Chabad rebbe, *Sefer Hamamorim Eter 5670,* pp. 115–117.

responsible. They lack the capacity of *da'at,* the ability to connect a truth to their own behavior. And therefore, children are,
to a certain extent, exempt from punishment until they reach
maturity.[88] Being mature means that one knows that actions
have consequences. One's knowledge and understanding of life
be-come personal and real, as opposed to being abstract and
external. When one attains *da'at* one is aware of being causal in
life and the responsibility that it entails. One makes moral distinctions and is empowered to act upon them.[89]

Personal reality resides in *da'at.* Until opinions, notions,
ideas, and concepts reach that level, they remain abstract,
theoretical, and inconsequential.[90]

Knowledge is the concretization of thought. The formation of absolutes and convictions, making thoughts real. *Da'at*
prompts a complete dedication of one's intellect, emotions, and,
ultimately, of one's actions. At the conclusion of the daily
prayers we say the "Aleinu." There we pray, that "You shall
know this day, and take unto your heart that the Lord is God in
heaven . . . ," and then we pray for a time when "All the inhab-
itants will recognize and know that to You every knee should
bend." When one knows this truth, it is not an abstraction;
rather, one is filled with a total certainty and conviction. One's
intellect, emotions, and actions integrate and respond accordingly. With *da'at* one acquires all;[91] the troika is complete.

---

88. Rabbi Shalom DovBer, the fifth Chabad rebbe, *Kuntras HaTefilah,*
chapter 5; The Lubavitcher Rebbe, *Sefer Hamaamorim, "Meluket,"* vol. 1, p. 35.

89. The Talmud asserts that if there is no *da'at* there cannot be distinctions. Jerusalem Talmud, *Berachot,* chapter 5, *halacha* 2. *Da'at* is the ability to
decide. See: RaBBi Shalom DovBer, the fifth Chabad rebbe, *Sefer Hamamorim
Eter 5670,* p. 133; *Sefer Hamamorim 5678,* p. 147.

90. See: Rabbi Yoseph Yitzchak, the sixth Chabad rebbe, *Sefer
Hamaamorim 5706,* pp. 77–78.

91. Talmud *Nedarim,* 41a; Midrash *Tanchuma, "Parshat Vayikra,"* the
beginning; *Midrash Rabba,* Leviticus, *parsha* 1, chapter 6.

Da'at is the completion of the thought process internalized into one's emotions and then actualized through one's deeds.

Kabbalah speaks of two levels within *da'at* itself: *da'at elyon*—upper, superior *da'at*—and *da'at tachton*—lower, inferior *da'at*.

Until now *da'at tachton*, the lower *da'at*, was explored. It is that which connects and acts as an intermediary between the cold intellect and warm emotions.[92] There is, however, also a higher level of *da'at*, *da'at elyon*. It also serves as a connecting point, not between the brain and the heart, but rather, between the levels of intellect, namely between *chochmah*, the male, and *binah*, the female.[93] *Da'at* promotes and engenders a unity between the male and the female by alleviating certain intrinsic differences and distinctions. It acts as a conduit causing the seminal infusion of *chochmah*, the male, to become impregnated in the womb of *binah*, the female.

In Kabbalistic literature *da'at* and *keter* are interchangeable.[94] The Hebrew word *keter* means a crown. It is a level that transcends intellect, as a crown that sits above the head. The concepts of *keter* and *da'at* represent alternative expressions of

---

92. Rabbi Schneur Zalman of Liadi, *Tanya*, chapter 3; *Tanya: Iggeret HaKodesh*, epistle 15, "*Likutei Torah*," 3:88c; Rabbi Menacham Mendel, the Tzemach Tzedek, the third Chabad rebbe, *Derech Mitzvosecho*, "*Ha'amanot Elokut*," chapter 2; Rabbi Shalom DovBer, the fifth Chabad rebbe, *Sefer Hamamorim Eter*, p. 115.

93. Rabbi Moshe Cordovero, *Pardas Rimonim*, *shar* 3, chapter 8; *shar* 8, chapter 17; *shar* 9, chapter 6; Rabbi Schneur Zalman of Liadi, *Tanya: Iggeret HaKodesh*, epistle 15. "*Likutei Torah*," part 3:88c; *Torah Or*, "*Parshat Mishpatim*," p. 75a.

94. The Kabbalah teaches that when *da'at* is counted in the Ten *sefirot* then *keter* is not, and when *keter* is counted *da'at* is not. See: Rabbi Chaim Vital the *Eitz Chaim*, *Shar Mochan DeTzelem*, chapter 5; Rabbi Schneur Zalman of Liadi, *Likutei Torah*, "*Parshat Emor*," p. 39b. See also: Rabbi Yoseph Gikatalia, *Shaarei Orah*, *shar* 5, p. 126; Rabbi Moshe Corodovero, *Pardess Rimonim*, *shar* 3, chapter 8; Rabbi Yoseph Ergas, *Shomer Emunim*, part 1, chapter 67.

the same force that enable a person to endure and sustain diametrically opposed states, concurrently. *Keter* is the metalevel
that allows the person to house the fundamental paradoxes of
life. *Keter* encompasses and connects the various dimensions of
reality, while *da'at* bridges and connects the various dimensions
of intellect.

Earlier, *da'at* was identified as the power to differentiate,
the ability to decide and to choose. *Da'at elyon,* the higher level
of *da'at,* is creative, contextual, inductive, and comprehensive. It
is in this domain that one chooses one's purpose in life, which
aspect one invests oneself in, and the like. There is a contextu-
alizing quality to the choice that has a spiritual source or under-
pinning. *Da'at tachton,* while sourced by *da'at elyon,* has its own
mechanism and operates on a lower level. It operates in the
domain of decisions and options, which implement the choices
of *elyon.* What schools do I go to? What am I going to work at?
Who are my friends? and so on. All important questions but
essentially made at the level of options (even when there aren't
any). It is deliberative and subject to mutation, but it is basically
aligned with the context established already with *da'at elyon.*

Choices that are made on *da'at elyon* are done at a seminal
level, rooted in a logic indigenous to the individual, and perhaps
seemingly irrational. Operating in *da'at elyon* one may simply
say, "I know this is the way it should be done," and that is it. A
person establishes that this is the way, without grounding that
choice in a rational thought process. There is, however, a vast
difference between being stubborn and the state of *da'at.* Being
stubborn in life, not being willing to listen to other people's
opinions and not changing even the slightest bit, means to surrender to one's weakness of heart.[95] The hallmark of the heart

---

95. Rabbi Yoseph Yitzchak, the sixth Chabad rebbe, *Sefer Hamaamorim
5688,* p. 85.

is its rigidity. The heart says, "This is the way I feel it should be done and that is final." Intelligence says, "This is the way I understand it should be; convince me otherwise." *Da'at* is of a different order. One feels a higher force's guidance, a power that is beyond the intellect.[96] Sometimes, it is only much later that one finally understands the reasons for one's choices. What one cannot fathom with logic one can feel with *da'at*.[97]

Having established what ChaBaD stands for, we are now prepared to explore *hitbonenut* meditation. The primary objective of this discipline is to train the meditator to master his thoughts and enable him to fill his mind with deliberately chosen thoughts. In *hitbonenut* one's intellectual apparatus, *chochmah, binah,* and *da'at,* the three primary domains of intellect, are utilized to develop thoughts into fruition. This type of intellectual meditation includes the rational linear intelligence, which through the meditation becomes broadened and expanded, so that it too can be a vehicle capable of comprehending and contemplating thoughts that are lodged in infinity.

In the later stages, through the melding of the mind and the heart, one's emotions are aroused. Emotions that originate in the heart, without being aroused by the intellect, can be external and superficial. Emotions that stem from the intellect are real and everlasting. So, by choosing a thought that speaks of the Creator's omnipresence, and meditating on it, the intellect arouses the heart to profound ecstasy.

---

96. Rabbi Shalom DovBer, the fifth Chabad rebbe, *Sefer Hamaamorim Eter 5670*, pp. 133–134; Rabbi Yoseph Yitzchak, the sixth Chabad rebbe, *Sefer Hamaamorim 5688*, p. 85.

97. Rabbi Yoseph Yitzchak, the sixth Chabad rebbe, *Sefer Hamaamorim 5700*, p. 156.

Yet, ecstasy that is felt in the heart is but one type of ecstasy. Ultimately, the ambition of the meditation is to reach the highest level of ecstasy attainable, and that is to become one with the Infinite. The Kabbalah speaks of three levels of ecstasy. The lowest being the one felt in the heart. Where intellectual contemplation of the mind arouses emotions of the heart. A pang of longing is awakened in the heart, which desires to be close to the Source of life. A higher degree of ecstasy is feeling emotions in the mind, intellectually sensing an allure and desire to be close to one's Source. The highest level of ecstasy available is when the meditator has no awareness of his feelings. The meditator attains a level of *deveikut*—adhesion, and oneness, where feelings of separation disappear, until awareness itself disappears, even the awareness of being in ecstasy.

The first step of *hitbonenut* is when, through the meditation, the emotions of the heart are awakened to rapture. The meditator harnesses all three of his intellectual capacities, *chochmah, binah,* and *da'at,* and uses them as tools to kindle his emotions. The purpose of the meditation is to feel what one is meditating about. For example, if one is meditating on the light of the Creator filling the universe, then once the emotions are aroused, one feels this Godly energy within the universe. These feelings are termed *yenika,* literally translated as a suckling. Like a young mammal who receives its nourishment by sucking and absorbing its mothers milk, these feelings are nourished and enhanced by the intellect. The measure of the feelings is contingent on how one has meditated. It can only suckle from the intellect as much as the intellect produces.[98] Once the emotions are externalized, they exist as separate entities from the intellect. Yet, as sucklings, they remain dependent on the intellect for their nourishment and survival.

---

98. Rabbi Schneur Zalman of Liadi, *Torah Or,* "*Parshat Bereishit,*" p. 4b; "*Parshat Yitro,*" p. 68c; Rabbi Shalom DovBer, the fifth Chabad rebbe, *Sefer Hamaamorim Eter 5670,* p. 134.

Emotions produced at this level are those of passion and longing, emotions of love that burn with intensity. On this level, the *deveikut* has not yet been attained. Here there still exists a you, who is in love; there is another existence other than the One who is loved. One may feel the greatest passion, feelings may be overflowing, yet there still remains a you who is experiencing these emotions. These emotions are felt. There still exists separateness, that is, a person who is feeling.

Emotions of the mind are a higher level of *hitbonenut*. These feelings are called *ibur*—impregnation.[99] The emotions of the mind do not exist independent of the intellect, but they are analogous to a fetus ensconced in its mother's womb. The emotions of the heart now become elevated to the mind.[100] Here passion and rapture of the heart is not felt, what is experienced is organized and collected inclinations of the mind, a proclivity of sort toward the subject of the meditation.[101] A more profound degree of *deveikut* is reached at this level. One's *yeshut*—existence, beingness—is less pronounced than as when one's emotions are displayed. Yet, no matter how subtle one's *yeshut* is, there still exists separateness. There still remains a meditator who feels the experience, albeit a feeling of the mind.

A supreme state of *hitbonenut* meditation is called *mochen degadlut*—intellect of maturity and of greatness.[102] In this advanced meditative state the meditator does not experience feelings. On the contrary, the experience is so hypnotic that he loses himself in the meditation. There is no longer an "I."

---

99. Rabbi Schneur Zalman of Liadi, *Torah Or,* "*Parshat Yitro,*" p. 68c. Rabbi Shalom DovBer, the fifth Chabad rebbe, *Sefer Hamaamorim Eter 5670,* p. 134.

100. The second Chabad rebbe, Rabbi DovBer, *Aimrei Binah,* p. 69.

101. Rabbi Shalom DovBer, the fifth Chabad rebbe, *Sefer Hamaamorim Eter 5670,* p. 134. See also: Rabbi Schneur Zalman of Liadi, *Tanya,* chapter 16.

102. Rabbi DovBer, the second Chabad rebbe, *Toraht Chaim Shemot,* p. 161b; Rabbi Shalom DovBer, the fifth Chabad rebbe, *Sefer Hamaamorim Eter 5670,* p. 135.

Emotions can only function in a condition of separateness. There needs to be an other who can receive and respond to the emotions.[103] For example, the emotion of hate amplifies this sense of separateness. It reinforces the idea that it is me or you. While the emotion of love expresses one's willingness and desire to overcome separateness and alleviate the boundaries that exist between me and you, so that it can be me *and* you. So, too, in meditation. When emotion exists, separateness also exists between the meditator and the meditation. Once, however, the meditator reaches higher meditative states, he no longer feels. And thus through the meditation, he joins and becomes one with what he is meditating on, that is, becomes one with the Source of all reality.

A suitable comparison, which enables us to better understand these three levels of *hitbonenut,* is love. To simplify the issue we will posit that there are three types of love. The first is love that is acquired. For example, love one has for a spouse, or for that matter, love one has for any good friend. The second is love that is natural. Such as the love one has for one's family, love for one's parents, parents to children, or siblings between themselves. The third love is the one a person has for himself.

Love that is acquired is generally passionate and exciting, one that burns with a raging intensity; yet the people who are in love forever remain separate from each other. The beauty of such love is that it transcends the differences between them. At times it is the very differences that stoke the emotions. This type of love, which overcomes distance and bridges gaps, continuously needs to be renewed and rekindled.

On the first level of *hitbonenut,* the meditation evokes emotions. The emotions are felt intensely and passionately. These emotions bridge the abyss separating finite man from infinite Creator. It is a feeling of overcoming differences.

103. Rabbi Sholom DovBer, the fifth Chabad rebbe, *Sefer Hamaamorim 5678,* p. 12.

Natural love is a love that one has innately and spontane-ously, as the love for children, parents, siblings, and so on. This kind of love differs from that which is acquired, in that it is not passionate and exciting. Rather, it is what it is called, tranquil love, being a function of natural instinctive feelings. There is less distance that needs to be overcome, and therefore, these feelings are more subdued and calm.

On a higher level of *hitbonenut,* the emotions that are born are not externalized; they remain in the mind. The emotions are not as conspicuously passionate, but this is not because the meditator is on a lower spiritual state. On the contrary, it is because he has become more at one with the meditation, and thus his *yeshut*—existence—is less pronounced, and his feelings are less felt.

Love of oneself seems to be a paradoxical statement. If love is a bridge that unites, then how does love for oneself manifest? In truth, however, the profoundest love one has is for oneself. It is the glue that integrates a human being spiritually and psychologically. It is not love, as a feeling or a craving;[104] rather, it is of a different order; it is a state of being. The difference between a feeling and a state of being lies in their nature and how they are experienced. Feelings are fleeting and temporary. To be sustained, they need to be rekindled and continuously remembered. And they are evocative, depending on an outer stimulus. A state of being is constant and contextual. It is, whether remembered or not, and is the source of all feelings and actions. It is a place to come from. It is that which is being expressed, and it is at one with the expresser.

The highest level of meditation is when one reaches a complete *bitul, bitul* being the apogee of *deveikut,* where there

---

104. Emotions cannot be *felt* for oneself. See: Rabbi DovBer, the second Chabad rebbe, *Aimrei Binah* (1) p. 20b; *Birchat Chasanim,* p. 22a. See also: the Maharal, Rabbi Yehudah Loew, *Nesivot Olam, Nesiv Ahavat Hashem,* chapter 1.

is the complete nullification of a sense of self,[105] not even having a sense of being in ecstasy.[106] There is the total eclipse of feeling, awareness, and thought. The "I" is transcended. And there is no room for self-awareness.[107]

These states of meditation are ordinarily ascended one rung at a time. At first one experiences feelings of the heart, then of the mind, and finally one transcends feelings altogether. Emotions, the love or fear one feels in the heart, are the wings of spiritual growth, assisting one in taking the first steps toward living a more meaningful, transcendent life. Yet, they are only the tools and not an end unto themselves. The objective is reaching the destination of transcendence by becoming closer to and then finally one with the Infinite.[108]

As described earlier, the *deveikut* one attains, shifts the beingness of the meditator. With this *deveikut* comes a new way of seeing called *he'staclut,* which is more accurately defined as gazing.[109] There are three ways that a person apprehends reality on an ocular level. One is looking, which is a purely biological function. The second is seeing, where whatever is looked at

---

105. Rabbi Yoseph Yitzchak, the sixth Chabad rebbe, *Sefer Hamaamorim 5701,* pp. 126–127.

106. Rabbi DovBer, the second Chabad rebbe, enumerates five levels in Divine ecstasy (within the Godly soul), the highest being ecstasy without any self-awareness. See: Rabbi DovBer, *Kuntras Hispalut, "Maamorei Admur Hoemtzoee Kuntresim"* (New York: Kehot, 1991), chapter 4. This text has been translated into English by Louis Jacobs, *Tract On Ecstasy* (London: Vallentine Mitchell and Co. Ltd., 1963).

107. Rabbi DovBer, the second Chabad rebbe, *Derech Chaim, "shar Hatifilah,"* p. 176.

108. Ibid.

109. The word *he'staclut* means more than just seeing an object; it connotes a complete undisturbed concentration, gazing intensively. See: Rabbi Chaim Yoseph David Azulay, *Ayin Zocher, marrechet hei* (50), p. 64; *Yad Melachei,* chapter 179. *Biur HaGra,* Rabbi Eliyahu of Vilna, *Orach Chaim,* chapter 229. Rabbi Yitzchak Blazer, *Or Yisrael, Sharei Or,* p. 31. *Torah Temimah,* Genesis, chapter 27:1.

is interpreted through the prism of the viewer's cumulative prejudices, bent, and contextual thinking. In short, the event is recreated by the mind in its own image. The third, gazing, can only occur in a condition of complete *bitul*. The gazer, having limited the internal static, the *yesh,* that prevents him from being with life and with God, can now experience and be at one with the object being viewed. Gazing is a doing, born out of a way of being, but which in turn allows existence to be in the (perfect) way that it is. In meditation it translates into losing existence,[110] and becoming one with the Infinite.[111]

King Solomon sings in Song of Songs of the passion between lovers. The song is interpreted by the sages of the Talmud to be an analogy of the love that exists between the nation of Israel and God.[112] He sings: O' my dove trapped in the clefts of the rock.[113] Doves derive pleasure and arouse desire for one another by gazing at each other. When a human being meditates on creation, gazing lovingly on the infinite's light that fills and imbues the universe, he derives immeasurable spiritual delight. This is called *he'staclut,* gazing with pleasure.[114] This spiritual bliss is so supernal that the meditator reaches a level of *kelot hanefesh*—an ascension of the soul, an eclipse of the

---

110. Rabbi Schneur Zalman of Liadi, *Maamorei Admur Hazoken: Inyonim,* p. 134. Through *he'staclut* a person reaches a level of *kelot hanefesh,* where the soul literally leaves the body. Rabbi Shalom DovBer, the fifth Chabad rebbe, *Kuntras HaTefilah,* chapter 1.

111. Rabbi Yoseph Yitzchak, the sixth Chabad rebbe, *Sefer Hamaamorim 5701,* p. 113.

112. Mishnah *Yodayim,* chapter 3, Mishnah 5; Midrash Rabbah, "*Shir HaShirim,*"*parsha* 1, chapter 11; Rambam, *Hilchot Teshuvah,* chapter 10, *halacha* 3.

113. *Shir HaShirim,* chapter 2, verse 14.

114. Rabbi Schneur Zalman of Liadi, *Likutei Torah, "Shir HaShirim,"* part 5, p. 41d.

physical, to the extent that at times the body expires and the soul literally transcends corporeal dimensions.[115]

Every thought is comprised of body and soul. The body of a thought is the *hitbonenut*—the intellectual aspect—while the soul is the *he'staclut*—the gazing or perception of the idea.[116] As stated earlier, the sequential order of *hitbonenut* is as follows: First the initial germ is revealed in *chochmah*, then developed in *binah*, and finally in *da'at* it becomes absorbed. Hence, *chochmah* precedes *binah*, and *binah* precedes *da'at*. Once, however, the thought is fully absorbed, the procedure begins to operate in reverse. One meditates in *binah*, and through *binah* one reaches *chochmah*. Ultimately, via *binah* one attains the highest degrees of *chochmah*, the level of *ayin*—the *nothing* that is beyond the *something*, nothingness being the divine that is beyond human comprehension and imagination, beyond being attainable through intellect.[117]

To connect with *ayin* one must become *ayin*.[118] In order to arrive at this level of *ayin* the meditator himself must be in a state of *ayin*. A meditator who is self-conscious and aware of his experience, aware that he is in ecstasy, cannot fully operate at the highest levels of *chochmah*, the *ayin*. By reaching the *ayin* within oneself, revealing the soul, the level of transcendence and *bitul*, one is then able to be with the Source of all life, the *ayin*, that creates and sustains all existence.

---

115. Rabbi Shalom DovBer, the fifth Chabad rebbe, *Kuntras HaTefilah*, chapter 1.

116. Rabbi Yoseph Yitzchak, the sixth Chabad rebbe, *Sefer Hamaamorim 5701*, p. 99.

117. Rabbi Schneur Zalman of Liadi, *Likutei Torah*, "*Parshat Bamidbar*," part 3, p. 17a.

118. Rabbi DovBer, the *maggid* of Mezritch, *Maggid Devarav Leyokav*, *Likutei Amorim*, "*Or Torah*," chapter 151, p. 34b. When one has reached a level of *ayin* there can be no emotions expressed, even the emotion of love. See: Rabbi Yisrael, the Maggid of Koznitz, *Avodat Yisroel*, "*Chanukah*," pp. 71–72.

With this attainment one's relationship with his Creator becomes ever more vital and alive. When a person feels himself as *yesh*—a separate existence who was created—his relationship with his Creator is then in the past tense. I was once created, but now I exist independently. If, however, a person regards himself as ayin—nothingness—he then feels, that at each and every moment he is continuously being created from *ayin*—the divine nothing—to *yesh*—something. This places his relationship with the Creator in the present tense, and it is continuously being renewed. It is not an impassive, stale relationship, dependent on memory. Rather it is alive, vibrant, and ever growing, a relationship being lived in the present.[119]

On the ultimate level one contemplates the *ayin* itself. It is an extremely advanced meditative state, where the meditator, through the power of *chochmah*, reaches the *ayin*. The consequence of this meditation is complete *bitul*. One loses the *yeshut* and becomes entirely absorbed in Godliness. There is no *thingness* to focus on, and paradoxically, there is no *thingness* contemplating.[120] Yet, incomprehensibly, when languaged, it is nothingness meditating on itself.

To recapitulate: *Hitbonenut* meditation includes various stages. Initially, it entails choosing, consciously and deliberately, a spiritual thought, and using the entire spectrum of the intellect, wisdom, understanding, and knowledge, to fully develop the thought over an extended period of time. Since *hitbonenut* is a spiritual quest to know and to feel via the mind, one's emotions are engaged, through the meditation. From there one moves on to a state where one's emotions are too intense to express themselves in the heart. In time a higher level is reached where

---

119. Rabbi Levi Yitzchak of Berdichov (1740–1809), *Kedushat Levi,* "*Parshat Bereishit,*" the beginning.

120. Rabbi DovBer, the second ChaBad rebbe, *Shar HaYichud, Ner Mitzvah Vetorah Or, Shar HaYichud,* chapter 5.

the meditator attains *deveikut*—oneness, where the *yeshut*—beingness—is lost in the greater existence of the Infinite. This is the apex, as the meditator and that which he is meditating merge and become unified with the oneness of God.

Earlier there was discussion as to the various pitfalls and spiritual dangers associated with meditations that attempt to reach beyond normal levels of consciousness. By desiring transcendence one may experience a *ratzu beli shuve*—a withdrawal without return—as the sage who gazed and died, or one can go insane, as the sage who gazed and was stricken and so on. Without the proper preparation, one may have trouble rebounding into normal earthbound reality. A person needs to be well-grounded emotionally, physically, and spiritually before tapping into powers that can overwhelm his homeostasis. Without the proper balance, the experience may cause only confusion and uncertainty.

These difficulties are less common with the *hitbonenut* style of meditation, notwithstanding that at the highest levels of meditation transcendence is reached. The difference however lies in the route one takes. In *hitbonenut,* transcendence is attained via the conscious mind and not by circumventing it. The path is methodical and incremental. *Hitbonenut* uses the intellect to transcend itself. In its linear approach, *hitbonenut* meditation builds on the previous attainment and secures it, enabling one to proceed in safety. This approach allows the individual to integrate and own his experiences, which then prepare him for the next stage of growth. For this reason, the difficulties associated with transcendental meditations are to a certain extent averted in this type of meditation.

Ratzu beli shuve, withdrawal without return, can occur when an experience comes too suddenly, and one is not equipped for it. If one moment, the meditator feels confined, and a moment later he feels liberated and released, the abrupt change and shift of consciousness may cause a withdrawal, and in the extreme case death. Therefore, meditation that skips all the inter-mediate steps between confinement and total release, can be dangerous. The Torah tells us that when Sarah heard the news that her (only) son Isaac was going to be offered as a sacrifice, she died.[121] The information was too overwhelming, and it came too suddenly.[122] However, when the experience comes more slowly, there is time to integrate. Although the ultimate goal of meditation is transcendence, the intellectual approach, as in *hitbonenut,* is to a degree safer and more conducive to growth.

Experiencing transcendence can also lead one to believe in one's omniscience and invincibility. Without adequate preparation, an experience that occurs too rapidly can leave a person with a distorted sense of reality. It can be a shock to the nervous, psychological, and spiritual systems. Even with preparation there is always a risk in accelerating one's spiritual development by leapfrogging over certain systemic elements. *Hitbonenut* meditation includes and develops all the components of the human being. It recognizes that ignoring the intellectual aspects of a person is counterintuitive to the desired result. In a three-dimensional universe one must retain the ability to navigate conventional reality. It is the nature of the mind / ego to cause mischief when it is not taken into account. By including the mind, and not circumventing it, and acclimating it to the

---

121. See: Midrash *Pirkei D'Rebbe Eliezer,* chapter 32; Genesis, chapter 23, verse 2; Rashi's commentary as explained by Rabbi Shabsai Bass (1641–1718), *Sifsei Chochamim,* ad loc.

122. When Jacob heard after many years that his son Joseph was still alive, the Torah says (Genesis, chapter 45, verse 26) *va'yafeg libo,* which is generally translated as *and his heart rejected it.* . . . (See: Rashi and Rabbi Shlomo ben Meir, the *Rashbam,* ad loc.) However, it can also be translated as *and his heart stopped.* The sudden overwhelming news caused his heart to skip a beat, and faint. (See: Rabbi Moshe Ben Nachman, the Ramban, Rabbi Ovadiah Sforno, *Sforno.* See also: Rabbi Avraham Ibn Ezra, *Eben Ezra.*) The Ramban here explains that overwhelming information can cause fainting, which is likened to death.

acceleration, the total person is being brought along with nothing left behind.

The accretion of experiences via the intellect creates a critical mass resulting in new paradigms, allowing one to function in this world and simultaneously empowering one to transcend it.

CHAPTER
10

Divine Ecstasy: Achieving the State of No Self-Awareness

In mystical thought, the supreme state of ecstasy is where one has little to no self-awareness of the experience. The meditator, being in a condition of *bitul*, has transcended his ego and has reached the *ayin*. A Chassidic master once observed[1] that Adam, prior to eating and internalizing a fruit from the tree of knowledge was in a perpetual state of meditation. His entire being was involved and preoccupied with meditating on the Creator. There was no part of him that was separate from the meditation, and he never felt himself to be meditating. Later on, however, it says: "Behold, man has become like the Unique one among us."[2] Man had become distinct, unique, and separate. Now, man operates with the consciousness of separateness. So while meditating he is aware that he is meditating.

If the desire is to reach the level of *ayin*, then a fitting meditation is to contemplate the divine *ayin*, the power beyond creation, and from whence creation emanated. The *nothing* that

---

1. Rabbi Simchah Bunem of Pshischah (1765–1827). See: Eliezer Shtainman, *Be'er HaChassidut, Chachmei Ha'Chassidut* (Israel: Mochon Kemach), p. 155.

2. Genesis, chapter 3, verse 22.

preceded the *something*. In order to meditate on this ayin, it would assist one to know how this level of *ayin* is spoken about in Kabbalistic literature, and how the *ayin* relates to the Kabbalistic view of cosmology.

God in the Kabbalah is called the *Or Ein Sof*—The Infinite Light.[3] Unlike the mathematical or philosophical definition of infinite, which is something that is unmeasurable and nondimensional, the infinite that is God is beyond these definitions. In mathematics, the word infinite means beyond grasp or measurement; yet the infinite of something finite is by its very definition a finite entity. For instance, infinite refers to an infinite quantity of finite numbers, as in, one, two, three, and so on, ad infinitum. God's infinite, however, is beyond all conceivable limitations.

This type of infinity that is unique to God, defies the linguistic distinctions that we interpret reality with. However, we facilitate our own discourse (the only discourse we know) when speaking of God, by describing what God is not.[4] We interpret the infinite in finite terms, by saying what God is not.

---

3. The name *Ein Sof* first appears in the teachings of the early Kabbalists. See: Rabbi Moshe ben Nachman, the Ramban, in his commentary to *Sefer Yetzirah,* chapter 1, Mishnah 1. See: *Kisvei HaRamban,* vol 2, p. 453; *Ma'arechet Elokut,* chapter 7, p. 82b; Rabbi Yoseph Gikatalia, *Shaarei Orah, shar* 1, p. 8. See also: *Zohar,* part 2, p. 239. For an earlier source for the term *Ein Sof* other than in the Kabbalah, see: Rabbi Shlomo Eben Gabriel (1021–1069), *Mokor Chaim* (Tel Aviv: HaMenorah, 1984), *shar* 1, chapter 4, p. 10. There is an argument with regard to the *Ein Sof.* Rabbi Moshe Cordovero asserts that the *Ein Sof* applies to God's essence of being. See: *Pardas Rimonim, shar* 3, chapter 1; *Or Ne'erav,* part 6, chapter 1, p. 43. However, Rabbi Menachem Azaryah De Fano argues that *Ein Sof* applies to God's *will,* to God's first cause, and there is no term for God's essence. God is above being infinite. See: *Pelach Harimon, shar* 4, chapter 4; *Yonot Elim, Hakdamah,* "*Me'inyon Ein Sof.*" See also: Rabbi Shalom DovBer, the fifth Chabad rebbe, *Yom Tov Shel Rosh Hashono 5666,* p. 166; Rabbi Chaim of Volozhin, *Nefesh HaChaim, shar* 2, chapter 2.

4. Though the Torah speaks of God's attributes, being kind, righteous, and so on, these references are only speaking of what God does, i.e., how

In fact, even this description is a definition of God being beyond definitions, of being beyond our grasp. The moment we language God, we have transmogrified God's unique essence, for God is also beyond the definition of being *ein sof*—infinite.[5]

This leaves the human mind with an anomaly. Since the Infinite is beyond all limitation and definition, and the finite world created exists by definitions, then, given the limitations of human comprehension, it seems to us that there exists an abyss between the Creator and creation, between the infinite and the finite. This would hold true of the spiritual worlds, as well, for however sublime and lofty those worlds may be, they are still finite by virtue of having been created.

Another anomaly pertaining to creation is that since the Creator is *ein sof,* how is it that finite creatures emerged into existence? How can there be a transformation from the infinite *ein sof* to the finite *sof,* from absolute oneness to multiple diversity? This idea violates our normal pattern of thinking, and the mind is left with the intolerable, the paradox.

The question is not directed toward the Infinite's capabilities. After all, we know God to be all-powerful and limitless, and it is *not* antithetical to God's capabilities to be reducible and even contentual, for just as God can be infinite, God can also manifest as finite.[6] The question is, how does a finite creation maintain its existence in the presence of the infinite? How do we

---

Godliness is manifested in creation, but are not descriptions of what or who God is.

5. See: Rabbi Eliyohu of Vilna, *Sifra DeZeniuta*, "*Likutei HaGra, Sod HaTzimtsum,*" p. 38a. Rabbi Schneur Zalman of Liadi writes that for a human being to say that God is beyond finite comprehension is so removed from what God truly is, it is as if one would say that a deep thought is so deep that it cannot be grasped with one's hands. It is self-explanatory, that for someone to say on a thought that it cannot be grasped with hands is simply foolish. The same is true with God. God is beyond any definition, even the definition of being infinite. *Tanya, "Shar HaYichud VeHaEmunah,"* chapter 9.

6. Rabbi Meir Ben Gabbai, *Avodot Hakodesh,* part 1, chapter 8.

perceive this world to be finite in the presence of God, the infinite? In other words, the infinite should subsume the finite and not allow the finite to emerge into a defined entity? And conversely, the finite should find it intolerable to exist with the infinite?

To overcome these difficulties, and to make creation more humanly comprehensible,[7] the Kabbalah explains that God created the finite through a construct called *tzimtzum*—contraction.[8] Creation was not a slow process of evolution from infinite to finite, from spiritual to physical, but rather, creation occurred via a quantum leap. God (figuratively speaking) hid the *ein sof*—the endless light—and through the withdrawal allowed for the concept of finitude to be revealed and to emerge. God withdrew the light into its source, and thus caused others to come into existence. Once there was a finite light, there began a course of evolution from this light. Initially, the divine finite light resided in higher spiritual realms and then ultimately descended into something defined and limited, our physical world.

This process is what the Kabbalah calls *seder hishtalshelut*— a course of spiritual evolution. Reification is the culmination of a process that begins as pure energy and ultimately becomes thing. In its last stage, the energy becomes converted into form and matter. Therefore, all of creation is one continuous loop,[9] linked by a thread of finite light that weaves from the first manifestations, through all the spiritual worlds above, and

---

7. Rabbi Shalom DovBer, the fifth Chabad rebbe, *Sefer Hamaamorim 5658*, p. 120. See also: Rabbi Yoseph Ergas, *Shomer Emunim*, part 1, chapter 53.

8. The roots of the idea of *tzimtzum* are found in the Zohar. See: *Zohar*, part 1:15a; *Zohar Chadash*, "*Vaetchanan*," 57a. It was the Arizal, Rabbi Yitzchak Luria, who was the first one to expound on the idea of *tzimtzumim*. See e.g.: *Etiz Chayim, Mevoh Shearim, Shar Ha'akdamot*. (See also: *Midrash Tanchuma*, "*Parshat Vayakhel*," 7; *Midrash Rabbah* Leviticus, *parsha* 29:4. Where the word *tzimtzum* is used with regard to revelation.)

9. Rabbi Schneur Zalman of Liadi, *Torah Or*, p. 25c.

finally, into this physical universe. Now, though it may appear that this world exists independently, in truth, it is but one of many worlds. This universe is the last in the link, and therefore, spiritually, the furthest removed from its source. The matter on the physical world is in effect a compressed and contracted version of the energy of the Infinite. However, since we human beings are part of that physicality and are matter, all that we perceive with our physical sensors is also matter.

It appears that this solution is not complete, and a fundamental question remains unresolved. If *tzimtzum* really occurred, then we are led to say that there is a limitation to the Creator's omnipotence. It would appear that a basic requisite for finitude to exist is the suspension of the subsuming power of the infinite. Conversely, if *tzimtzum* is only a chimera (and it is the way humans perceive creation), then how is it that this finite world can exist and not be overwhelmed by the infinite? From our perspective these two forces cannot coexist; it does violence to the normative rules of the physical universe of which we are a part. How then are we to negotiate these seemingly antithetical realities?

The answer lies with the Kabbalistic theory of relativity. The truth or the facts of the *tzimtzum* depend on the perspective of the observer. In the eyes of the Infinite all that exists is Infinitude. Therefore, the *tzimtzum* is not an actual withdrawal of the Infinite leaving an empty space devoid of Godliness, but as the prophet says, "The whole earth is full of God's glory."[10] *Tzimtzum* is not a real contraction for God.[11] Rather, it is a

---

10. *Isaiah* 6:3. See also: *Jeremiah* 23:24. *Midrash Rabbah* Deuteronomy 2:28, as interpreted by Rabbi Chaim of Volozhin, *Nefesh HaChayim, shar* 3, chapter 3.

11. See: Rabbi Yoseph Ergas, *Shomer Emunim,* part 2, chapters 35–39; Rabbi Menacham Azarya De Fano, *Yonot Elim,* chapter 2; Rabbi Schneur Zalman of Liadi, *Tanya,* "*Shar HaYichud VeHaEmunah,*" chapter 7; *Likutei Torah,* "*Hosofot Vayikra,*" p. 51b; Rabbi Chaim of Volozhin, *Nefesh HaChayim,*

concealment of the infinite light from the lower levels. The infinite is a context in which everything can and is contained, things, people, concepts, events, and so forth, indeed the whole creation. There is no contradiction because it is, so to speak, big enough to contain every contradiction, paradox, and anomaly. There is no alternative to the *ein sof*. In the Infinite perspective there is no separate existence. It is man who perceives the *tzimtzum* as a (real) contraction, because a person's evaluative and discerning powers are trained for the physical universe. Man thinks spatially, and thus his mind interprets the Infinite as shrinking. But the Infinite is of a different order, and exists in a different reality. Man can only imagine existence in a context of limitations and separations. In man's eyes there is an actual withdrawal of the light, leaving a great void, and allowing the world to emerge into existence. For humankind the world exists as a discrete independent entity. For *yeshut*—separateness—is the reality of man.[12]

From our finite limited perception we affirm that that which is tangible and can be apprehended with our physical senses is real. If we can see it or touch it then it is a *yesh*—a reality. The creative animating energy that lies beyond our senses we call *ayin* because for us it is not real and is as nothing. Conversely, in the Ultimate's reality, the creative animating force is the only existence. What we call *ayin*, God calls *yesh*. The Infinite is the true existence. The created world, which seems to operate as an independent entity, is a chimera, an illusion of man's perception, while in truth, it is the real *ayin*.[13]

---

shar 3, chapter 7; Rabbi Menachem Mendel, the Tzemach Tzedek, the third Chabad rebbe, *Derech Mitvosecho*, "Shoresh Mitzvat HaTefilah," chapter 34; Rabbi Baruch of Kosav, *Amud Ha'avadah*, "Hakdamah," p. 1b, 62b. See also: Rabbi Avraham Azulay, *Chesed LeAvraham*, part 7, chapter 1.

12. Rabbi Schneur Zalman of Liadi, *Tanya*, "Shar HaYichud VeHa-Emuna," chapters 3 and 6; *Iggeret HaKodesh*, epistle 20.

13. See: *Tikunei Zohar, tikun* 69; Rabbi Schneur Zalman of Liadi, *Siddur*

A celebrated Chassidic master, Rabbi Pinchas of Koritz, once said: The world is analogous to a book that can be read forward and backward. One can read creation in the sequence of *ayin* into *yesh,* and thus relate to the physical creation as a genuine existence. Or, one can read the book from the end to the beginning, and realize how all of creation emerges from the divine *ayin.*14

Now, this indeed can be a good point to meditate on, to fully comprehend how all existence emerges from the *ayin,* and the fact that it is only in man's limited perception that the physical is real, while in the infinite's perspective, the *yesh* that we call reality is absorbed in the *ayin.* Meditating on the concept of "there is no other,"15 and nullifying the idea that there *is* . . . and finally realizing that all that exists is the Infinite.

There are two ways to meditate on this issue. One is to meditate on the core concept, that the *yesh* is subsumed by the *ayin,* and with the power of imagination envision the physical metamorphosing into the spiritual, picturing how one's own *yesh* is absorbed in the *ayin* and filling the mind with this image. Another way is to meditate on the details of the issue, attempting to comprehend the concept better by giving it practical meaning and drawing parallels to one's own life, seeing how the idea is reflected in there, making the idea more real and less

---

Im Dach, p. 44b; Rabbi Shalom DovBer, the fifth Chabad rebbe, *Sefer Hamaamorim 5678,* p. 86; Rabbi Yoseph Yitzchak, the sixth Chabad rebbe, *Sefer Hamaamorim 5703,* p. 179.

14. Rabbi Pinchas of Koritz. See: Eliezer Shtainman, *Be'er HaChassidut, Al Harishonim V'al Ha'achronim* (Israel: Mochon Kemach), p. 261.

15. Deuteronomy, chapter 4, verse 39. This idea should not be confused with the theory of pantheism, where God is equated with nature, and the law of the universe is God. For though the world is Godly it is not God. God is all reality but is also *more* than it. The world is included in God. See also: *Midrash Rabbah* Genesis 68:9; Exodus 45:6; *Midrash Tanchuma,* Parshat Ki Tissa, chapter 27; *Midrash Tehilim,* chapter 90.

abstract. The detailed method uses the intellect while the other method bypasses the intellect, and uses the imagination.[16]

Both these methods have their distinct advantages. Meditating on the details of how the *yesh* is nullified in the *ayin,* one feels the *ayin* as more imminent and more powerful. When the concept of the meditation is contemplated slowly and the details are digested meticulously, one level at a time, then the experience feels more real. The ideas of the meditation feel closer and are of more relevance to the meditator. However, when meditating on the general concept of how the *yesh* is absorbed in the *ayin,* one can penetrate the core of the idea, piercing to the essence of the light. Ostensibly, it is less intellectually exhausting to meditate on the general than on the specifics.

Yet, many masters prefer the detailed approach, they assert, that when a truth is attained without the involvement of the intellect, those truths are but imaginary and illusionary. The insights that are gained and the clarity one assumes perceived, are in effect, just a mirroring of one's own imagination.[17] Consequently, when emotions are aroused through the avoidance of the intellect, they are usually expressions of the ego, accompanied by feelings of superiority, frivolity, and the pursuit of bodily pleasures, even when one does manage to pierce the veil of ego, penetrate the coarseness of matter, and feel the energy within.[18] He may even experience the nothingness and attain *bitul.* Yet, if this level of *bitul* was attained by bypassing the intellect (intellect being the raison d'être of man), then the

---

16. Rabbi Schneur Zalman of Liadi, *Maamorei Admur Hazoken,* "In-yonim,"* p. 133.

17. The Rambam writes that when a human being aspires to comprehend something that is beyond his intellectual capabilities, he will experience false imaginations and distortions of truth. See: Rambam, *Moreh Nevuchim,* part 1, chapter 32.

18. Rabbi Schneur Zalman of Liadi, *Maamorei Admur Hazoken,* "In-yonim,"* p. 134.

impression will not be of a permanent nature, and the feelings aroused will fade soon thereafter.[19] When, however, the experience is attained by meditating on the details, that is, through utilizing one's intellectual capacities, the impact is more real. The meditation can be a transformative one, engendering a positive effect on the lower levels of one's psyche.[20]

When one arrives at these levels by circumventing the intellect, the high of the experience may not have durability. Additionally, the meditator may confabulate by thinking that he has attained a new level of growth, when in actuality he is just having a pleasant imaginative trip. In this context of circumvention, where the objective is to reach *ayin,* the goal becomes an oxymoron and unworkable. In this modality the seeker will always be perpetuated, no matter how long or arduously he tries to eliminate separateness. It remains unattainable because the meditator's *yesh* survives. To actively seek nothingness would seem to be a contradiction in terms, for if there is a someone who is searching, then by its very definition there is separateness.

The premise of the detailed approach is that by taking incremental steps via the intellect, the *ayin* is reached automatically. When what is sought is a comprehension of the *ayin* with the intellect, and one is not actively seeking to find the *ayin,* nor searching to attain *bitul,* then reaching the *ayin* is a natural ultimate outcome. The attainment is in the next step. However, when the attempt is to go for the *ayin* from the outset, then all that one gets is one's own *yesh*—beingness and ego.[21]

Within the meditation of the *ayin* there are two levels. One

---

19. Rabbi DovBer, the second Chabad rebbe, *Shar HaYichud,* "*Ner Mitzvah Vetorah Or,*" part 2, *shar HaYichud,* chapter 4; See also: *Toraht Chaim,* "*Bereishit,*" p. 112b.

20. See: The Lubavitcher Rebbe, *Igrot Kodesh,* vol. 19, p. 195.

21. Rabbi Schneur Zalman of Liadi, *Maamorei Admur Hazoken,* "*Inyonim,*" pp. 133–134.

is where the meditator contemplates the emergence of the *yesh* from the *ayin,* fathoming with the mind the subsuming of the *yesh* in the *ayin.* Another is to meditate on the *ayin* itself. The latter is a highly advanced state of meditation, where the meditator uses the power of *chochmah*—pure undivided intellect to meditate. "Who is wise?" asks the Talmud. One who sees the creator, within creation."[22] The thrust of the *ayin* meditation is the actualization of this maxim. When a meditator operates on a level of *chochmah,* he can actually see the inner Godly energy vibrating within creation. He can then allow the image to fill his mind and become ingrained into his consciousness. The consequence of such meditations is complete *bitul* and loss of a sense of separateness.[23]

Ultimately, the distinguishing criterion between reaching the *ayin* and feeling *yeshut,* albeit on an elevated level, is self-awareness. If the meditator even feels the slightest twinge of excitement, then he should know that his ego is involved in the experience. In this way, the ecstasy is sensual and on some level selfish. However, if there is no self-awareness, then the ecstasy is simply divine.[24] If the meditator feels that he is experiencing *bitul,* then that is the greatest indication that he is not. Only when there is no self-awareness is there genuine *bitul.*[25]

---

22. See: Talmud *Tamid,* 32a, as interpreted in Chassidic thought. See: Rabbi Schneur Zalman of Liadi, *Tanya,* chapter 43. See also: Rabbi Yisrael Ba'al Shem Tov, *Tzavoas Horivash,* chapter 90.

23. Rabbi DovBer, the second Chabad rebbe, *Shar Ha Yichud,* "Ner Mitzvah Vetorah Or,*" part 2, chapter 5.

24. Rabbi DovBer, the second Chabad rebbe, *Kuntras Hispalut,* "*Maamorei Admur Hoemtzoee: Kuntresim,*" chapter 1.

25. Rabbi Shalom DovBer, the fifth Chabad rebbe, *Beshoo Shehikdimu 5672,* part 1, chapter 214; Rabbi Yoseph Yitzchak, the sixth Chabad rebbe, *Sefer Hamaamorim 5706,* pp. 118–119.

CHAPTER
11

The *Ayin* of
Jewish Meditation
Versus the Nothingness in
Other Meditations

One of the peak achievements of a meditational experience is to attain a level of *he'staclut,* gazing. Here the meditator, having lost his self-awareness, has the ability to gaze. Gazing is a function of beingness in which oneness occurs. There is no interaction, as there is no "there," but then in that state there is no "here," either. Through the meditation the meditator attains a level of oneness with the meditation, and becomes unified with the *ayin,* fusing with the divine energy (within the thought), and creation. It is the nullification of normative internal and external reality, depriving the ego of any attachments. At this state, there is an eclipse of the ego and one experiences ecstasy without self-awareness.

Those familiar with Eastern thought may be inclined to draw parallels between this advanced state of *ayin* consciousness and the emptiness and nothingness popularized in the East. In Eastern thought, the ultimate reality, the name of which varies from one discipline to the next, *Sunyata, Brahman, Tao,* and so forth, are all fundamentally expressing the same concept: nothingness and emptiness. Emptiness, according to Eastern thought, is the essence of all life and the source of all form and matter. And while there are certainly some similarities between the nothingness taught in the Kabbalah and the one taught in other disciplines,[1] nonetheless, on the whole, the Kabbalistic notion of nothingness and the concept of emptiness expressed in Eastern thought are as different as east and west itself. They are expressing diametrically opposed views of life and of the role that a human being plays upon this earth.

Reaching a level of *ayin* within oneself, cleansing oneself of

---

1. The *Zohar* teaches that the great sages of the East inherited their wisdom from Abraham. As it is written "And to the children of his concubines Abraham gave gifts, and he sent them . . . to the land of the East" (Genesis, chapter 25, verse 6). Originally these teachings were pure, though, later on they were drawn to many (idolatrous) sides with this wisdom. See: *Zohar,* part 1, pp. 100a-b. According to the Talmud, the gifts Abraham gave the children of his concubines were mystical names of impurities. See: Talmud *Sanhedrin,* 91b; Rashi on Genesis, chapter 25, verse 6. See also: *Zohar,* part 1, 99b, 133b, and 233a; Rabbi Menasha Ben Israel, *Nishmat Chayim, maamor 3,* chapter 17. Being that the original source of Eastern philosophy was Abraham, thus, the name *Brahman,* which is from the word *Abraham,* is used. See: Rabbi Menasha Ben Israel, *Nishmat Chayim, maamor* 4, chapter 21.

Incidentally, there are various etymological similarities between the two. For example, the Eastern word *ram,* which means exalted, is similar to the Hebrew word for exalted *rom. Veydah,* which means knowledge, phonetically is similar to the word *dai'a (Da'at).* And there are many more.

The same is true with Western (ancient) philosophy. The Torah says," . . . Which is without Blemish" (Numbers, chapter 19 verse 2), which the *Zohar* interprets as, "This is the Greek wisdom" Zohar, part 2, p. 236. According to Rabbi Menachem Recanti the *Zohar* is alluding to ancient Greek philosophers prior to Aristotle, whose views to some degree, were similar to that of the Torah. See: Rabbi Yoseph Ergas, *Shomer Emunim,* part 1, chapter 3; Rabbi Menasha Ben Israel, *Nishmat Chayim, maamor* 4, chapter 21. See also: Rabbi Yehudah Halevi, *The Kuzari, maamor 2,* chapter 66; Rabbi Moshe Isserles, the Ramah, *Toraht Ha'olah* (Tel Aviv: Yeshivath Chidushei Harim, 1999), part 1, chapter 11; Rabbi Aharan Berechyah of Modena (????–1639), *Ma'avar Yavak* (Vilna: 1880), *maamor 3,* chapter 33. In fact, legend has it that many of the ancient Greeks received these teachings from the Jewish sages and prophets. See: Rabbi Meir Eben Aldavia, *Shivilei Emunah, nosiv* 8, p. 352; Rabbi Menasha Ben Israel, *Nishmat Chayim, maamor* 4, chapter 21. The Kabbalah teaches that the wisdom of the creator permeates the entire field of knowledge, and thus, what is known to the mystics through the Kabbalah was

ego and transcending the sense of I, can be translated in two different ways. One says that by losing the sense of the false self and transcending ego, one uncovers the *real* self. The other approach says that by relinquishing and transcending ego, one finds oneself humbled in the greater existence of the Infinite, thereby being redefined as an empowered and expansive human being.

The following Chassidic tale may shed some light on the issue. Once, some years back, there was a group of pagan worshipers, who were engaged in black magic. It was believed that they possessed metaphysical powers and could, through their rituals, create negative energy. In their town there lived a righteous man, who once, by chance, stumbled on the path of these pagans. Seeking to take revenge on this noble man, they decided to impose on him an impure spirit, which would lead him off his virtuous path. One day, when the man awoke with feelings and ideas that seemed foreign to him, he decided to pay a visit to his rebbe.

Upon hearing his story, the rebbe handed him an apple and told him to proclaim, "I do *not* want to eat the apple." The Chassid, being a righteous person, and not desiring to tell a lie, insisted that he really did fancy to eat the apple. This went on for quite a while, the rebbe requesting him to say, "I do not want it," and the Chassid insisting he really did. Finally, the Chassid, out of frustration, acquiesced and proclaimed, "Yes, I do not want to eat the apple." Hearing his declaration, the rebbe told him to immediately recite a blessing and eat from the apple, even though by this time he no longer desired to do so. Once he ate from the apple, he was instantaneously cured.

---

known to the Greeks through philosophy. See: Rabbi Tzadok HaCohen of Lublin, *Likuttei Maamorim* (Bnei Brak: Yehadut, 1973), p. 55. See also: *Dover Tzedek,* p. 97b. Consequently, the Midrash contends, if a person tells you that there is wisdom among the nations, believe it. *Midrash Rabbah*, Lamentations, *parsha* 2, verse 13.

In this narrative, the rebbe instructs his disciple to con-
sume a part of nature, an apple, by acting contrary to his
nature, that is, eating the apple despite his not wanting to eat
it. By contravening his nature, he liberated himself from the
powers of nature, and by consuming nature (the apple), he
became a master over nature. Through this subterfuge, the
rebbe liberated him of the impurity. How is it that through
doing something against one's nature, one rids oneself of the
powers of the unholy?

The underlying point here is the recognition of the inherent
powers that exist within nature, and to a degree, that nature is
naturally more spiritually sensitive than the human being.
Understanding this concept will help one to decipher this
Chassidic tale, as well as to comprehend Judaism's point of
view on spiritual powers. The Kabbalah, as explained earlier,
teaches, that following the *tzimtzum,* the general contraction of
the infinite light, there began a process of evolution and devo-
lution, at first into higher spiritual realms, then into something
defined and limited, such as this physical world. This world
assumes that it created itself through natural forces and that
now it is sustained by these very same elements. The truth,
however, is that this world is only one of many interconnected
worlds. There exists a parallel spiritual universe to ours, and
this physical sphere is sourced and is a direct transformation of
a higher spiritual universe. Everything physical is in reality a
manifestation of its spiritual counterpart. All entities, which
have an existence in the spiritual worlds, are projected into our
physical universe by adjusting to the limitations of time and
space.[2] Every existence in this world is a reflected image of a

---

2. Rabbi Moshe Isserles, the Ramah, *Toraht Ha'olah,* part 2, chapter 1. See
also: Rabbi Yoseph Yitzchak, the sixth Chabad rebbe, *Sefer Hamaamorim 5711,*
pp. 8–9. *Midrash Rabbah,* Genesis, *parsha* 10, chapter 6; *Zohar,* part 1, p. 251a;
part 2, p. 171a; part 3, p. 86a.

spiritual entity.[3] For example, the stork is called a *chassidah*, a kind creature, for it displays the attribute of *chesed* by sharing food with other birds.[4] It is a physical manifestation of the cosmic attribute of *chesed*. The way the stork behaves below correlates to the design that was determined above.

From the foregoing one might infer that the stork is a virtuous animal. In actuality, except for man, morality does not exist in nature. Animal behavior is instinctive rather than chosen, and the way animals interact with each other is a direct manifestation of the will of their Creator. Animals generally do not possess the intelligence that allows for a deviation from nature. They are instinctual creatures functioning as the Creator designed them without the benefit of a moral code or that of free will. Without the latter, behavior cannot be characterized as good or evil. Animals simply act out of the innate traits that were intended for them.

Animals maintain a harmony with their own nature and nature at large, violent occurrences notwithstanding. They are inherently closer to nature, and do not entertain feelings of alienation. An animal operates according to his nature, while man can (if he wills) be at odds with his nature. Animals, to the best of our knowledge, are integrated creatures, where action and being are one. There is no inner conflict present in nature. For this reason, animals possess a greater innate spiritual sensibility than man.[5] Being that their actions are more aligned

---

3. A human being can fathom what is above by observing what is below. Above is the source while below is its branches. *Safer Hayashar, shar* 1.

4. Talmud *Chulin*, 63a; Leviticus, chapter 11, verse 19; Rashi, *Chassidah*. (Interestingly, there is an argument whether a *chassidah* is a kosher animal. See: Rabbi Yoseph Caro, *Biet Yoseph*, "Yoreh Deah," chapter 82.)

5. Animals do not possess an evil inclination, *Avoth D'Rebbe Nathon*, chapter 16:3. See also: Rabbi Menachem Ben Shlomo Meiri, *Chibur HaTeshuvah* (Jerusalem: Kedem, 1976), *Meishiv Nefesh, maamor* 2, chapter 9, p. 411. The Maharal, Rabbi Yehudah Loew, writes that a human being possesses

with their nature, which by extension is the will of the Creator, they are therefore inherently more spiritually sensitive.[6] According to the Talmud, when an evil spirit roams a city the dogs bark, and when a holy spirit looms, they laugh.[7]

These energies of nature can be harnessed by a human being, but only if he chooses to operate with the consciousness of an animal[8] and becomes a part of that nature. These spiritual powers are called *koach hatumah*—impure powers. They are the powers that are contained within nature.[9] It is believed that through advanced meditative techniques, the practitioner can tap into these energies that are not bound by dimensionality and experience a level of expanded sensitivity. He can observe the immediate future,[10] experiencing a prophetic vision that is sourced in the unhallowed.[11] Yet, the route a human being

---

a soul, which is a part of God, and the soul is on a much higher level than these spirits, thus, a human Being does not feel the presence of these spirits (he is not impressed), while the lower creatures are indeed impressed by these spirits and feel their presence. See: *Be'er Hagolah* (Bnei Brak: Yehadut, 1980), *be'er* 5, p. 98.

6. See: Numbers, chapter 22, verse 23; Rashi, *VaTaira*. The vision of animals is not an actual seeing, rather it is a *feeling of a presence*, which only an animal can feel. See: Rabbi Moshe Ben Nachman, the Ramban, and Rabbeinu Bachya on Numbers, chapter 22, verse 23; Rabbi Yitzchak of Acco, *Meirat Einayim*, "*Parshat Balak*," chapter 22, verse 23. See also: Rabbi Menachem Recanti Parshat Balak, *Levush Malchut*, vol. 7, p. 41b.

7. Talmud *Baba Kamma*, 60b. In the standard version of the Talmud it is written that dogs *cry* when an evil spirit roams. In other versions it is written, they *bark*. See: Exodus, chapter 11, verse 7, the commentaries, *Daat Zekeinim* (Tosefot, 12–13th centuries) and Rabbi Chaim Ibn Attar, *Or HaChaim*.

8. To literally live with an animal. See: Rabbi Meir Ben Gabbai, *Avodot Hakodesh*, part 4, chapter 26.

9. See: Rabbi Moshe Isserles, the Ramah, *Toraht Ha'olah*, part 3, chapter 77.

10. See: *Safer Hachinuch* (author anonymous; attributed to Rabbi Aharon Halevi of Barcelona, thirteenth century), mitzvah 510.

11. Rabbi Meir Ben Gabbai, *Avodot Hakodesh*, part 4, chapter 26.

chooses to attain these powers is entirely dependent on his own discretion.

A human being is unique among all the creatures that roam this earth in that he alone has the freedom to choose. Man has the ability to choose to be virtuous or to choose to be the opposite.[12] A human being is a fusion of an angel and a beast,[13] having the potential for both. Being born with an propensity toward positive behavior does not necessarily translate that one's behavior will be that way, for a person may choose to ignore it. Neither does being born with an inclination toward bad behavior predestine one to live an immoral life. Predilections are compelling forces of nature, but they are not destiny. Even if one is born with a certain inclination, one has the capacity to overcome and act according to his choices.[14] While man can soar above the angels,[15] he can also descend to the level of beasts.

The path one desires to take en route to the attainment of spiritual powers is solely dependent upon the person. One can behave as an animal and shorten the spectrum of creativity available to one created in the image of God. One can choose to

---

12. The RamBam calls the belief that a human being has the freedom to chose, "the foundation of the Torah." Rambam, *Hilchot Teshuvah,* chapter 5, *halacha* 3.

13. Talmud *Chagigah,* 16a. Midrash Rabbah, Genesis, *parsha* 8, chapter 11.

14. Rambam, *Shemone Perokim,* chapter 8.

15. Rabbi Chaim Vital, *Sharei Kedusha,* part 3, *shar 2;* Rabbi Yehudah Loew, *Tifferet Yisrael* (Israel: 1980), chapter 33, p. 96. See also: *Gevurat Hashem* (Israel: 1980), chapter 67, p. 312; *Nesivot Olam, Nosiv Hemet* (Bnei Brak: Yehadut, 1980), chapter 3, p. 205. See also: Rabbi Chaim of Volozhin, *Nefesh HaChaim, shar* 1, chapter 10; Rabbi Eliyahu HaCohen, *Sheivet HaMusar,* chapter 2:5, p. 53 and chapter 11:14, p. 174. Rabbi Meir Simchah of Dvinsk, *Meshech Chochmah,* "*Parshat Beshalach,*" p. 116. Others write that this is also the opinion of the Rambam. See: Rabbi Yitzchak Aizik of Komarna, *Aimrei Kodesh* (Israel: Heichal Habracha, 1997), *Derech Emunah,* p. 113.

live life by surrendering one's freedom of choice, living in the consciousness of animals, which is essentially limited to being reactive. And though in their search they may indeed find "magical powers," these powers are devoid of Godliness, and in fact, are a barrier in one's quest to reaching the Transcendent. Or one can conduct oneself as a human being, rationally, and intentionally, and connect with the source and creator of nature and truly become transcendent.

Man is a creature that has choices. While acknowledging that he is part animal, man possesses a spiritual creative aspect. This means that he can choose the paradigms, philosophies, and symbols that shape his life. The subsequent integration of his life is then based on how aligned his actions are with his choices.

The aptitude of choice is a God-like gift.[16] When a human being chooses to live life deliberately and by choice, he is manifesting the God-like potential in his own life. And when his choice is to live in harmony with his own nature as a human being, and align with the Creator's design for human beings, then he can aspire to transcend the strictures of the animal self and enter the endless. It is incumbent on man, if he desires to utilize his full potential, to exercise his spiritual instincts of choice, as animals employ their natural ones.

Tamei is the word the Torah uses to indicate a state of impurity. This word stems from a term that implies a relinquishing of independence.[17] Connecting with the powers of *tumah*

---

16. The power of free choice is a God-like power. The ability to do whatever is desired without being compelled in a certain direction can only come from God, who is truly free (and the creator of all limitations). See: Rambam, *Hilchot Teshuvah,* chapter 5, *halacha* 1; as it is interpreted by Rabbi Schneur Zalman of Liadi, *Likutei Torah,* "Parshat Emor," 38b. See also: Rabbi Yehudah Chayit on *Ma'arechet Elokut,* chapter 8, p. 106a; The Lubavitcher Rebbe, *Likutei Sichot,* vol. 30, p. 203. See also: Genesis, chapter 3, verse 22. Rashi, *Sforno,* ad loc.

17. See: Rabbi Shamson Refoel Hirsh (1808–1888), *Vayikra,* chapter 19,

means that one is functioning at a level of subjection, restriction, and subservience, lacking free will, and operating without choice. The practitioners of black magic aspired to abandon their capacity of free thought and personal feelings by means of vigorous body gyrations, incantations, ingesting narcotics, and the like. By doing so, they believed they would become infused with these powers.[18]

The ancient Greeks worshiped the pagan deity Dionysus. The worshipers of this deity would work themselves into a frenzied state through wild dancing and song. In this state of intoxication, one of the practices was to tear an animal open with bare hands and then drink its blood. Other ancient pagan practices involved human sacrifices, the drinking of human blood, lewd indulgences with holy prostitutes, and so forth. The Torah makes mention of the ancient Phoenician cult known as Baal. The Torah writes of them: "They cut themselves . . . with swords . . . until the blood gushed out."[19] They would mortify their bodies with all forms of orgiastic rites. These rituals were performed to induce a state of nonconsciousness, and thereby the surrender of the freedom to choose. By losing themselves, so to speak, they were able to tap into the powers of impurity, thereby experiencing oracular visions, clairvoyance, and the like.[20]

The difference between achieving purity and holiness, and attaining unholiness and impurity is to serve two different

---

verse 31. (English translation by Yitzchak Levy, *The Pentateuch: Leviticus* (Judaica Press: Gateshead, 1989), p. 561.)

18. See: Ibid.

19. Kings 1, chapter 18, verses 26–28.

20. The Rambam writes that ancient oracles and prophets would drink blood to obtain prophetic visions and insights. Rambam, *Moreh Nevuchim*, part 3, chapter 46. See also: Ramban, Leviticus, chapter 17, verse 11. They would also fornicate with animals to induce a state of prophecy. See: Rabbi Moshe Alshich, Exodus, chapter 22, verse 17.

masters and to live in two different universes. To serve in the universe of purity and holiness is to interact with the limitless, both in scope and potential. Adversely, the impure serves the senses, the temporal, and the limited in man. Impurity is reached by surrendering one's freedom and succumbing to the animal within. Holiness and purity is attained when one elevates oneself by committing to the path of harmony with the transcendent, and then acting in alignment with that commitment. And as a result, the animal aspect of the human being is also harnessed to serving that commitment, thus creating an integrated human being. This is the universe of holiness, a universe of limitless growth and being.

On the whole, the aforementioned practices are for the most part extinct, especially in the industrialized societies; however, on a more subtle level, many of these ideas are still found in the East.[21] When the masters of the East speak of being in sync with one's nature, they are talking of being in touch with the forces of nature. Eastern thought teaches that in advanced stages of meditation, one can transcend the false sensation of ego and selfishness and become at one with one's own true nature, and by extension, one with the whole of nature. Eastern thinkers, however, do not believe in a supernatural being, a transcended force that is beyond nature and who creates it. And therein lies the major difference between Judaism, which is a religion based on revelation and monotheism, and Eastern thought.

One of the methods in Eastern philosophy to achieving nothingness is by first selecting an object for meditation and then filling one's mind with the image, thereby clearing the mind of all other thoughts. Initially, the meditator observes that the

---

21. See: *Zohar,* part 1, pp. 100a–b. According to the *Zohar* many of the ideas of the East are *Avodah Zatah*—idol worship.

object inherently exists. But progressively, as the consciousness shifts, the reality of the object changes. What was a solid three-dimensional thing is perceived differently. For example, the realization sets in that solidity is only valid in a certain part of the range that is physical reality. The atom, the basic building block of matter, is overwhelmingly devoid of content. By extension, everything, including the meditator, is part of the emptiness and nothingness. Ultimately, what we call the self is the space in which life occurs.

The meditator aspires to become one with universal consciousness, which, according to Eastern thought, is an extension of one's own consciousness, and is all there is. Beyond the mask of the *maya*—the illusion that there exists the many—is oneness. When one frees oneself of the spell of *maya,* one realizes that all phenomena that one perceives with the physical senses are, in fact, part of the same reality. Everything, including oneself, is a component of this one reality. The aim is to realize that we are ephemeral beings inextricably related to all of creation, and meditation is performed so that we can become aware of this. This way one can get in touch with one's own true nature, and thus by extension, with the entire universe.

The level of nothingness that is taught in Eastern philosophy is but another name for the word *yesh.* The underlying creative force of nature is found within nature itself. And though it may be referred to as a formless creative force, a nothingness that gives rise to all matter and form, it is not a supernatural "being," a transcendent "entity" that creates nature. Rather, it is a part of nature that creates. Nature itself is the creator. Generally, in the East there is a type of pantheistic view of God, where the laws of nature are equated with God, and God with nature. The essence of the Eastern mystical experience is to go beyond the universe of distinctions and opposites and reach a state where reality exists undivided.

Indeed, one can reach a degree of elevation, where diversity

and dichotomy cease to exist, but ultimately, one only transcends self to attain another level of self. The levels apprehended are all within the natural order, for according to
Eastern thought there is nothing beyond that. The Eastern
concept of nothingness is meant to be taken literally. Nothing
exists. Not only is everything empty of an independent sub-
stantial existence and nothing exists in and on itself, but furthermore, there is really nothing that truly exists.

This is a major point of divergence with Jewish thinking.
The Torah teaches that *ayin* is the true existence of reality, and
it is the divine essence of all creation. So there is a *something*
within creation; it is only that this something is what we paradoxically call *nothingness—ayin*. Consequently, the transcendence the Torah aspires to teach is a transcendence beyond
one's nature and beyond nature itself. The Infinite is transcen
dent, and to reach that level one must also live life transcen-
dently. What is more, Judaism having observed and recorded
biblically the perverse nature of mankind refuses to license a
person's quest for enlightenment without the grounding of law.
Judaism realizes the contradictions, conflicts, and the paradoxes within the human soul and nature, and therefore con-
cludes that not every impulse is pure.

A more subtle difference between the two approaches can
be observed with regard to the different responses to foreign
thoughts that may enter the mind in a meditative state. When
one is meditating and an extraneous thought arises into consciousness, Eastern thought instructs the meditator to welcome
the thought, allow it to be, and let it pass. In contrast, classic
Jewish thought teaches that when one is in the middle of praying or studying (i.e., in a meditative state) and a foreign thought
occurs, one should resolutely make an effort to resist thinking
about the thought. Judaism addresses the inner duality within
human nature and believes that most people operate in this
universe of division and distinctions. Therefore, there is a clearly

defined law that distinguishes between what is good for man and what is not, between right and wrong, and between the light and the darkness. Hence, when an inappropriate thought occurs during one's meditative state, one should attempt to push it aside, although sometimes it is best when removed gently.

Early Chassidic masters proposed another way in which to deal with uninvited thoughts. They argued that when a foreign thought enters one's consciousness, one should aspire to elevate and sublimate the thought. For example, if the thought is of a desire for a physically beautiful object, one should contemplate the origin of the desire. One should reflect and consider that the aesthetics and the beauty of the object is but a manifestation of a divine force that created it to be so desirable. Therefore, he should redirect and rechannel his desires to the source of the beauty that is within the object. And then, rather than experience a fascination for the physical object, he is attracted to the underlining energy within it, that is, the Creator. He dismantles the husk that surrounds the thought, and sublimates the core of the thought to its source.[22] Once again, one is not told to tolerate or maintain the foreign thoughts as they appear, but rather to think about them in an elevated manner.

Yet, many Chassidic masters felt that to engage in foreign thoughts, even for the purpose of elevation, should only be performed by those of us who have completely neutralized and sublimated the selfish self and operate with little or no ego. For

---

22. See: Rabbi Yisrael Baal Shem Tov, *Keter Shem Tov,* chapter 171; *Tzavoas Horivash,* chapter 87; *Baal Shem Tov Al HaTorah,* "*Parshat Bereishit,*" pp. 20–21; *Amud HaTefilah,* p. 143; The maggid of Mezritch: *Magid Devarav Leyokav,* "*Likutei Amorim Or Torah,*" chapter 37; "*Likutei Yekarim Or Haemet,*" chapter 194, p. 2; Rabbi Moshe Chaim Ephraim of Sudylkov, *Degel Machanah Ephraim,* "*Parshat Behaalotecha,*" p. 177; Rabbi Nachum of ChernoByl, *Meor Einayim,* "*Parshat Shemot,*" p. 62; Rabbi Yakov Yitzchak Horowitz, the seer of Lublin, *Zikhron Zot,* p. 141. See also: Rabbi Eliyahu ben Moshe Di Vidas, *Reshit Chachmah,* "*Shar Ha'Ahavah,*" chapter 4, in the name of Rabbi Yitzchak of Acco.

most, however, such undertakings can be spiritually degenerat-
ing, and can cause more harm than good.[23]

Trading the limited for the limitless, the finite for the infinite, by transcending one's nature is the ultimate objective of
meditation. Yet, if the meditator truly desires to reach the *ayin*
that is buried beneath the *yesh,* he must live himself on the level
of *ayin*—nothingness. He must transcend his own sense of self
and operate with little or no self-awareness. In other words, in
order to penetrate the concept of nothingness, one needs to live
a life of *bitul.* Only by experiencing *ayin* in one's own life, can
one comprehend and be at one with the cosmic level of nothingness.[24] *Ayin* is attained when one transcends the illusionary
separateness of self and becomes submerged in the greater existence of the Infinite.

Salomon Maimon, an 18th-century Kantian philosopher,
traveled throughout Europe in search of knowledge. On one of
his stops he went to a Chassidic court. In his autobiography, he
recounts his impressions of Chassidim. He writes that he was
utterly wowed. The rebbe, whose face shone with radiance, displayed great brilliance in Torah scholarship. The rebbe used the
entire spectrum of Torah thought to illustrate his points.

---

23. See: Rabbi Schneur Zalman of Liadi, *Tanya,* chapter 28. See also:
Rabbi Tzvi Elimelech of Dinav, *Derech Pikudecha,* Hakdamah 7, p. 26. Rabbi
Klunimus Kalman, *Maor Vashemesh,* "Parshat Re'eh," p. 581; Rabbi Tzodok
HaKohen of Lublin, *Komtez HaMincha,* chapter 16, p. 26. The Baal Shem Tov
teaches that when a meditator is in a state of *d'eveikut,* and a thought arises into
consciousness, then it can be assumed that this thought is a minor form of *ruach
hakodesh*—divine inspiration. See: Rabbi Yisrael Baal Shem Tov, *Keter Shem Tov,*
chapter 195, p. 25b; *Likutei Yekarim,* chapters 12 and 48; *Or Haemet,* p. 205;
Baal Shem Tov Al HaTorah, "Parshat Ekev," p. 557. Yet only one who has achieved
a most elevated state, where there is only oneness in his heart, can be certain
that the thoughts that occur are expressions of transcendence and are not manifestations of the ego.

24. Rabbi DovBer, the second Chabad rebbe, *Shar HaYichud,* "Ner
Mitzvah Vetorah Or,*" part 2, "Shar HaYichud," at the end of chapter 5.

After a while, he began to realize that all the teachings of the rebbe were aimed at articulating one point. The one idea that the rebbe sought to teach was the concept of *bitul*—self-nullification.[25] From his words one can understand what it was and what it is that preoccupies a Chassidic master.

The idea of *bitul* runs deep within the hearts of all Kabbalists. In fact, the word used to connote mystical thought is Kabbalah, which by definition means to receive.[26] In order to study Kabbalah one must open oneself to greater awareness, emptying and ridding oneself of all previous spiritual clutter, so that one can become a proper receptacle to receive. To a degree, this truth extends to the entire oral Torah, called Talmud. The word Talmud stems from the Hebrew word *talmid*—student. To learn Torah one must humble oneself and be willing to be taught. One must be a space to receive knowledge. A Torah scholar, even the greatest and most learned, is traditionally called

---

25. See: Salomon Maimon (1753–1800), *Safer Chayei Shlomo Maimon* (Tel Aviv: Mossad Biyalak, 1953), pp. 144–145.

26. The word Kabbalah connotes a tradition that was received from a generation previously. See: Rabbi Moshe ben Nachman, the Ramban, Introduction to Torah, *Ramban Derashah Al Divrei Kohelet* (Jerusalem: Mossad Harav Kook, 1982), p. 190; Rabbi Joseph Albo, *Safer Haikkarim, maamor 2,* chapter 28; Rabbi Yoseph Ergas, *Shomer Emunim,* part 1, chapter 11. The term Kabbalah has come to mean a particularly mystical thought. Rabbi Moshe Ben Yakov of Kiev printed a letter attributed to the Rambam, in which the Rambam refers to mystical thought as Kabbalah. See: *Shoshan Sodot* (Koretz: 1784), p. 31a. See also: Rabbi Avraham Abulafia, *VeZot L'Yehudah* (Jerusalem: 1999), p. 24; Rabbeinu Bachya, Genesis, *"Parshat Vayishlach,"* chapter 32, verse 10; Rabbi Shimon Ben Tzemach Duran, *Magen Avot,* part 2, chapter 3, p. 22a; Rabbi Shem Tov Ben Shem Tov, *Sefer Ha'emunot, shar 4,* chapter 7; *shar 5,* chapters 2 and 3; Rabbi Yoseph Yavatz, *Avot,* chapter 3, mishna 12; Rabbi Yoseph Yavatz, Psalms, chapter 26, verse 1; Rabbi Eliyahu ben Moshe Di Vidas, *Reshit Chachmah,* Introduction; Rabbi Meir Ben Gabbai, *Avodat Hakodesh,* part 2, chapter 13; Rabbi Yoseph Shlomo Delmedigo, the yashar of Candia, *Safer Eilam,* p. 61.

a *talmid chocham*—a student of wisdom,[27] for they are forever willing to remain students, and they are always prepared to learn something new.[28] This is indeed a true mark of *bitul*.[29]

Experiencing *bitul* means taking leave of the ego and living in oneness, aligning one's desires, thoughts, emotions, and activities with the essence of one's transcendent self. Yet being that the inner consciousness of a human being is "part of God," *bitul* does not negate a person's existence. On the contrary, one finds oneself through *bitul*.[30] Reaching a state of *ayin* is to submit one's natural base instincts to one's Godly-consciousness, ex-changing the limited for the limitless. Through this, we become truly free and empowered, developing into powerfully effective cocreators, engendering a world imbued with harmony and inner peace.

Kabbalah teaches that there are levels beyond the *ayin* and that *ayin* is not the Ultimate. With regard to creation, the Kabbalah speaks of two types of energies, the Infinite's energy manifested as an immanent all-pervasive force and an energy seen as a transcendent power.[31] *Memale kol almin* is a light that permeates and is invested in the universe. It is the energy that animates and sustains the universe in an intimate way, similar to the soul that is vested in the body.[32] It is a finite light,[33] that fills

---

27. See: Talmud *Baba Kama,* 41b; Tosefot, *Lerabot, Gittin,* 60a; Rashi, *Ha'Reuyin.*

28. Rabbi Chaim Ben Betzalel, *Safer HaChaim, Safer Zechuyot* (Jerusalem: Machon Sharei Yoshar, 1996), chapter 1, p. 38.

29. A title of humility. See: Rabbi Chaim Yoseph David Azulay, *Ayin Zocher, marrechet chet* (4).

30. The Lubavitcher Rebbe, *Sefer Ha'maamorim Meluket,* vol. 5, p. 302.

31. Kabbalah teaches panentheism not pantheism. All is included in God, not all is God. See: chapter 10, footnote 13.

32. Talmud *Berachot,* 10a; Midrash *Rabba,* Leviticus, *parsha* 4, chapter 8, Midrash *Tehilim,* chapter 103.

33. Rabbi Schneur Zalman of Liadi, *Tanya,* chapter 51.

creation.[34] *Sovev kol almin* is the light that encompasses and hovers over creation.[35] It is a divine infinite light[36] that is beyond being revealed and manifested in a physical three-dimensional universe. Hence, the light of the Creator both pervades and envelopes creation.[37]

These two manifestations, the finite and the infinite light, are both not the essence of God. The quintessence of God is termed *atzmut*—innermost essence. It is God beyond the finite but also beyond the infinite[38] and even beyond being defined as the

---

34. See: Rabbi Saddiah Goan, *Emunot VeDeyot, maamor* 2, chapter 13. The Midrash teaches that the reason God appeared to Moses in a thornbush, a boron tree, is to demonstrate that God's presence is found even in the (seemingly) lifeless. Midrash *Rabba*, Exodus, *parsha 2,* chapter 5; Midrash *Rabba*, Numbers, *parsha* 12, chapter 12; Midrash *Rabba*, "Shir Hashirim," chap re 3, verse 9; *P'siktah D'Reb Kahana*, chapter 1.

35. See: *Zohar, Raya Mehemna*, "Parshat Pinchas," p. 225; introduction to *Tikunei Zohar*. In a famous medieval poem titled *Shir Hayichud* the creator is praised as being *sovev* and *memale*. This poem is attributed to Rabbi Shemuel HaChassid (circa 1115–?). The poem is reprinted by Rabbi Yakkov Emdin in the back *Sidur Beit Yakov* (p. 466). Rabbi Schneur Zalman of Liadi explains that the concepts of *sovev* and *memale* should not be taken literally with spatial connotations, for they are both strictly related to the degree of their revelation and manifestation in the universe. The divine light that is revealed within the physical is referred to as *memale*—filling the world. For it can be observed and felt in the physical. While the influence that is not as revealed, that does not manifest itself in the world, is called *sovev*—encompassing. (Though, they are both truly contained within this world.) *Tanya*, chapter 48.

36. Rabbi Schneur Zalman of Liadi, *Tanya*, "Igeret Hakodesh," chapter 3; *Shar Hayichud V'Ha'emuna*, chapter 7.

37. See also: Rabbi Yom Tov Lipman Heller (1579–1654) *Safer Ha-Nitzachon*, "Parshat Vaetchanan," on the verse *VeYodatah HaYom;* Rabbi Avraham ben David Herrera (1570–1635), *Shar HaShamayim, maamor* 4, chapter 6; Rabbi Chaim of Volozhin, *Nefesh HaChaim, shar* 3, chapter 2.

38. See The Lubavitcher Rebbe, *Sefer HaMaamorim Meluket*, vol. 2, p. 235.

source of the *ein sof*—the endless infinite light.[39] Furthermore, the mere fact of saying that God is above is itself a definition. The only way we can utter a description of God is through observing the manifestations which we identify as Godly. Any description given (even that God is beyond) is not describing who God is, only how God manifests.[40]

What we do know is that *atzmut* manifests as finite and infinite energies,[41] and is contained in both of them simultaneously, existing as a contradiction, as an oxymoron.[42] *Atzmut* is revealed within the finite—*yesh* —and the infinite—*ayin*

---

39. See: The Lubavitcher Rebbe, *Sefer HaMaamorim Meluket,* vol. 2, pp. 285–286.

40. The Lubavitcher Rebbe, *Maamor Shabbat,* "*Parshat Nitzavim,*" 5748–1988.

41. Rabbi Meir Ben Gabbai, *Avodot Hakodesh,* part 1, chapter 8. See also: Rabbi Shalom DovBer, the fifth Chabad rebbe, *Sefer Hamaamorim 5678,* p. 419.

42. See: The Lubavitcher Rebbe, *Likutei Sichot,* vol. 12, pp. 74-75, footnote 30. God's ability to exist in a contradiction was manifested in time of the Temple in the holy of holies. The Talmud says that the measurement of the ark did not occupy any physical space in the holy of holies (Talmud *Yuma,* 21 a; *Baba Batra,* 99a; *Megillah,* 10b). Though it had a measurement, the measurement did not occupy any space in the Temple. The ark was a demonstration of a presence that existed within and above the dimensions of space simultaneously. This phenomenon was a demonstration of *atzmut* whose existence is not defined by our perception of what existence is. See: The Lubavitcher Rebbe, *Sefer HaMaamorim,* "*Meluket,*" vol. 4, p. 137, p. 340. God is not limited to human capacities, God can exist in an oxymoron. See: Rabbi Shlomo Ben Aderret, *Teshuvat HaRashba, teshuvah* 418. Though, there were philosophers who argue that to say that God exists in such a form is irrational and senseless. See: Rabbi Joseph Albo, *Safer Halkkarim, maamor* 1, chapter 22.

The argument whether this can be said of God appears to be an argument between the rationalists and the mystics. To the philosopher this description defines logic, while to the mystic this phenomenon, the paradox of existence, can be observed even within nature. See: Rabbi Shalom DovBer, the fifth Chabad rebbe, *Sefer HaMaamorim 5678,* p. 420; The Lubavitcher Rebbe, *Sefer HaMaamorim,* "*Meluket,*" vol. 1, pp. 60–61.

concurrently. For *atzmut* is beyond *yesh* —physical existence—and beyond *ayin*—nothingness, spirit. The power to be finite is displayed in the *yesh,* while the capacity to be infinite is manifested in *ayin.* Humans call the infinite *ayin*—nothingness—for it is beyond human comprehension, and thus considered to them as nothing.[43]

The human mind operates as a three-dimensional apparatus. It assumes that the physical, the dimensional, is not Godly, and that everything that is beyond the physical, beyond dimensions, the *ayin,* the spiritual, is God. Or at the very least, closer to God than the physical. In truth, both the *yesh* as well as the *ayin* are creations and not the creator. *Atzmut* is beyond being as well as beyond nonbeing

Having established this premise, we can begin to decode the enigma of physical reality. There has been a question asked perennially for millennia: Is the world of appearance, a world apprehended with our physical senses, a genuine reality? Or is it only an illusion of the senses, as many philosophers (especially of the East) claim, and in fact, having no objective existence.[44]

Alma deshikra—a world of fallacy is the way the Kabbalah refers to this physical universe.[45] What the human eye observes as objective separate reality is but an illusion of the truth.[46] The

---

43. See: Rabbi Moshe Corodovero, *Pardess Rimonim, shar* 23, chapter 1; Rabbi Schneur Zalman of Liadi, *Tanya,* "*Igeret Hakodesh,*" epistle 20.

44. In Western philosophy the proponent of this idea was George Berkeley (1685–1753). He argued that the existence of material objects is dependent on them being perceived. And thus, he denied the existence of nonmental physical reality. Matter is a cluster of ideas, man's or God's. See: George Berkeley, *Principles of Human Knowledge/Three Dialogues* (Penguin, 1988). "No idea can exist unless it be in a mind," Second Dialogue, p. 163.

45. Rabbi Schneur Zalman of Liadi, *Maamorei Admur Hazoken, Maarazal,* p. 336. *Hayam Yam,* the eleventh day at *Elul.* See also: *Midrash Rabbah.* Leviticus. Parsha 26. Chapter 7.

46. Rabbi Yisrael Baal Shem Tov, *Keter Shem Tov,* p. 6; Rabbi Schneur Zalman of Liadi, *Tanya,* "*Shar Hayichud V'Ha'emuna,*" chapter 3.

criterion applied by humans for things being real is whether they can be apprehended with the physical senses.[47] That which can be sensed is real. However, in the creator's perspective the world is *ayin*—nonexistence—and *yesh*—matter—is in reality subsumed in the *ayin*—the Godly energy.[48] In the view of the creator, the physical is not defined as being a *yesh*—a separate existence—but as an *ayin*. The infinite energy that creates the *yesh* is the authentic reality.

Despite this assertion, the universe is not a figment of the human imagination, and it is not merely an illusion. The Torah opens with the words: "In the beginning God created the heavens and the earth."[49] By stating this, the Torah affirms the authenticity of a physical universe.[50] However, physical reality does not exist the way man perceives it, as a separate independent entity; rather, the physical dimensional universe is but another expression of The Oneness. Just as the spiritual worlds manifest the infinite power, so too the physical world manifests the finite. Yes, undoubtedly, the physical universe exists with all the finite limitations and dimensions of time and space, but it is not an entity separate from its creator; rather it is a manifestation

---

47. Rabbi Shalom DovBer, the fifth Chabad rebbe, *Sefer Hamaamorim 5643*, p. 39.

48. Rabbi Schneur Zalman of Liadi, *Tanya*, "Shar Hayichud V'Ha'emuna," chapter 6.

49. Genesis, chapter 1, verse 1.

50. The authenticity of the physical reality can be proven from the many laws of the Torah that pertain to the physical and the laws that regard the physical as a real existence. See: Rabbi Shmuel, the fourth Chabad rebbe, *Sefer HaMaamorim 5629*, p. 143; Rabbi Shalom DovBer, the fifth Chabad rebbe, *Sefer HaMaamorim 5643*, p. 95. It should be noted that there are Kabbalists who assert that the entire Torah can only exist in the vacuum of the *tzimtsum*. On a level that is beyond the *tzimtsum*, even the reality of Torah does not exist. It is the blueprint of creation, but beyond that there is only Oneness. Hence, the world indeed is an illusion to man. In the perspective beyond *tzimtsum* there is only God. See: Rabbi Tzodok of Lublin, *Likutei Maamorim*, p. 195.

of that which is beyond it. The finite nature is but one display of the Creator.[51]

Paradoxically, *atzmut*—the essence of all reality—is especially manifest in the our universe, as opposed to all other worlds. This world is unique in that it is physical, hence laboring under the notion of separateness, and therefore it does not

---

51. See. *Kuntras Inyano Shel Toraht HaChassidut,* printed in the back of *Sefer Ha'erchin* chapter 17. The Kabbalah teaches that the numerical volume of the word for nature in Hebrew *hatevah* is eighty-six, the same numerical volume of one of the names of God, *Elokim.* See: Rabbi Meir Eben Aldavia, *Shivilei Emunah, nosiv* 1, p. 45; Rabbi Moshe Corodovero, *Pardess Rimonim, shar* 12, chapter 2; Rabbi Eliyahu ben Moshe Di Vidas, *Reshit Chachmah,* "Shar HaTeshuvah," chapter 6, "Shar Ha'Ahavah," chapter 11; Rabbi Yeshayah Halevi Horowitz, *Shenei Luchot Habrit,* "Shar Ha'otyot," p. 89a. (Parenthetically, it seems that Rabbi Yeshayah Halevi had a different version of the *Zohar* than ours. In the *Zohar* this numerical equation is mentioned.) Rabbi Yisrael Baal Shem Tov, *Keter Shem Tov,* part 2, p. 24; *Baal Shem Tov Al Ha Torah,* "Parshat Bereishit" Rabbi Schneur Zalman of Liadi, *Tanya,* "Shar HaYichud VaHa'emuna," chapter 6, *Likutei Torah,* part 4, p. 22b; Rabbi Yakov Yoseph of Polonnye, *Toldot Yakov Yoseph,* "Hakdamah," p. 3. Rabbi Moshe Chayim Ephraim of Sudylkov, *Degel Machanah Ephraim,* the beginning; Rabbi Nachum of Chernobyl, *Meor Einayim,* "Likutim," p. 190; Rabbi Elimelech of Lizhensk, *Noam Elimelech,* "Parshat Lech Lecha," p. 12; Rabbi Avraham Yeshoshua Heschel, *Ohev Yisroel,* "Parsaht Vayyetze," p. 40; Rabbi Baruch of Kosav, *Amud Ha'avadah,* p. 108b; Rabbi Tzvi Elimelech of Dinav, *Bnei Yissochar,* "Maamorei HaShabatot," *maamor* 8, p. 21a, "Maamorei Chodesh Tishrei," *maamor* 4, p. 15a.

The author of *The Second Kuzari,* the philosopher Rabbi David Nitu (1654–1728), once delivered a lecture in a London synagogue. During his lecture he declared that nature is a divine manifestation. This caused a great stir in the Jewish community in London (they believed his ideas bordered on pantheism). So they resolved to ask one of the leading Rabbis of Europe, the Chacham Tzvi, Rabbi Tzvi Ashkenazi (1660–1718) for his opinion on this issue. The Chacham Tzvi responded by affirming that this idea was a Jewish idea and a most authentic statement. See: *Responsa, Chacham Tzvi,* chapter 18. The son of the Chacham Tzvi, Rabbi Yakkov Emdin, writes of the entire episode with his father in his autobiography. See: Rabbi Yakkov Emdin, *Megilat Safer* (Israel: Jerusalem Jewish Classics, 1979), p. 55. See also: Rabbi

overtly sense its connection with the creator. Every other world recognizes whence it emanated. For example, the spiritual world of *yitzirah* knows that it evolved from the world of *beriah,* and *beriah* from *atziluth,* and so forth, while only in this physical world is there the possibility for one to feel as if the world had created itself. Atheism is a phenomenon that can only occur in this universe. The reason is that all universes exist in the realms of *seder hishtalshelut*—the spiritual evolution—where there is a causal progression and a continuous flow of energy from one world into the next. They are all openly interlaced in a sequential progression. However, the physical is not obviously a link in the chain of the spiritual, the *seder hishtalshelut.* Therefore, only a power that is above being caused by something else, above the *seder hishtalshelut,* can source such a world. That energy is *atzmut,* which has no antecedent causality. Only *atzmut* has the power to create something that seems to be an autonomous entity. Only *atzmut* whose being is an imperative and whose existence is derived from essence, has the ability to source a creation that is unaware that its existence depends on a creator and who feels that it had created itself.[52]

The singularity of physicality, in the spiritual scheme of creation, is that it lives in the illusion that it is self-referential and independent of a creator. *Atzmut*—the prime cause, which is in fact self-referential and self-generative—infused within creation the notion of independence as a concomitant to the notion of separation. This feeling is important, as it is the context for freedom of choice. Choice is born of freedom and independence, lest it be meaningless.

In a time of *galut*—spiritual concealment—the concept of *atzmut* within this world is expressed in atheism, in that the

Chaim Yoseph David Azulay, *D'Vash L'Phi* (Jerusalem: 1962), *marrechet tet* (1).
52. Rabbi Schneur Zalman of Liadi, *Tanya,* "*Igeret Hakodesh,*" epistle 20.

world does not point to a creator. However, when redemption is achieved, *atzmut* will be manifest in its true form; every man will see how the *yesh*—physicality—is derivative of the real *yesh*—the Ultimate existence.[53] Man will behold, the essence of God that permeates and is within all creation.

In conclusion, there are three ways a human being can perceive reality. The first is the perception prior to meditation, where one views the universe as it appears to the naked eye, where the *yesh* is the only genuine existence. The next level is the perception that comes with meditation, where one realizes that the *yesh* is but a facade for its inner energy, its true existence, the *ayin*. And the highest perception attainable is to view reality in the same way *atzmut* views reality, to see beyond the *ayin* and realize that God is within the physical as much as God is above it. Ultimately, one comes to the understanding that the purpose of his creation is so that in the physical world he can acknowledged God as the source and master, thereby creating a dwelling place for God here on earth.[54] Revealing the *yesh* of physicality as in actuality the *yesh* of *atzmut,* is to come full circle and return to where one began, in earthbound reality.

A poet once wrote: "We shall not cease from exploration, and the end of our exploration will be to arrive where we started and know the place for the first time." Through meditation one beholds the reality that one has always seen, as if for the very first time.[55]

---

53. Rabbi Dovber, the second Chabad rebbe, *Biurei HaZohar,* "*Parshat Beshalach,*" p. 43c; The Lubavitcher Rebbe, *Sefer HaMaamorim Meluket,* vol. 1, p. 6; See also: Rabbi Schneur Zalman of Liadi, *Maamorei Admur Hazoken, Maarazal,* p. 483.

54. See: Rabbi Schneur Zalman of Liadi, *Tanya,* chapter 36.

55. Rabbi Nachman of Breslov writes that following his meditation the world seemed to him like a new world. See: Rabbi Nachman of Breslov, *Chayei Moharan,* chapter 107.

CHAPTER
12

Character Refinement—
Meditating to Achieve
a Better Self

The quest to better oneself is a lifelong journey, the destination being the development into a person whose entire personality bespeaks transcendence and refinement of character. Character refinement, the transformation of character flaws to virtuous personality traits, play a pivotal role in the Jewish experience. Many believe it to be, in fact, the very foundation of Torah.[1] The Torah, in its entirety, was given only to refine man, the Midrash states.[2] Yet character refinement is one of the most arduous tasks one will encounter in a lifetime of challenge. Where does one begin? How does one presume to rid oneself of that which feels like second nature, and more so, to transform that second nature entirely?

In contemporary Jewish thought there appears to be two predominant styles of meditation, of which the objective is

---

1. Mishnah *Avot,* chapter 3, Mishnah 17; Rabbeinu Yona, ad loc; Rabbi Menachem Ben Shlomo, the Meiri, in his commentary on *Kiddushin,* 41a; Rabbi Simcha Zissel Ziv of Kelm, *Kisvei Ha'Saba M'Kelm* (Bnei Brak: Sifsei Chachamim, 1984), p. 151. Rabbi Chaim Vital calls good behavior the seat and foundation of all Mitzvot. See: *Sharei Kedusha,* part 1, *shar 2.*

2. *Midrash Tanchuma,* "Shemini," chapters 7 and 8. Midrash *Rabba,* Genesis, *parsha 44,* chapter 1; Midrash *Rabba,* Leviticus, *parsha* 13, chapter 3.

character refinement. One is known as the way of *mussar*, the other is the Chassidic approach. While these disciplines are both geared to the perfection of one's character,[3] the Chassidic masters take this further. Philosophically, they maintain that the main motive of character refinement is for the instinctive characteristics of man, one's second nature, so to speak, to become Godly.[4]

Though they both converge in their aim, they differ greatly in their approach. *Mussar* philosophy dictates that negative traits must be combated head on. A *mussar* meditation involves the study of a devotional work, namely, a book on ethics, as one carefully contemplates each negative trait within himself in an attempt to reach self-improvement. One singles out each attribute individually and meditates on its negativity, with the intent of perfecting oneself by eradicating that same trait.[5] Chassidic philosophy proposes that negativity may be annihilated by overwhelming it with positive energy. Meditation on

---

3. The Baal Shem Tov says the purpose of the creation of man is to transform his natural temperament and refine himself. See: *Keter Shem Tov*, chapter 24, p. 4b; *Baal Shem Tov Al Ha Torah*, "*Parshat Bereishit*," p. 41. See also: Rabbi Yakov Yoseph of Polonnye, *Ben Porat Yoseph*, p. 53, 169; *Tzafnat Paneach*, p. 27b. The aim of the *mussar* movement is for character refinement. See: Rabbi Yisrael Salanter, *Or Yisrael*, pp. 82–85. Rabbi Yitzchak Blazer, *Chocvei Or*, *p.* 14; *Safer Or HaMussar*, part 2, article by Rabbi Yitzchak Blazer, pp. 189–190. See also: *T'nuat HaMsusar*, vol. 1, p. 274.

4. A saying by Rabbi Shalom DovBer, the fifth Chabad rebbe. See: *Beshoo Shehikdimu 5672*, part 2, chapter 376, p. 773; *Sefer Hasichoss: Toras Sholom*, p. 185. See also: *Migdal Oz* (a compilation on Chassidic thought edited by Y. Mondschein) (Israel: 1980), p. 144. See also: *Kuntras Inyano Shel Toraht HaChassidut*, printed in the back of *Sefer Ha'erchin* Vol. 1, chapter 1.

5. A master of the *mussar* movement, Rabbi Yoseph Yuzal Horowitz (1848–1920) writes that perfecting one's character must be done through the details of each characteristic, concentrating on each trait in particular. See: *Madregot Ha'adam*, part 1 (Jerusalem: Chemed, 1970), pp. 107–110.

the beauty of the soul causes the imperfections of one's character to slowly dissipate and disappear.[6]

An individual without experience of the Chassidic discipline
may surmise that this route of positivity does not, in fact, completely eradicate the negative and is merely a superficial camou-
flage, concealing the negativity that continues to exist within
one's personality. A prominent master of the *mussar* movement
once argued that while Chassidim merely cover over their faults,
mussar teaches the person how to eradicate and purify their inner
makeup.[7] Yet the Chassidic masters have vehemently disagreed,
arguing that any negotiation and handling of negativity, in any
which way and for whatever reason, is by its very nature a negative undertaking. Negative energy is contaminating, and one
who "wrestles with a muddied person is bound to become soiled
himself."[8] The approach of Chassidic philosophy, therefore, is to
train the human mind to think and dwell solely on the positive
aspects of life, to surround oneself with positive energy, and thus
through the focus on the positivity, the negativity will eventually
disappear entirely.

The differing views of these two approaches are quite
apparent within our daily lives as well. Take, for example, the
effort to lose weight. A person may implement and make use of
these methodologies in this struggle. The person struggling to
lose the weight knows that weight gain is caused by foods that
are high in fat content. If one follows the philosophy of *mussar,*
one will meditate on the negative implications of eating fatten-
ing foods and will visualize it as an enemy that desires their

---

6. See: *Migdal Oz,* p. 423. The Lubavitcher Rebbe, at a Chassidic
gathering the last day of Passover 1957 and at a Chassidic gathering on
Simchat Torah 1955.

7. A saying attributed to the founder of the *mussar* movement, Rabbi
Yisrael Salanter. See: Hillel Tzeitlen, *Al Gevul Shnei Olamot* (Israel: Yavneh,
1997), p. 273.

8. See: Rabbi Schneur Zalman of Liadi, *Tanya,* chapter 28.

destruction. One holds back and refrains from indulging by dwelling on the negativity. The Chassidic method, on the other hand, would be to shift one's consciousness and redirect one's attention toward the positive. In this case, one would meditate on how healthy one can be and how invigorated one can feel, if one eats nutritiously.

Rabbi Avraham the Angel, a noted 18th-century Chassidic master, once remarked that the "Seven Year War" introduced new paths in the understanding of divine service. The battle tactics introduced by Frederick the Great taught Reb Avraham how he too could be victorious with his own inner battles. In times gone by, combat was a hand-to-hand affair and was fought head-on. The common course of battle was for each army to divide its soldiers into three camps, one flanked to the right, another to the left, with the third placed in the center. When the time came to engage in battle, they would attack the opposing force straight on. Frederick devised a new plan of action; rather than each individual camp attacking the opposite camp, all three divisions would surround one of the enemy's three divisions and overwhelm it from all directions. On a personal level, one may want to eliminate the negative trait of anger by engaging it in a thorough resistance and in the process upending much mental and psychological energy. Using Reb Avraham's method to overwhelm the enemy one marshals the positive energy within oneself, conjuring thoughts of love and acceptance and arousing inner feelings towards God and consequently submerging the negativity in positive energy, eventually eradicating the negativity entirely.[9]

The Baal Shem Tov once explained the difference between the Chassidic approach to refinement and the classic approach of

---

9. See: Rabbi Avraham the Angel (1739–1776), *Chesed Le'Avraham* (Jerusalem: Machon Sifsei Tzadikim, 1995), pp. 197–201; *Migdal Oz*, pp. 390–392; *HaTamim* (a compilation of Chassidic thought and related issues), booklet 3, p. 120a.

mussar with the following metaphor. Imagine, he said, you catch a thief in the midst of robbing your home. Without premeditated thought you scream and howl until the thief bolts. Now, though the immediate danger is resolved, the larger issue is not. Who is to say that this same thief will not return the very next day, if not to your home, then perhaps to that of your neighbor? There is, however, another method, and it is final and preemptive. You grab the thief by his collar and persuade him to become an honest man and to never steal again.[10]

A master of *mussar* once chanced upon his students calmly engaged in *mussar* study and immediately rebuked them for their complacency. "Is this the way to handle a thief? Where is the passion and intensity in your studies?"[11]

In *mussar* the emphasis lies on the impending negativity of the act. One perceives the immediate negativity of the behavior, and through screams and shouts one rids oneself of it. Yet, taking the time and exercising patience in handling this same negativity, overwhelming it with the positive, as it were, will accomplish something far more dramatic and enduring, namely, the metamorphosis of the negative into something deeply positive.

The path of the Chassidim is a path of light,[12] to overwhelm the darkness in one's inner psyche with the soul's power of illumination.[13] *Mussar* philosophy dictates that the physical should be looked upon as the enemy.[14] Chassidic thought maintains that there is no inherent contradiction or dichotomy,

10. The Lubavitcher Rebbe, *Likutei Sichot*, vol. 2, p. 474. Rabbi Yoseph Yitzchak, the sixth Chabad rebbe, in the name of Rabbi Schneur Zalman of Liadi. See: *Sefer HaSichot 5696*, p. 131.

11. See: *Safer Or HaMussar*, part 2, p. 166.

12. Rabbi Yisroel DovBer of Vilednick, *Shearith Yisroel*, p. 152.

13. Rabbi Yoseph Yitzchak, the sixth Chabad rebbe, *Igrot Kodesh*, vol. 3, p. 547.

14. A person must know that his animalistic soul is his greatest enemy. See: Rabbi Eliyahu Dessler (1892–1953), *Michtav M'Eliyahu* (Bnei Brak:

for within everything that exists one will find Godliness. Chassidism aspires to teach its adherents to find the holiness inherent in all of creation, even that which hides itself within the physical and the mundane.[15] The masters of *mussar* instruct their followers against the daily trivialities of the mundane. They admonish their students *not* to eat and *not* to sleep. The Chassidic masters, on the other hand, train their disciples, *how* to eat and *how* to sleep, encouraging these very same mundane acts as energy-sustaining for the ultimate objective of divine service.[16]

A Chassidic master once offered the following metaphor: There once lived a mighty king who ruled over the entire world. This mighty king wished to test the loyalty of his subjects. He sent a trusted servant on a journey throughout his kingdom and charged the servant with the job of stirring revolutions in the various lands within the kingdom. The servant set out on this journey, encountering success in some countries, while in other countries, loyal to the king, they drove him away. In one land, however, where the people were wise, they saw through their beloved sovereign's scheme and realized that it was but a ploy to test their loyalty.

The evil inclination is this imposter servant. There are those who welcome him, joining in his revolt. There are others who view this evil inclination as the enemy and go all out in battle against it. There are still others, those who sense the deception and identify the evil for what it is, merely a mask. For these wise people, the war is won without battle. By revealing the identity

---

1964), book 3, pp. 43–44. See also: Rabbi Bachya Ibn Pakudah, *Chovot Halevavot,* "*Shar Yichud Hama'ase,*" chapter 5.

15. Rabbi Shalom DovBer, the fifth Chabad rebbe, *Sefer Hasichoss, "Toras Sholom,"* p. 7.

16. Rabbi Yoseph Yitzchak, the sixth Chabad rebbe, *Safer Hasichot Kayitz 5700,* p. 152.

of the enemy and introducing a greater light, the mask of evil begins to melt away.[17]

The difference between these two approaches essentially stems from where one is coming from, namely, which emotion one lives by. In *mussar* the fear is most emphasized,[18] while in Chassidic thought the emphasis is on love.[19] To a degree, fear is a function of the ego. It is the ambiance in which the ego thrives. The ego is the false self that lives in a constant state of survival. It is that which accumulates, schemes, and discards trust out of its fear of annihilation. It is insatiable in its insecurity, thus more is never enough. Confronting the ego is to give it more energy.

---

17. Rabbi Yakov Yoseph of Polonnye, *Toldot Yakov Yoseph*, "*Parshat Vayakhel*," p. 252. See also: *Baal Shem Tov Al Ha Torah*, "*Parshat Bereishit*."

18. See: Rabbi Yisrael Salanter, *Or Yisrael*, p. 57. See also: *T'nuat HaMsusar*, vol. 1, p. 259.

19. See: Rabbi Baruch of Mezhibuzh (1757–1810), *Butzina De'Nehurah* (Bronx: Yeshiva Ohr Mordechei, 1956), p. 12, *Sham, Kuf Zayin; Ba'al Shem Tov Al Ha Torah*, "*Parshat Mishpatim*," pp. 368–369; *Hayom Yom*, twenty-sixth of Addar 1 and twenty-sixth of Shevat. See also: Rabbi Yakov Yitzchak Horowitz, the seer of Lublin (1745–1815), *Zikhron Zot, Zot Zikhron, Divrei Emet* (Israel: 1973), *Zikhron Zot*, p. 129; *Divrei Emet*, p. 147. In *mussar* there is much discussion of punishment, retribution, hell, and so on, all with the intention to arouse fear. In Chassidic thought, however, such talk is scarce, if any. Now, although there is a mitzvah to fear God (Deuteronomy, 6:13), and to a degree, fear is the first step in serving God (See: Talmud *Shabbat*, 31b; *Zohar*, part 1, p. 7), nonetheless, as the Kabbalah points out, there are two levels of fear. There is *yirah ila'ah*—higher fear—and *Yirah Tata'ah*—lower fear. (See: Rabbi Schneur Zalman of Liadi, *Tanya*, chapter 41; Rabbi DovBer, the second Chabad rebbe, *Derech Chaim, Hakdamah*.) Lower fear is a fear of being harmed and punished. (That is a fear that is an extension of one's ego, afraid to be hurt.) Higher fear is not actually fear of harm; rather it is a sense of awe and marvel, being overwhelmed by the Infinite's presence. Such fear stems from a person's *bitul*. It is a mark of a level *of d'eveikut*. See: *Divrei Emet*, p. 133. See also: Rabbi Nisan Ben Reuven, *Derashot HaRan*, *derush* 7, p. 120; Rabbi Yoseph Albo, *Safer Haikkarim*, *maamor* 3, chapter 32. Rabbi Yeshayah Halevi Horowitz, *Shenei Luchot Habrit*, *Asarah Ma'amarot*, *maamor* 3–4, p. 215.

By driving it into hiding, it will act surreptitiously, strategically, to ensure its own concepts of reality. It will sacrifice the human and the true transcendent self for what *it* considers most important. It thrives on fear. The Chassidic philosophy has a powerful strategy to neutralize fear and its parent, the ego. It harnesses the most formidable power of the universe, the power of love. Through love entire new paradigms are brought into consciousness. Where fear predominated and suffused the space, there is now a universe permeated by love, inspired by the most positive, life-affirming power, that is, the Infinite. In the new arena of such magnitude, faults, fears, and ego become infinitely less significant, and with time, entirely disappear.[20]

Now that we have explored the various methods and techniques for meditation, it behooves us to recall that "These are all the words of the living God."[21] There are no two souls alike, and what inspires one may not be the source of inspiration for another. Each individual person should search within himself and find what it is that moves him, and then follow that path with all the energy and emotion he possesses. In the words of the prophet, "Each one on his own beaten track shall go forward."[22]

---

20. The source of all negative traits is the ego. See: Rabbi Eliyahu ben Moshe Di Vidas, *Reshit Chachmah, Shar HaYirah,* chapter 4. Rabbi Elimelech of Lizhensk, *Noam Elimelech,* Parshat Tazria, p. 175. The desire a person has for physical pleasures, which offer self-perpetuation and aggrandizement, stem from one's preoccupation with the ego. (See: Rabbi Yoseph Yitzchak, the sixth Chabad rebbe, *Sefer HaMaamorim 5680,* pp. 1–14.) Therefore, by revealing the soul that is transcendent (see: Rabbi Schneur Zalman of Liadi, *Tanya,* chapter 19), the *source* of one's negative traits will subside and then slowly disappear.

21. Talmud *Eruvin,* 13b; *Gittin,* 6b.

22. *Yoel,* chapter 2, verse 8.

CHAPTER
13

Eight Steps to Meditation

The previous chapters detailed the various processes of meditation. From the purely practical preparatory steps to the highly esoteric aspects of meditation, we have explored Jewish meditation in its depth and breadth. Yet meditation cannot be fully appreciated without the actual process of meditating occurring. Experiencing meditation, one can fully grasp its extraordinary powers and the difference it can make in our daily lives. Toward this end, I have included a guide comprised of the basic techniques of meditation, designed to facilitate your ability to meditate, and allow you to get into it.

1) Check *your* level of commitment. It is axiomatic that the degree of success is commensurate with the degree of commitment. Also know, however, that whatever that level is, it's okay.

2) Find a location that is conducive to conducting a process that is incompatible with disturbances and interruptions. Make it *your* space by familiarizing yourself with it and establishing it as a safe and comfortable place, because you say so. It is okay to change your location if it doesn't work.

3) Choose a focal point, be it a thought, a verbal, a visual, or even a body movement, and concentrate on it. Notice the intruding thoughts that arise, allow them. If persistent *gently* remove them. In the beginning you may experience discomfort, perhaps headaches, know that they are part of the process. (It is okay to take an aspirin, but in time you'll make headaches disappear.)

4) Seek the right time in which to meditate. This is determined by the constraints of your schedule and the availability of your energy. Use your common sense.

5) There are countless thoughts, verbal or visual mantras that can be employed; the Shema, or the chant Ribbono Shel Olam, are good and simple examples. When using the mantra-style meditation remember that a mantra can either be a meaningful word or a very short phrase, its purpose is to focus, empower, and inspire during the meditation. Try one on for size, discard it if the fit is wrong, then try another until you achieve an optimal level of comfort. Then use it.

6) If by now you haven't invented excuses to quit, and you continue the practice, you may begin to see some salutary changes. Your body may begin to register with you as more than just a vehicle that transports you. You are in touch with your breathing, your heartbeat, your limbs, and you marvel at the complex engineering miracle that you are, and perhaps an awe dawns for The Engineer. You also begin to control the functions of this machine so that it's not just running on automatic.

7) Having established a routine, you begin to observe that after each session of meditation you feel refreshed physically and mentally. You might even feel a craving for the serene state you experience during and after each session.

Conversely, the resistance you may still experience occasionally is normal, and has to be included with affection. Do not judge yourself harshly.

8) Using meditation as an active method to advance spiritually, not just for physical and mental well being, requires intentionality and refocusing on specifically spiritual subjects. Undertaking the spiritual path is arduous and not done frivolously. It is a life-altering commitment. Be patient and persevere.

In conclusion, it is significant to keep in mind that the importance lies in the journey rather than in the destination. Here you win even when you don't attain the ultimate goal. The paradox is innate within the meditation. The meditator becomes more by being less, and achieves more control by having less of it. This does not make sense in the universe of consistency and linear thinking. Welcome to the higher universe of spirituality, where anomaly is logical, and parody reasonable. Good luck.

Index

About the Author

Rabbi DovBer Pinson is a renowned Jewish scholar, teacher, and author. His books include *Reincarnation and Judaism: The Journey of Soul*, *Inner Rhythms: The Kabbalah of Music*, and *Toward the Infinite: The Way of Kabbalistic Meditations*. Rabbi Pinson is an acclaimed speaker and has lectured in both scholarly and lay settings throughout the world. Rabbi Pinson resides in New York with his wife and two children.